Therese

Neijraln

A PORTRAIT BASED ON AUTHENTI<

BY JOHANNES STEINER

✝

Therese

ACCOUNTS, JOURNALS AND DOCUMENTS

Neumann

ba house DIVISION OF THE SOCIETY OF ST. PAUL • STATEN ISLAND, N.Y. 10314

Originally published in German under the title *Theres Neumann von Konnersreuth* by Verlag Schnell & Steiner, München.

NIHIL OBSTAT: DONALD A. PANELLA, M.A., S.T.L., S.S.L.
Censor Librorum

IMPRIMATUR: TERENCE J. COOKE, D.D., Vicar-General
New York, New York
October 21, 1966

Library of Congress Catalog Card Number, 66-27536

Designed, printed and bound in the U.S.A. by the Pauline Fathers and Brothers as part of their communications apostolate.

CONTENTS

Part III: Evaluation — 217

Purpose and Principles of This Book

Since Therese Neumann first received the sacred stigmata in 1926, a host of publication has appeared, representing the most divergent positions. Far too many confused accounts, legendary reports by local figures, and obviously false information have distorted a great number of these works. There has as yet appeared no suitable continuation to the exact and scholarly biographical work of Fritz Michael Gerlich, whose two volume account closes with the year 1929.

Therese Neumann died in 1962; today it is possible to present documentation, both written (oral) and photographical, which was not open to publication during her lifetime. It is also possible to achieve the position of clearer perspective that is possible only after death.

Chief among these new materials is a concise collective biography which appears as the joint work of several of Therese Neumann's "close relatives." The picture is rounded out by letters from Therese herself, which give real insight into her interior life, and by the opinions of persons who knew Therese Neumann over the course of many years.

It is impossible, and not the intention of the author, to cast light on all the questions that have risen about Konnersreuth—the time is too soon and the book too small. Theologico-mystical questions are constantly vying with medical considerations. Quite properly, the Church has refused to recognize any definitive value in visions and apparitions which are bound up, or could be bound up, with a particular endowment or talent, which are different in each individual, as well as in their expression and experience. The deciding factor is personal conduct and personal application. And thus the main question is whether or not Therese Neumann made special or even heroic efforts in following Christ. Only in this light can the wealth of charismatic phenomena have any power to convince.

This book is the authentic story of Konnersreuth. It is not a resumé of other books; nor is it an attack or a defense, like so many other books that treat the subject. It is rather an objective statement of facts, based on immediate and first-hand sources of information, and refraining from polemics wherever possible.

The chief sources:

1. The primary source is Therese Neumann herself. Gerlich's biography is based primarily on her own statements; her words are, to a large extent, the basis for Father Naber's journals, and the author of this volume has also drawn extensively upon her own statements.

2. Father Josef Naber, spiritual director and confessor, ninety-three years old at the time this book was written, was assigned to the parish Church at Konnersreuth from 1909 to 1960 (since resigned), and in this position he was spiritual advisor to Therese Neumann and immediate representative of the Church's authority in the parish. He was a prime source for Gerlich and is even more so for the period elapsed since the publication of Gerlich's work. During the 34 years that the author was a regular visitor in Konnersreuth, Father Naber often spoke about what had happened there and made it possible for the author to have access to reports of visions, periods of elevated calm, and mystical Communion; he put his own written records at the author's disposal during the preparation of this volume and, throughout the time of its composition, constantly offered new and more complete details.

For all this cooperation and encouragement, the author wishes to express his heartfelt gratitude. Father Naber's own attitude towards the events at Konnersreuth are expressed in the following words: "My point of view, from the beginning, was this: I must make a very careful observation of these extraordinary experiences to see if there is anything to offend the teaching or morality of the Church. If there is, then I must take a stand against them, mercilessly; if there is not, then I can let affairs take their own course, lest man, in what he falsely thinks to be his wisdom, should meddle dangerously in the plans of God."

3. Many of the statements in this book are the result of first-hand accounts by the parents and family of Therese Neumann. From her mother, for example, I gleaned information about Therese's birth and early childhood, from her father, about his (at least subjectively justified, as we shall see) refusal to have her taken in for observation. I am especially indebted to her brother Ferdinand. The documentary part of this book owes its existence to his close cooperation. Whereas it was generally impossible to take pictures in Konnersreuth, Therese gave him the privilege, as her brother, of taking occasional photographs and recordings. This she did on the advise of her spiritual advisors who wanted to be assured of proper materials for the subsequent documentation of her story. During her lifetime, however, she never allowed these records to appear publicly.

4. The most historically exact and painstakingly written work is the two-volume book by the late state archivist Dr. Fritz Gerlich, in 1929. This book describes Therese Neumann's life story up to that point of her life with an exactness that extends to every detail: it was the fruit of many months of direct interrogation of Therese Neumann and her immediate acquaintances. Still, in one or another individual point, Gerlich is not complete. Therese later admitted that, since Gerlich was both a layman and a Protestant, she simply could not tell him everything. In 1948, after Gerlich met a violent death in the concentration camp at Dachau, the author of this volume had planned to have

his book republished. But Therese Neumann let it be known that she would prefer no further publications about her life and experiences during her lifetime. And thus the plans were laid aside.

5. A good part of the material for this book goes back to the information supplied by the "Eichstätt Circle." In this connection, Francis Xavier Wutz, professor of Old Testament exegesis, is deserving of first mention. He was the "germ cell" for Therese Neumann's association with Eichstätt. Not immediately interested at the outset, he made a side-trip to Konnersreuth in 1926, on a visit to Waldsassen, in order to get his own views on the general impression of the events at Konnersreuth. He was quite surprised and deeply moved by what he saw, and, when he heard her Aramaic words, be became interested on purely professional grounds as well.

Since he was a man of direct and energetic spirit, he quickly won confidence in Konnersreuth; thus it happened that Therese's sister, Ottilie, went to work as his housekeeper. When the two younger brothers, Ferdinand and Hans entered the school in Eichstätt, they were able to live with Dr. Wutz and thus Therese herself made frequent visits there, generally during the Easter season. It was like a second home for her.

Since many of Dr. Wutz's colleagues became close friends of Therese Neumann, Eichstätt (easier to reach, in its position in the middle of Bavaria, than Konnersreuth) became the spiritual center for the members of the so called "Konnersreuth circle," a friendly group which numbered, in 1930, in addition to those already named, the Abbess of St. Waldburg, Maria Benedicta von Spiegel, Prince Erich of St. Waldburg-Ziel, Father Ingbert Naab and Father Kosmas, O.F.M. Cap. Many a time—twenty years ago as a young collaborator of Gerlich's—I met Gerlich at Eichstätt between 1930 and 1933, drawing new security and strength and ideas for his war against National Socialism.

Of the university professors who were prominent in the circle, canon lawyer Dr. Josef Lechner and Dr. Francis Xavier

Mayr, professor of chemistry, biology, and geology, deserve mention: many a brick for the building of this volume comes from their hands. As a development of the close relation between Eichstätt and Konnersreuth, but also as an outgrowth of their normal concern and interest for the Church's prerogatives in Konnersreuth, it must be noted that the bishops of Eichstätt, Konrad Preysing (later Cardinal of Berlin), his successor Michael Rackl, and the then Bishop Joseph Schroffer, all showed genuine interest in Therese Neumann.

6. The author was himself introduced in Konnersreuth in 1929 by Father Ingbert Naab and Dr. Fritz Gerlich, and has since maintained unbroken and close contact with Konnersreuth. After the war it was possible to make the connections even more intensive since the author's professional needs brought him into the neighborhood of Konnersreuth several times a year, and frequently for rather extensive visits. Thus he had an opportunity to speak with Therese Neumann herself and to acquire first-hand information to correct or round out the work of Gerlich's biography.

The concise biographical account that thus results will serve as a first introduction to a reliable narrative of Therese Neumann's life. In order not to take up too much room, the biography had to be curtailed in many areas, and thus, in the section that deals with the mystical phenomena, only a few characteristic examples can be offered. As regards the visions, of the more than a hundred known to the author that appear in the course of each Church year, only two of the most important will be explicitly described for the present. The author is working on a project that will make the content of the rest of the visions available to the general public as well.

A scientific and properly documented text, however, demands not only years of working and re-working, but also the perspective of distance, standing apart from the experiences described, so that all the documents that demand a closer scrutiny (or are reserved for Church examination) can be properly

1 *Therese Neumann*

evaluated. A continuity of effort is thus set in motion with the publication of this edition. The final results will take into account all the valuable acts and documents in the archives at Regensburg—their availability for future research is surely only a matter of time. This brief biography is only a preparation for what is to come, not a substitute in any way. It is only a brick for the bigger building.

Wherever the author has incorporated his own observations and comments, in the quotation of someone else's words, excepting in the case of footnotes or remarks contained in parentheses, these observations are noted by the word: author.

Part One

Therese Neumann's Life Story

Foreword

In our day, many people avoid using the word "Savior" for
the Second Person of the Blessed Trinity. It seems too childish,
or perhaps too pietistic, or even too old-fashioned. Therese Neumann—on the unanimous admission of all who knew her—was a
childlike and pious soul all her life long. Excepting for formal
prayer, I have never heard her use the word Jesus Christ or
even Lord. She always spoke of Him only as Savior.

Now the word Savior is nothing more than a translation of
the name Jesus. "You shall call his name Jesus (that is Savior)
because he will save his people from their sins" (Matt. 1, 22).
Therese Neumann's preference for the word Savior as opposed
to all the other names for Jesus is the result not only of her
own subjective feelings, but also of her inner spiritual orientation. Natives and visitors at Konnersreuth seemed to feel this
about her, and, letting themselves be drawn into the experiences
to which they were a witness, they seemed to realize that this
expression is a statement not only of the power and grandeur
of God, but also of his love and gentleness: they began to use
the word Savior themselves. Whenever Father Naber, whenever Gerlich and others who have known her well, whenever
the author of this volume comes to speak the name Jesus, in
his own language, the word that involuntarily rises to his lips
is Savior. So it will be throughout this volume.

Home and Early Years

Therese Neumann was born between Good Friday and Holy Saturday, April 8-9, 1898, just before midnight. She was born in Konnersreuth, the first of eleven children (one of whom died shortly after birth), the daughter of Ferdinand and Anna Neumann. On Easter Sunday, April 10, she was received into the community of the Church in Holy Baptism. The general poverty of her birthplace, situated between the Fir Mountains and the Bohemian Forest, and the poverty of the Neumann family in particular, with its many children, forced them to a sense of economy and yet a freedom from real want that we can scarcely imagine: they were spontaneously grateful for all God's free gifts: for the warm rays of the sun, for the changing harmonies of color in the skies and on the countryside, for bird and flower. Therese was intelligent, industrious, and pious. Her report card upon leaving school, April 30, 1914: Religion and practical instruction, very good; reading and arithmetic, "almost very good"; composition and penmanship, good. Over-all grade—very good. It was not till later in her life that Therese admitted having had a face-to-face vision of our Savior at her First Communion, as well as her repeated experience of sacramental Communion without a priest.[1]

Her earnest wish and desire was to go to Africa as a nursing sister to the colored missions, as soon as her brothers and sisters

---

1. Gerlich makes no mention of this. See the section on sources.

were grown up enough so that she would no longer be needed at home. She had already made her plans for entering the Missionary sisters of St. Benedict at Tutzing.

Then came the First World War. Her father was drafted and during a furlough he presented her with a little picture of St. Therese of Lisieux that he had brought back from France. Back at home, the women had to do the work of their absent husbands. Therese was healthy and strong and hired out as a working girl for a farmer in Konnersreuth in order to earn her own keep and save a little money from her meager wages for the support of her brothers and sisters. She was so well developed that she could do the hardest man's work. In 1916 her employer and his hired man were drafted; Resl (as they called her) and two of her sisters who had meantime taken employment were entrusted with the management of the entire farm. "In the fields I was always happy: knitting, sewing, needlework, embroidery—that I didn't like." But she never lost sight of her desire to be a missionary sister after the war.

Sickness

But things worked out differently. On March 10, 1918, a fire broke out at a neighboring farm. As one of the strongest hands in the neighborhood, Resl took her position on some bales of hay where she took the full buckets the others were bringing from the well and quickly raised them up over her head to her employer who poured them over the side walls of an adjoining shed that was threatened by the flames. It was here that she met with an accident that determined the course of her later life: she dislocated her spine. Subsequent medical examination revealed that the second and third lumbar vertebrae had been wrenched out of normal position. The consequent pressure on the central nerve fibre (a pressure which could not be relieved) caused great pain in the small of her back and soon developed a "furry" feeling in the legs, lack of balance, and serious falls, until, as a result of the progressive laming, Therese was forced to become bedridden in her parents' home. Attempts to alleviate her condition in the hospital at Waldsassen were fruitless. This was in 1918.

By mid-March of 1919 her condition was further aggravated by total blindness. Therese's suffering and anxiety over her chronic ill health were now increased by her realization that not only would she now be economically dependent on her family, but would also be costing them a good deal of time and work, caring for her as an invalid. Her father and mother never complained: they bore up under her misfortunes just as Resl herself, with great resignation. They made every effort to secure proper medical attention, but no improvement in her case was to be hoped for. These seven years of patient suffering and sickness matured Therese for what was to come. She bore up under it all with a truly heroic disposition.

From the time she received the holy picture from her father, Therese had been drawn to Sister Therese of Lisieux on account of her child-like piety and the fact that she had the same name as the great Saint Theresa of Avila. Frequently, and then daily, she said the prayer of the Little Flower to the Child Jesus— the prayer was printed on the holy card. When she prayed these words on April 29, 1923, Therese dreamed that someone was touching her pillow. She woke up and could see again. At once she pounded her cane on the floor of her room. When her sister Crescentia came running in, Therese recognized her voice first. Her outward appearance had changed greatly; during the more than four years of Therese's blindness she had grown quite strong.

Therese said nothing about her cure; she wanted to save the good news for her mother. Her mother came and wanted some proof of the sudden cure; she held out a bouquet of white blossoms at which Therese's expression visibly changed. Zengl had to go and call Ottilie. Resl greeted her with the words: "My, but you certainly have gotten big since I last saw you!" Her father had been to Neustadt that day, a Sunday, in order to see a nature healer. He had visited the man several times before, offering him his entire week's earnings if he could supply some successful treatment for Therese. Since the medical efforts had thus far produced no effect, the family had been turning everywhere for help. Now, as he was coming home that evening, Therese immediately noticed that her father had grown grey; but she did not mention this fact in his presence. Therese could also read once more, even the fine print in the diocesan prayer book. The joy in the Neumann family was great indeed.

Her lameness, however, had not been healed; the spasms grew worse. Muscular contraction set in on the left leg and her left foot was drawn up against her right thigh. As a result of this contortion Therese had to lie on her back; this led to extensive bed sores on her back and legs. Her left foot was infected for a half year and the ankle bone was exposed. The doctor feared he might have to amputate the foot (April, 1925). Therese's mother was unalterably opposed to this and refused to allow the operation. In the beginning of May, Therese had her sister Zenzl put a rose petal that had touched the relics of the Little Flower at Lisieux, into her bandages. Shortly afterwards, she experienced an improvement in the foot. The bandages were opened and the rose petal had stuck fast to the infected area, which was completely healed. Fresh skin had grown over the wound.

On May 17, 1925, Resl's parents (they were downstairs at the time) heard her suddenly cry aloud in pain. They ran up to her room and, to their utter consternation, they saw Therese staring fixedly and almost blankly straight ahead. Suddenly she sat up without any help. Her mother, completely amazed, lifted up the blankets and saw the left foot straight and healthy alongside the right foot. Therese called for the priest, but when they asked her if they should send for him, she made no answer.

They sent for Father Naber. When Resl came to herself, he asked her, "Resl, where have you been?" Instead of answering him, she said: "I can sit up now and even walk." They would not believe her, but when she asked for a dress, they gave her one. She got up and took a few steps, to everyone's amazement.

Father Naber asked her once again where she had been; when everyone else had left the room, she told her confessor that she had seen a beautiful light, and a voice came out of the light asking her if she wanted to be cured. She answered that it was all right with her whatever came from God, that he was the one best fitted to decide. The voice asked her once again: "Wouldn't you like to be able to get up this very day and be able to walk and take care of yourself again?" She answered, "I want anything and everything that comes from God. I am happy with all the flowers and birds, or with any other suffering he sends. And what I like most of all is our dear Savior himself." Then the voice told her: "Today you may have another little joy. You can sit up; try it once, I'll help you" (Gerlich I, 87).

Then she was lifted up by her right hand, with "something cold," and felt a very painful tearing and wrenching on her vertebrae, and a "crack, as when something snaps in two." (This was when she uttered the cries of pain that brought her parents rushing up to her room.) Then the voice continued: "You can walk, too, but you still have very much and very long to suffer, and no doctor can help you, either. Only through suffering can you best work out your desire and your vocation to be a victim, and thereby help the work of the priests. Through suffering you will gain more souls than through the most brilliant sermons." Who this "I" was the voice did not say.

These closing words prompted Fr. Naber and another priest to whom he related the whole incident to look in Scripture. They also thought of St. Therese of Lisieux, since the cure had been worked on the very day of her canonization. The words were actually to be found in her own autobiography, the Sixth Letter to the Missionaries.

In the days that followed, Therese's parents wanted her to rest as much as possible and spend her time at home. On the feast of Corpus Christi, June 11, 1925, in response to her incessant pleading, she was brought to Church for the first time since her accident. This was the first time she had left her home since 1918. Half the town gathered in the market place and accompanied her joyfully and triumphantly home. Her father escorted her on his arm, and she used a cane in her other hand. The wounds had been suddenly healed on May 17, and the underlying physical causes of her lameness had all been cured, but her legs were still weak after so many years of being constantly bedridden.

On September 30, 1925, the anniversary of St. Therese's death, Resl lay awake at night and prayed the litany in her saint's honor. The same wonderful light appeared again, and the friendly voice told her that she would now be able to walk without any outside help. As soon as she fully realized the meaning of this new communication, she got up—it was after midnight—and walked around in her room for a quarter of an hour. When the Church bell rang next morning, she went downstairs to greet her astonished parents, and then ran off to Church.

On All Saints' Day and All Souls' Day, in 1925, Therese spent almost all day and night in Church, reciting the indulgence prayers. As a result, she caught a severe cold, and once more she was confined to her bed. A constantly increasing agony of pain soon developed, accompanied by a very high fever. The doctor was finally called in, on November 13, Dr. Seidel. He diagnosed the case as acute appendicitis, about to rupture, and asked for permission to operate at once at the Waldsassen hospital. Then Resl asked St. Therese for help, to keep her mother from crying so, and had them put the relic over the part that hurt. First she had asked the priest whether or not such a request was tempting God. He said there was nothing wrong in asking St. Therese to help her, without an operation, if this was God's will for her. Therese Neumann, who was writhing in her agony of pain, as the priest described it, began to pray: "St. Therese, you can help me. You have often helped me before. It is all right with me, but you can hear how my mother is carrying on."

As she rose with a beaming countenance, the light appeared to her again, and the voice began to speak (Gerlich): "Your perfect resignation and joy in suffering pleases us. And so that the world will know that there is a higher plan at work, you will not need to be cut open now. Get up and go right to Church and thank God. Right away, right now. But you will still have a lot to suffer and you will be able to cooperate in saving many souls. Your own self you will have to constantly keep dying to, more and more. And keep your childlike simplicity, always." Together with the appearance of the light, a hand had reached out towards her. Her father got the impression that Therese was holding out her hand as if she wanted to grasp something but could not reach it; he asked his daughter what it was. She answered that a hand had appeared to her and that she was trying to take it in her own, but she could not. It was a slim, white hand (Gerlich I, 98).

When Resl came to herself, she related the words she had heard and ended up by asking for her clothes. Her mother refused, saying that it was too dark and cold outside. But Therese remembered the words: "Right away, right now," and insisted on having her way; finally the priest took her side and they let her go. Resl got up and went to the Church, completely free of pain and fever. The whole incident, from the doctor's first arrival until her return from the Church, took place within one hour, from 6 to 7 p.m. The following night, the swelling and infection went down all by itself.

"The next day about noon, Father Naber and Therese Neumann took the bus to Waldsassen to Dr. Seidel's sanitarium; he was amazed to receive their visit. He explained that it did occasionally happen, but only very very rarely, that the infection in acute appendicitis empties out naturally through the intestines. But even then the cure of such a patient required more time than normal operation and recovery" (Gerlich I, 99-100).

We might well suppose that Therese Neumann frequently reflected on the words addressed to her both on May 17 and on November 13, and that she was perfectly resigned to the sufferings that had been predicted. She was prepared for suffer-

ing. This attitude is evident already in her very mature answer
to the question of May 17, when she was asked if she wanted
to be well or not: "Everything is all right with me, living or
dying, whatever our dear Savior wants; he knows best." An
even clearer evidence of this resignation is to be found in the
letters which she wrote from her sickbed after she had been
healed of her four years' blindness, in 1923 (see page 110).
Already in these years she knew how to find meaning in suffering. Since she could not be of any service to the human community by her activity, she hoped at least by offering up her
sufferings to be a useful member of the Mystical Body of Christ.
From that time onward, her whole life's history must be regarded as heroic.

From her later life, there is one more sudden cure to report.
On August 15, 1940, during a vision of the Assumption, all
the results of a serious stroke suddenly disappeared. A fuller
account can be found on page 178.

° "Dear Sister! The dear Savior has restored my eyesight. Greetings from,
Your friend, Therese."

Lack of Nourishment

Therese's nourishment intake dwindled constantly in the course of her sickness. From Christmas of 1922 onwards, Therese Neumann could take only liquid nourishment because of a strained throat muscle; from August of 1926, and then only on the insistence of her mother, she was able to swallow only two spoonfuls a day. From August onward, she no longer had any feelings of hunger, and instead experienced a strong aversion for food and drink. From Christmas of 1926 she finally refused to take any further nourishment at all. She took only Holy Communion, every day, and a few drops of water. From September of 1927, Father Naber no longer even gave her water. From this time until the end of her life, a period of 35 years, Therese Neumann lived without taking any food and any drink: daily Communion was her only nourishment.

Christ's sacramental presence was never dissolved in her, except for some particular cases and circumstances; it remained until shortly before the next Communion. She could always feel when the sacramental presence was ended and she always immediately insisted on receiving Communion again.[2]

Therese's lack of nourishment intake has been attested to under oath, by Therese herself, by her parents and family, and by all the people who knew her during those years. "Frequently she would be spending the whole day with the workers in the field or in the garden, under the hot summer sun, and didn't have the least feeling of thirst" (Ferdinand Neumann, brother). Besides these witnesses, all the people at whose home she was a guest, often for several days at a time, throughout the course of her life, can also vouch for the fact that she never took any nourishment. In such a matter it would be a very serious error to consider the solemn statements of people

---

2. Report of Fr. Naber; examples can be found in the Second Part, See pp. 194 to 214.

who were bound by conscience as false, and thereby insert an element of deceit or illusion into the testimony. It is wrong to question the credibility of people who respect the truth and are known to have been witnesses to the facts, without overwhelming indications to the contrary, particularly when their statements have all been in perfect harmony on such a wide variety of details.

In connection with her lack of nourishment intake, her elimination processes were also suspended. In a previously unpublished journal kept by Fr. Naber, we find the following entry, under date of March 1, 1931 (Second Sunday of Lent): "Vision of Christ's Transfiguration." [3]

Therese related how she had left hunger and thirst behind on Mt. Tabor on the occasion of her first vision of Christ's Transfiguration (August 6, 1926). I had the impression, on that occasion, that from that day on she experienced no need of food or drink, surviving on liquids alone. Solid food she had not tasted now since the beginning of 1923. From August 6 of 1926, up to Christmas of this year, Therese would take some liquids only on the insistence of her mother—the amount would probably amount to about a cup a week—but even then she was inclined to vomit after drinking the liquids. She used to fool her mother, as she tells it, by pouring the liquids over some flowers, but they always died.

"From Christmas of 1926 until some time in September of 1927, she would take only an occasional sip of water, together with Holy Communion; since I felt that she could not otherwise swallow the particle of the host that I insisted on limiting her to—on account of the great difficulty she had in swallowing, due to her sore throat muscles. From September of 1927 she never had even the least bit of food or drink, not even a drop of water. Her elimination processes, from bowels and bladder

---

3. The Second Sunday of Lent and the Feast of Christ's Transfiguration on August 6th have the same Gospel selection (Matt. 17, 1-9 — Author).

—they had been growing more and more infrequent (a little water every two weeks and every two or three months, accompanied by the greatest pain and effort, a little fluid matter from the bowels)—completely ceased at the beginning of the year 1930.

"Whenever she was asked what she lived on, Therese would say, quite simply, "On our Savior." She meant "On Holy Communion." Her life was a literal fulfillment of the Lord's words: "My flesh is meat indeed and my blood is drink indeed." The fact that Therese lost all sense of hunger and thirst precisely on the Mount of Transfiguration, upon contemplation of the glories of the Lord, reminds me of the words of Scripture: '*Satiabor cum apparuerit gloria tua.*'"

(Thus far the account of Father Naber, March 1, 1931.)

Special Proof of Her Lack of Nourishment Intake

In July of 1927, with her own full consent, and with the permission of the Ordinary of Regensburg, Therese Neumann was strictly and painstakingly under observation by a medical commission and four Mallersdorf nurses, who were under oath. The Ordinary had first of all determined, from competent medical sources, how long a man could possibly be expected to live in a normal manner without food and drink; and, especially with reference to drink, he had been advised to observe a test for eleven days. He finally decided upon a 15-day period.

During these 15 days, there were always two of the four nurses, under oath, watching Therese very closely, in strict observance of their ecclesiastical and medical instructions. The water she used to rinse out her mouth was measured, all her eliminations were strictly controlled and measured. Samples were taken from the blood that flowed in her stigmata, and it was chemically examined. She was subject to all manner of very painful personal examinations, which, in her opinion, were not understood as being part of this thorough medical observation, without even being asked for her prior consent. It was ten years before she had the courage to describe it all even to her own parents.

During the course of the observation an attempt was also made to blind her by using carbon arc lamps with a light intensity of 5,000 watts during her normal Friday ecstasies. The lamps were focused directly on her open eyes during the ecstasies. If Therese had been normally sensitive to light, these experiments would have easily been the cause of serious visual disturbances for the once blind patient. But Therese did not even blink. This was proof that she was completely insensitive to external influences when she was in a state of visionary contemplation—as later proved to be the case.

There is no evidence of even the least nourishment being taken during these fifteen days. At the beginning of this examination, her weight was 121 pounds, but after her Friday sufferings it dropped to 112.5 one time and 115 another time, and at the end of the examination, without benefit of food or drink, it was once again 121 (Cf. Mayr, p. 243). Therese Neumann's average weight did not appreciably decline during the later years of her life; she appeared to grow even stronger in proportion to her age and general development.

During her Friday sufferings she always lost considerable weight (up to 8 pounds, as verified by the above account): but by the middle of the following week, and without any nourishment at all, her weight was always back up to her normal average. Such a marked deviation in weight could hardly be regularly absorbed by a normal organism even with the help of special nourishment, at least not repeatedly and not without causing some severe disturbances.

The Third Reich took official notice of the fact that Therese required no nourishment, at least to the point that, during the days of food rationing, she was issued no ration cards stamps. The officials further honored her request to substitute a higher ration of soap coupons to meet the increased demands of her extra Friday wash. This arrangement was continued, even after the war, until the end of rationing.

Stigmatization and Passion Visions

The cures already mentioned and the gradually dwindling need for nourishment which had developed into complete lack of nourishment intake by Lent of 1926, were suddenly joined by other new experiences: the beginning of her historical visions and—connected with her visions of Christ's sufferings—the impression of the stigmata. Therese had had no conception of the very nature of stigmatization, and had no wish to experience it. As she admitted years later, this would have seemed to be "sinful arrogance" on her part. Against the possible charge of autosuggestion in this area, we thus have Therese Neumann's own declaration.

On the night of Thursday, March 4, 1926, and on Friday, March 5 (she was lying on her bed without any particular thoughts and without realizing that it was Thursday), she suddenly saw Christ kneeling in the Garden of Olives, and heard him praying. Suddenly he looked at her ("He took a good look at me"). In the same moment she felt such a sharp pain in the region of her heart that she thought she was going to die. At the same time, blood began streaming down from the spot that hurt. She kept on bleeding lightly until noon Friday. On the next two Fridays the vision was repeated, this time lasting until the scourging and crowning with thorns, and the side began bleeding again. On Passion Friday, March 26, 1926 she also saw the carrying of the cross and a fall beneath the cross.

The wound in her heart bled and a wound broke out on the back of her left hand.

On Good Friday of 1926 (April 2) she saw the whole way of the cross for the first time, from the Mt. of Olives to the final moments on the cross. They sent for Father Naber, and he came with the oils, in order to give her the anointing of the sick. He reports (April 21, 1926): "... When I visited her on Good Friday afternoon with another priest, she was lying there like an image of the martyrs, her eyes all caked with blood and two streaks of blood across her cheeks; she was as colorless as a corpse." It is characteristic of Resl that she always tried to hide her wounds—on Good Friday the right hand and both feet also began to bleed—from her parents and Father Naber; with the aid of her sister Kreszenz, she managed this even on Good Friday.

On Holy Saturday, when they changed her bedding, she was no longer able to hide the wounds. Her parents were excited and hurried off to Father Naber. He brought Holy Communion early Easter Sunday morning. When he left he told her parents to take the bandages off her hands and feet and ordered Resl to show her wounds. She was very much opposed to this plan, but she obeyed his orders. "Seeing this unexpected sight, Father Naber was extremely impressed and excited, as were her parents the day before, and it was a long time before he managed to fully recover his normal equilibrium" (Gerlich I, 105). Early that Easter Sunday morning, Therese had had a vision of the risen Savior.

An immediate attempt was made to cure these wounds, first with home remedies, and, when these produced no effect at all, with medical help. Dr. Seidel, from the Waldsassen sanitarium, examined Therese and established that the wound in her side was 3⅕ centimeters long. He admitted that he had never seen the likes of it throughout the many years of his professional practice. He applied medication and bandaged the wound, but the more he tried to heal it, the worse the pain grew. The hands and feet also began to swell. Therese, who lay

there in such terrible agony that three men from Konnersreuth who saw her said: "What a terrible ordeal!" now asked
the Little Flower for a sign. If the wounds were to be healed
with the medication, that was all right with her, but if not,
then would the dear Lord please make her understand what
she was to do next (April 17, 1926, 2:00 a.m.).

Shortly after her prayers, she felt a loosening of the bandages. She awakened her sister "Zenzl" who was sleeping in the
same room, and asked her to take off the bandages. Then she
pounded on the floor with a cane (that was a prearranged
signal for waking her parents in their bedroom downstairs) and
showed them the wounds. They were bright red in color, but
a transparent growth of skin had formed over them, so that
from that time on Therese could wash her own hands and
feet. Dr. Seidel was astonished at the unnatural behavior of
the wounds; they were neither inflamed nor infected when left
alone, but any medical treatment resulted in the most agonizing
pain. He decided to make no further attempts to treat them.

Her natural shyness and her desire to avoid sensational
curiosity-seekers led Therese Neumann to wear fingerless gloves
at first, and later clothing with long sleeves, so that the evidence
of her wounds could only rarely be observed. This desire to
shun all curiosity and publicity was characteristic of Therese
for the rest of her life. To the best of her knowledge, no one
but the doctors, the nurses, and those of her family who helped
to care for her had ever seen the wound over her heart. A
theology professor, who had uncovered the wounds while
Therese was in ecstasy, was not allowed to visit her again.

As far as she was able, Therese made every effort to avoid
being photographed by people she did not know, and even
acquaintances whom she allowed to take her picture for a keep-
sake on some special occasion, had to promise that they would
not make the pictures public without her express permission.
The stigmata remained until the end of her life. On her death
bed, the wounds in her hands were covered.

The report of these events spread like lightning throughout

the world-wide press. A storm of sensationalism broke loose in Konnersreuth, most unwelcome to those who were immediately connected with the phenomena, and the public interest grew in leaps and bounds when it gradually became known that these Passion ecstasies were repeated every Friday (excepting for feast days and festal seasons). Many were attracted to Konnersreuth by the simple and righteous needs of their own soul; many came out of mere curiosity and were so moved that they went to church, to pray and receive the sacraments. This strengthening of faith and confidence in God was one of the missionary lessons of Konnersreuth, as were all the difficulties and self-denial that this little circle of Christians, particularly Father Naber and the members of Resl's immediate family, had to face, and were so happy to face, in terms of the material sacrifices required to make the crowds of visitors at home, as well as the great expenditure of psychic strength and patience.

Therese Neumann's
States of Consciousness

1. Ecstatic States

a. State of Visionary Contemplation

In the last chapter we already spoke of one mental state that departed from normal human consciousness; the ecstatic state of visionary contemplation. This ecstatic state has other forms as well, which we shall discuss below.

b. State of Elevated Calm

Anyone seeing Therese Neumann in this state, which occurred after almost every reception of Holy Communion, and also appeared between her visions of suffering, to give her strength, would get the impression that she was already joined to Christ in full beatitude. She would sit up straight and almost immobile, her eyes closed, her face happy and relaxed, and, unlike her reaction during the visions, she could be spoken to. Her responses were lively, clear, and so tactful that many people who spoke with her under these conditions were deeply moved and even shared her serenity. The knowledge that Therese displayed in these conversations went far beyond the limits of what she was familiar with in normal circumstances. On these occasions she would speak something close to High German.

She would completely look through the person of her listeners, and many times she would make personal references to her listener's earlier experiences, always without reproach, and more or less to establish confidence, or she would answer a question before it had even been put into words and asked. It was possible to discuss problems with her that concerned the welfare of her own soul or other people's souls, as well as projects that were designed to promote the service of Christ; frequently she would even give some very personal bits of advice.

But it was wrong—it frequently happened this way—to interpret these bits of advice according to the individual's own desires. If the questioner was really convinced of the supernatural source of this knowledge, and realized that the answers came from a transcendent principle, then he also had to realize that the answers might very well involve an event that transcended the limits of human life and death (Gerlich's fate, for example): finally it is important to recall that this was not a case of oracular orders, with the giver of the oracle assuming full responsibility for the consequences, but rather personal advice, and that when it was taken and followed, the man who received the advice remained just as responsible in the eyes of the law and conscience as if a friend had given him normal advice.[4]

---

4. For example, when a social project — homes for the poor working class people — was spoken of as desirable and highly laudable in an answer Therese gave in such a state of elevated calm, this was not equivalent to saying (Cf. *Bildpost*, No. 13—March 31, 1963, "Durch den Rat der Resl in den Konkurs?") that the sponsors of the movement could simply go ahead and obligate themselves to heavy financial burdens. The project in question certainly did have idealistic goals, but it also had the unhappy consequence, as is all too clear today, of having been begun some ten years too soon. As a result, the sponsors were unable to get the official

Her answers obviously did not come from her natural knowledge or normal state of consciousness. Father Naber frequently discovered further explanations of her visions by conversation with her in this state. When she returned to normal consciousness, Therese had no recollection of what she had spoken of, and not infrequently the orders and advice she gave were worded as a reminder: "Tell Resl that she is supposed to write to such and such a person, or do such and such a thing, etc." Everyone she spoke to in this state was addressed as "*Du*" (the familiar German form of the second person pronoun). After some time, Therese would return to her normal state, generally with a great relaxing yawn.

Visitors were always careful to observe proper reverence for the Blessed Sacrament which Therese had received shortly before, when she was in this condition, and the conversations were always in keeping with the situation. Improper questions were never answered. This state of elevated calm could also be interrupted or broken. When she was asked once whether she would be canonized or not, her answer was: "Be happy that your foolishness is a sort of Purgatory" (Professor Wutz's account). In general, the circle of those who were admitted to her states of elevated calm was very limited. Father Naber always used to ask whether a given person was to be admitted— particularly when he was to leave a person alone with her in her ecstatic state.

As an example, let us once more take a case which clearly shows that the knowledge of ecstasy and the normal state of

---

permissions they needed to finish construction. This was a formality that the sponsors should obviously have checked into *before* they invested their securities unless they were willing to risk heavy loss. It would appear that the people concerned with the promotion of this project had been interpreting Therese Neumann's answers subjectively and thus they had assembled a party of sponsors in all good faith. When the people in Konnersreuth became aware of incidents such as this, questions of this kind were no longer permitted during Therese's periods of elevated calm.

her knowledge were completely distinct from each other, and thus her personal opinions could never influence the answers she gave in a state of ecstasy. Father Naber allowed me—it was in 1931—to accompany him as he brought Holy Communion to the Neumann home and address some questions to Therese in her state of elevated calm on subjects which I was commissioned to investigate and happened to be working on at the time. (Cf. later "The Straight Way.")

On the way to her home we heard the church bell tolling. I did not know who had died, and it seemed improper to ask the priest while he was carrying the Blessed Sacrament. But after Therese had received Communion, Father Naber left the room. I was alone with Therese in her state of elevated calm and had an opportunity to state my questions. After a lengthy conversation she said the following: "Benigna is right when she says that every man receives according to the measure of his trusting. Just look how the Professor has been helped." She then described at great length how Professor Wutz had been helped and concluded with these words: "Last night a man died. He was a good man, but he never wanted to learn anything about our Savior. The priest went to see him, but without success. Then Resl went to see him and he straightened everything out (that is, he received the sacraments—Author), and last night he died suddenly. My, how he has been helped!"

I was wondering why this last bit of information was directed to me. Then her ecstasy quickly passed and she returned to her normal state, and Father Naber came back into the room. Resl greeted him with the question: "Did that poor old lady finally die last night?" "What poor old lady?" asked the priest. "You know," Resl answered, "N.N." [I have not bothered to give the woman's real name.]. "No, no," he said, "She hasn't died yet." "Well, then," Resl continued, "who was it? There's no one else sick around here and I heard the church bells tolling right before you got here." Then Father Naber told her the dead man's name. She was astonished and kept repeating: "Is that so! There was nothing wrong with him, was there?" At this point I told them about what Resl had said in her ecstatic state and realized that she knew things in her state of elevated calm that she was completely ignorant of in her normal state, even things that completely contradicted her knowledge in the normal state. Later I discovered that the words she had quoted about trust were from something once said by Benigna Consolata Ferrero.

c. "Prayer of Quiet"

A further form of the ecstatic state is the "prayer of quiet" in which the soul, united with God, loses all sensation of time. This state was also verified in the case of Therese Neumann. I quote two examples from Father Naber's account.

"April 12, 1931 (White Sunday): During Easter Week Therese had no real pain in her wounds; she only felt that something special was there. On White Sunday evening, the pain started again, and the following night she was privileged to suffer in reparation again, this time for the non-Christian father of a First Communicant. In Easter week, when Therese was unable to go to church, she still saw our Savior every day at home, at the time of consecration, and quickly passed from a brief vision of the Savior into the prayer of quiet, which was the source of even greater happiness for her (she was in the state of elevated calm) than the vision of the Savior."

"May 24, 1931 (Pentecost Sunday): The previous night at about one o'clock, Therese had slipped into the church [they had allowed her to keep a sacristy key so that she could go in and out of the church for visits, even after the doors were locked, without being seen or disturbed—Author] and sat down on one of the choir stalls. There she had a vision of our Savior and passed into the prayer of quiet. It was not until they came to ring the Angelus that she slipped quietly away. Her longing for such quiet times alone with the Savior takes away all her fears, and makes her feel happy." [The length of time involved on this occasion was at least four hours. — Author]

d. State of Rapture

A special and very lofty form of the ecstatic state, which is only seldom verified in experience, was called by Father Naber the "state of rapture." This state came over Therese Neumann whenever she saw something particularly beautiful, for instance, a particularly colorful sunset or an overpowering landscape. (An example: When Therese was on her way back from a visit with Bishop Gregorius Schmid of Grünick in Chur, going across the upper Alps and she saw the Rhone glacier on her right, sparkling in the sun, and at her feet the upper reaches of the Rhone valley. Source: Professor Wutz.)

This state, according to Father Naber's report, "also came upon her when she heard a sermon about the love and goodness of the Savior. She would then sit or stand quietly, smiling happily, her hands crossed over her breast. On such occasions, as she explained it herself, she could no longer think, she could only feel the greatness and power of God and the Savior." The 93-year-old Father Naber says today that, in his opinion, "such a state of ecstasy is a little bit of heaven, and that that is the way the angels and saints will look when they contemplate God."

In his Notes we find the following entry under the date of June 1, 1932: "New spiritual visions have made their appearance since Christmas of 1931. Therese says that she cannot describe how these actually are. They come upon her whenever, in her visions, she sees the divinity of our Savior at work in his public life, in his speaking and activity; from consecration until communion, whenever she is privileged to see the Savior coming down from heaven onto the altar in all his glory, at the consecration time; and at other times too, whenever she is particularly conscious of the grandeur and power and beauty of God. Then her breast swells, she opens her mouth and her eyes and gasps for breath, or she sits quietly, smiling happily, her hands crossed over her breast. From time to time such a fullness of 'joy in the Lord' takes hold of her that she can hardly contain it; as she puts it, she can feel a certain measure of the grandeur and power of God and the Savior. This state visibly transcends the prayer of quiet, in which, without any discursive thinking, she simply loves the Savior and takes her joy in him; but this state is also to be distinguished from the elevated state of calm in which the Savior transposes Therese's body and soul into the sweetest calm and quiet, without disturbing their normal functioning in the least, excepting occasionally when Therese is to be the medium of transmitting some special message."

2. Childlike Prepossession

In addition to her normal states and the various forms of the ecstatic state described above, there was still another state, that of childlike prepossession regarding what she had just seen in vision. This state always immediately followed a vision or came between one vision and another. In this condition, Therese had a five-year-old's capacity for expression, although she still had an adult capacity for thinking. In this state she could be questioned about the content and course of the vision she had just had, whereas otherwise, in her normal state, she was reluctant to discuss it.

In this condition, she could never, throughout her whole life, recall the same visions from one time to the other, not even in the case of her visions of the Passion that were regularly repeated. From one vision to another, she could hardly believe that Jesus was crucified; from one vision to the other she took Judas for one of Jesus' friends, because he kissed Jesus, etc. But on the other hand, she found it easy to remember the same persons and places that she had seen in other visions. For instance, she recognized Bethlehem, in her vision of the slaughter of the Holy Innocents, as the place where "they wouldn't take the Mother in a few days ago." (Four days earlier she had had a vision of the Holy Family looking for a place to stay in Bethlehem: this strange association of two distinct visions makes us wonder, despite ourselves, whether this slaughter of innocent children is not to be viewed as a punishment for the hardhearted-ness of their mothers — Author.)

She also recognized the Jordan, in one vision, as the place of Christ's baptism, as the "running water where the three crossed with their people (the Three Kings)." Paul, whom she had seen in one vision violently arguing his point in the Apostolic Council, she referred to as the "Foot-stamper" in other visions; John the Baptist she called "the man with the animal-skin clothes"; Mary Magdalene "the handmaid"; Pilate as the "Idra-uminet" (dialect German for "I don't trust myself"), etc. The Blessed Virgin was always "the Mother," St. Joseph was always "the good man," John the Evangelist was "the young man." Those to whom she related her visions gradually learned to recognize these names and used them in asking her about her later visions.

3. Normal State

In her normal state Therese Neumann appeared to be intelligent, and it was possible to talk about many things with her and discuss a variety of problems, particularly since her acquaintance with such a variety of visitors from all over the world constantly kept broadening the circle of her knowledge.

In this normal state there was also evidence of normal human failings. In an effort to paint a true picture of this woman, these aspects must not be left out. Therese had a lively temperament; and people of such temperament naturally tend to be hasty in their conduct (to call it sudden temper would be a rather harsh judgment in Therese Neumann's case), that is, not able to conceal a sudden start of anger. As a result many visitors got the impression that she was distant and easily became impatient; many even thought she was without love.

But let us have a better look at the circumstances; who would not be a little impatient when year after year she had to listen to strangers, dozens and even hundreds coming and telling her their problems—and what problems!—every day. When people started running after her in the house, into the garden, even into church, when they came in busloads and brought their cameras and hid behind every corner and turn in the path to take her picture, when they tried to snap pictures even in the midst of a conversation. Who could possibly blame Resl for being somewhat unfriendly towards visitors that chased her into the sacristy when she was busy dressing the altars—the church doors were closed then—and disturbed her work, and having them asked to leave? Who could blame her for turning people away when they were forcing their way into her garden, frequently armed with telescopic-lense cameras, while she was tending to her flowers—for the Church once again?

Such an unyielding temperament and impatient reception obviously turned away almost everyone, earnest people and sensation-seekers alike. But when Therese noticed that a visitor had a real problem she could help him with, she was glad to give him her full attention, at any time of the day that it was possible to speak with him, and, once contact had been established, for as long a period as necessary.

Unfortunately, she soon realized that many visitors who were most eager for a chance to talk with her, had only one familiar answer to her questions about why they came: "We just wanted to see you," and Therese was justifiably angry when she heard this. Still, she kept working patiently against this principal fault of hers, her temper: "Whenever I have been hasty, I always went back quickly to our Savior, so that he could take it all away," and in another place she promises, "Savior, help N.N. and all next month I will be very sweet to all my visitors." Giving comfort and practicing the works of mercy were her whole being. We shall have occasion to discuss this further in the pages that follow.

Inner Life

The most exceptional element that stands out in Therese's normal state is her childlike pious character, her constant and intimate union with our Savior, an awareness that her visitors more or less strongly felt and shared; this was further evidence of the strength and joy that springs from being close to God. Many people came back from Konnersreuth with far different interior dispositions than when they went there; some for only a short time, like the seed that fell upon stoney ground (Luke 8, 13-15), but many were influenced for the rest of their lives. The accounts that follow in the Third Part of this book are a confirmation of this statement.

Therese Neumann had to suffer in almost super-human proportions. Her bodily sufferings, the constant sense of pain from the stigmata (excepting during Easter week), the bodily torments she experienced together with Christ every Friday, the pains and suffering occasioned by her works of reparation—these were all further intensified by the suffering within her soul: cooperation in the sufferings of our Savior and his Blessed Mother, sharing the sufferings of the sick, sharing in the sufferings and mental anguish of her visitors. People mocked her; "Savior, forgive them," was her answer whenever she heard a curse word.

Even in the great piles of mail that she got every day there were many insults, some of them anonymous. If they were directed against her personally, she paid no further attention to them. At least she paid no outward attention to them; inside she might have been very much hurt. But there were also many insults directed against God and the saints and sacred things. This disturbed her greatly. On an insulting postcard that she received in December of 1930 the traces of tears are still to be seen. The contents of this communication are quoted below, in an effort to show what kind of abuse gradually found its way into Konnersreuth.

"To Miss Therese Neumann, halfway a saint, at Konnersreuth, street address not needed, world-known. From: an impatient devotee. Postmark: Würzburg-Bamberg, December 14, 1930. Now then! How is Resl? Why don't we hear anything from you or about you any more? Are your miracles all over with? Don't you still have a little sore on your hand, your side, and another little sore on your foot and still eat in advance so you can go hungry better? What? Aren't you going to have a baby on Christmas Eve, the way the Blessed Virgin did; you can always say it was the Holy Spirit or the Angel Gabriel. Now, that would really be getting somewhere; then you'd be called a saint and pretty soon you'd be lifted up into heaven.

"Or you might not live in the end at all; we keep hearing that you've died. Until next Good Friday maybe, that's quite a while; by then maybe there'll be parliament elections again; now that'd really be something for you, you could run all over the place and hunt for voters. But do something different at least so we keep hearing about you. My wife has been asking me for some time now, 'What's with this Therese anyhow?' And whether it's true that the chaplain is really your sweetheart.... Greetings from — Your Franzl."

This coarse attack upon the honor of the Blessed Virgin obviously occasioned much more pain for Therese than the vicious attacks upon her own person. In Father Naber's journal, during the next few weeks, we find constant references to her acts of reparation for the sender of this mocking letter. In a state of elevated calm she revealed that this man had been bragging drunkenly about his wit in sending the postcard a few weeks later and then, while he was leaving his home, he lost his balance on the way out of his house and fell over a chair, with serious consequences (which are then described in individual detail). He was a joiner and lived near Würzburg; earlier he had been employed in a bank. He had no faith, but in the course of his recovery from his accident he began to think more seriously, especially after he developed a serious case of pneumonia and pleurisy in addition to the dislocations he had suffered in the fall; he realized the connection between his accident and his blasphemies and Therese promised that he would be converted; but she would have to suffer along with him.

Therese Neumann never liked to read things written about

herself, if she ever even read them at all. Still it was unavoidable
that she be consulted for an explanation of those cases in which
people were making attacks against her character. She accepted
all this with patience and resignation, but it was easy to see
that she was hurt when she had to answer the inquiries of
well-meaning people who wanted to know the truth about false
information and accusations that had been made against her—
not to mention the newspaper stories about the secret birth of
her illegitimate son, fathered by a fakir— answering such charges
as that her condition was the result of hysteria or a thirst for
publicity or suggestion or autosuggestion, if not outright deceit
on her part.

Even within Catholic circles, strange to say, much slanderous
information was spread about Therese: in 1950 a book in Ireland
(it was translated into German, at Einsiedeln, in 1953) written
by Hilda C. Graef, in which, in addition to several other mis-
leading and erroneous accusations, the author claims that, in her
Friday sufferings, Therese Neumann was covered with menstrual
blood (in the German edition this one accusation was not retained).[5] After the publication of this book I had an opportunity
to speak about it with Therese and she said, "I would be quite
willing to stand before our Savior with Hilda Graef and say,
'Savior, look at us, you know us, and I have no need to be
afraid of you.'"

Even in her early childhood Therese's deeply interior religious attitudes were well developed. There are classes of human
souls and human spiritual life whose innermost essence we
naturally tend to shrink from examining. But it seems to be
God's will that we should have an occasional insight into the
"heart chambers" of his specially favored ones, as an example
for our own inspiration. Thus, in her autobiography, the Little

---

5. Hilda Graef visited Konnersreuth only once and went to see
Therese Neumann at a time when Resl had very little time to spare and
was thus somewhat short and blunt in her dealings with the authoress
— Author.

Flower was ordered to lay bare the deepest secrets of her soul. And there are many similar examples from the lives of various saints.

Therese Neumann's death, and the argument developed above, make it possible to cite the following entry from Father Naber's diary without being accused of indiscretion: "December 21, 1930. Therese spoke of the past: 'When I was still a little girl, and had not yet received our Savior, I used to run to our old Pastor and put my hand softly and tenderly in his hands, and be happy in the thought that these hands, early this morning, held my dear Jesus and now I can touch them too. This always made me happy and I always ran back home full of joy, happy with my dear Jesus. I often used to think that if I were a boy I would be a priest too; then I would be able to hold Jesus in my hands. But if I had ever become a priest, our Savior would have had a bad time of it: I would have held him so tightly in my hands and kept caressing him all the time and people would have said, 'He never gets Mass over with, the slowpoke.' But they could say whatever they pleased, it was all for our Savior. And when I get to heaven, then I'll never have to go away from our Savior, I'll always have enough time for him, and I'll never have to leave him: I can love him always.' "

In connection with the above let me quote two statements that Father Naber noted as an expression of Therese's in her state of elevated calm: "Love is everything, love is the source of all virtue, even humility." And the other: "The Savior will one day judge us according to our love."

Therese's prayer life can hardly be described in any great detail. In this we are dealing with a subject that the individual himself is not inclined to bring out into the open and which someone else, particularly a layman, can hope to understand, to some degree, only on the basis of what shows on the outside. This was my impression: Therese Neumann's whole life was so bound up with God that her whole day was a prayer. She prayed the liturgy of the Church, the rosary, and several prayers from her prayer book, the diocesan prayer book, *God's Praises*—as far as formal prayer is concerned. Her Book of Psalms was always at her side. The way of the cross she found impossible to pray; it was too strong a reminder of her regular Friday sufferings. These reminders were so vivid that she regularly fainted.

Her impulsive ways, even in her prayer life, could be recognized by the fact that when she found something in her prayerbook that she did not like she simply crossed it out. She once showed me a book that she had received as a present that very morning from a priest who had visited her, the author of the book. The prayer read: ". . . Let us one day come to you in your kingdom": but the following words had been crossed out: "and glorify us then in the measure that we worked on earth to promote your greater glory." I had to laugh at this show of temperament on her part. But she said: "Well, it's true. That would really be something, that would—giving orders to our Savior and telling him how he's supposed to reward us!" These simple words, straight from her heart, show that, without really being aware of it, Therese had the same attitude that our Lord meant to inculcate in his parable of the laborers in the vineyard (Matt. 20, 1-15).

But much dearer than these prayers out of books were her personal prayers, her "talks with our Savior," whom she constantly asked for advice and kept before her eyes in everything she did. The prayer of praise was her favorite form of personal prayer: You are so kind, you are so good, you are so mighty, you are so forgiving. And she kept finding new forms of praise. Every time she carefully arranged a flower on the altar—and there were often hundreds of them in a single day—she would think: "You are blooming for our Lord," or "Be beautiful for our Lord." When her birds sang, she heard the praises of God in their singing.

She did not like to talk very much about thoughts like these. But in her conversation, in an attempt to cheer up the person she was talking to, and bring him into like "tune with God," she would frequently say a word or two that let people know what she was feeling. It is generally recommended for Christians to begin their day's work by a good intention every morning, so that everything they do throughout the day will be a prayer to God. Therese's daily regime was on a somewhat higher plane: hers was a "spiritual breathing." Her whole life was one long prayer.[6]

---

6. In this respect, cf. the account on p. 135 by Father Leo Ord: "Therese Neumann's Inner Life."

Charisms

Preliminary Note: The charismatic life of Therese Neumann cannot be treated in the framework of the chapter on her "normal states." There is a constant intermingling of all the states described above. If the reparatory suffering and awareness of the Eucharistic presence generally fall within the limits of normal states of awareness, the other charisms all pass over into the ecstatic states. That is why there is a separate chapter for them.

Charisms often referred to in the Greek plural form charismata, are the special gifts of the Holy Spirit's grace (*gratiae gratis datae*), some of which are mentioned, for example, in Mark 16, 17-18. In Therese Neumann's case the presence and activity of several such gifts can readily be verified. Stigmatization and lack of nourishment are already special signs, and the ecstatic states which we have described above were a still higher progression in mystical life. But still higher faculties came into play. It is my intention to mention them here, grouping them all together, as a sort of overall view, and then illustrate each of them with appropriate examples in the second part of the book. Thus, the present brief biography is limited to only a very few illustrations.

1. Visions

a. Historical Visions and Tableaux

After the first visions of Christ's suffering began to reoccur regularly in the Lent of 1926 (see page 32), Therese continued to have visions throughout her life, corresponding to the feasts and seasons of the Church year. Most of these visions were historical, based on the Gospels or the Acts of the Apostles, or from the Lives of the Saints, and sometimes they were also tableaux, for example: the Child Jesus transfigured in glory on a cloud, or the Holy Innocents transfigured into glory, or the Poor Souls, generally people she knew, begging for forgiveness, or the same poor souls, or other poor souls glorified in heaven after their time of purgation—particularly on All Saints' Day. Other visions transcended time and matter and passed over into the realm of the *invisibilia,* for instance, the vision of the Fall of the Angels. This visions was so impressive that Therese begged our Savior not to show her anything like it again. The vision was never repeated. The other visions kept repeating year after year, and the visions of Christ's sufferings were repeated even within each year. There were so many visions in the course of a year that it would take a special book to list and describe them all. Such a book is being contemplated: it will appear following the publication of the present work. (There were often as many as a hundred visions in the course of the Church year.) Among the most significant are her visions of Christmas, Three Kings, Transfiguration, Resurrection, Pentecost, Ascension, Assumption, and, most striking of all, the vision of Christ's sufferings, which was distinguished from all the others by the fact that in this vision Therese was privileged to suffer together with Christ, internally and externally.

In her visions, Therese would frequently see particulars that rounded out the accounts as sketched in the Gospels and frequently made the precise Gospel stories much more picturesque and striking. For example, the passage in Luke's Gospel (4, 28-30), that describes how Jesus was almost cast off the cliff in Nazareth. Therese saw, with fright, how they were ready to throw Jesus over the edge of the cliff into the precipice below, and then, with triumph, how he turned around in the air and walked back through them, so that the people were all amazed and shrank back from him. This picture gives us a better understanding of Luke's words: "But he passed through their midst."

Afterwards, when Therese was discussing this vision in her normal state, I asked her if our Savior had been passing through the air or hovering over the surface of the ground, and she answered with a smile: "Hovering naturally. The same way he walks on the water [Matt. 14, 25-26, vision on the former octave day of the feast of SS. Peter and Paul], not taking steps on the surface of the water—with the stormy up and down of the waves that would be impossible—but sort of hovering over the water." Interrogation would always produce particular details that rounded out the full picture of each vision.

In this ecstatic-visionary state, Therese was insensitive to all external influences and could not be spoken to. She would experience these visions with all her senses. Not only did she see; she also heard and could repeat what she had heard, frequently in the same intonation and in the languages it had been spoken in. Aramaic for example: "*Shelam lach, Miriam* . . . (Hail Mary)," the Angel's greeting. Or Greek: "*Zosin*" (They are alive! —the exclamation of the multitudes after John the Apostle had raised the two dead men to life in Smyrna—a locale where Greek was spoken). French, as well: "*Mon Dieu, je vous aime* (My God, I love you)"—words of the Little Flower shortly before her death. In one vision (June 13) of St. Anthony of Padua (who was visiting a friend near the northern borders of Portugal), she heard a remarkably nasal language. Later on, Father M. Strauss (Kinding), who had been a missionary for many years in Brazil, came to see her accompanied by a Brazilian doctor. When she heard them speaking to each other, she exclaimed: "I've heard that language before! That's what they were speaking with St. Anthony." (Professor Mayr's account)

She had, of course, never heard or studied any of these languages. Suggestion on the part of her visitors is ruled out by the fact that, during her visions, that is, on the first occurrence of hearing these languages, the visitors could not possibly know what she had seen or heard. There are also many examples of visions in which her interrogators expected something quite different from what she actually reported; for example, in her vision of Lourdes, which she reported without using any correct French at all. Her account was taken down phonetically and upon examination Professor Wutz and Dr. Gerlich were able to determine that the words corresponded to the Pyrenees dialect.

Her sense of touch and feeling was also at work in her visions. I happened to be driving home with her and Father Naber—it was 1952 or 1953—on January 13, in the evening, after we had been to see the Bernadette film, and in the car she had a vision of Christ's baptism (Gospel for the day—Commemoration of Christ's Baptism). We stopped the car as soon as we noticed that she was having a vision. In spite of the fierce cold, Therese loosened her shawl, and then quickly tightened it about herself again: "Heavens, but it's cold now," she exclaimed, "and just a moment ago the sun was burning so hot on my back."

There is also evidence of the fact that her olefactory sensation was at work. For instance, in a vision of the Blessed Virgin's empty grave (on the Feast of the Assumption), she dilated her nostrils and drew a deep breath. Afterwards she said that it smelled like the sweetest flowers. On the other hand, during a vision of Lazarus' being restored to life, while they were opening the grave, she made gestures of revulsion and turned her nose away and tried to exhale the foul smelling air ("Lord, he already smells").

Together with the charism of visions we listed two other groups of visionary experience which also appeared together with the historical and tableaux visions: visionary participation in Church feasts and her visions of particular judgment.

b. Visionary Participation at Holy Mass and Church Feasts

Therese Neumann frequently enjoyed the grace of being privileged to attend Mass in the parish Church at Konnersreuth, in vision, on occasion when her suffering made it impossible for her to leave her house. On such occasions she would see, not only the progress of the Mass, but also the Church decorations and the behavior of the people attending Mass. She always mentioned when there were any flowers that needed arranging or if the children had been a little bit unruly.

These visions were not limited to the times when she was actually present in Konnersreuth. She was regularly privileged, when staying in Eichstätt, to enjoy a visionary participation in the Sunday Mass in her parish church at home. On the first occurrence of these visions, Professor Wutz took down the sermon preached in Konnersreuth, as Therese reported it to him, and then asked Father Naber to tell him what he had preached about that morning. The notes he had taken and Father Naber's report of the sermon were in perfect harmony. What is more, Professor Wutz was able to advise Father Naber that here and there the flowers were beginning to wither, and once again Father Naber was able to verify the facts as reported by Therese.

In December of 1930 Father Naber happened to say Mass in Berlin and Therese, from Konnersreuth, was able to attend the services along with him. After he had returned, she described the Church to him and told him she noticed that he had a hard time getting the tabernacle open (cf. the account on page 182).

She also had a visionary participation of great Church feasts. For instance the opening of the Holy Year in Rome, the Promulgation of the Dogma of the Assumption of the Blessed Virgin Mary into heaven, the special celebrations in Lourdes, Lisieux, and Fatima, Catholic Days and special ecclesiastical congresses. At the World Eucharistic Congress in Budapest in 1938, her brother Ferdinand from Eichstätt, without her knowledge, had managed to make his way to Budapest (in those days it was legally almost impossible to leave Germany and participate in such a congress). In Budapest he met Cardinal Kaspar from Prague, who was a friend of the Neumann family, and through him managed to secure permission to take pictures in the immediate vicinity of the Apostolic Nuncio, Cardinal Pacelli. When he got back home to Konnersreuth, Resl told him, before he could even open his mouth: "You were in Budapest, I saw you there, you were always right out in front." (Ferdinand Neumann's account)

In the same way she was privileged to participate in the solemn closing of the World Eucharistic Congress in Munich in 1960. Every year on Easter Sunday she was, in vision, among the crowds who gathered in St. Peter's Square in Rome, to receive the Papal Blessing *urbi et orbi*. In this visionary experience, she was able to meet three popes: Pius XI, Pius XII, and John XXIII. The last time she had this vision was the year of her death, Easter Sunday, 1962.

c. Visions of Particular Judgment

Whenever Therese Neumann had been present at a death bed, and frequently even when she had not been present, a little time after the person's death, she would see his soul rise up from his body in a luminous form similar to the actual living body of the deceased; then she would see Christ coming to judge his soul. Christ was always accompanied by luminous souls, people who had been particularly close to the deceased during life, and had meantime been privileged to enter into eternal bliss. As a general pattern, these visions of particular judgment took the following course: the judgment vision all followed the same general pattern; the Savior would appear with his glorified body, radiating light, accompanied by incorporeal luminous forms, and look lovingly at the face of the deceased. The deceased's face would become more or less luminous and he would immediately understand that his present state was the result of absolute justice. The judge and retinue then disappeared, while the soul remained waiting there alone.

In some cases Therese would see the Savior at the very moment of a person's death, smiling with a heavenly light; the soul of the deceased would then become luminous and capable of following our Savior. She herself would then cry out in ecstasy,

"Come! Come!" and reach out her hands invitingly. In these cases she always experienced an exceptional joy afterwards.

She never witnessed the damnation of any human soul (the deceased to whom she had been called had always lived in the faith or else they had effected their final reconciliation with God before death). (Besides, it is only logical to suppose that our Savior would not let anyone on earth witness the mystery of such a terrible judgment.)

Father Naber, in his complete listing of Therese's visions of particular judgments, includes the following account: "The Savior looks at the departed soul with a friendly smile and returns into heaven, with his retinue; the departed soul can follow in this company if it has been found absolutely pure, or it will remain sadly where it is, until its longing for heaven has fully purified it. That will be their purgatory."

2. Vicarious Sufferings and Reparation

Reparation for both the living and the dead occupied a great part of Therese's activities throughout her life.

Vicarious sufferings and sicknesses are those sufferings and sicknesses which are undertaken for other people; the person who was originally affected recovers his health. Sufferings of *reparation,* on the other hand, seem to cooperate with Christ's redemptive work to remit sins; Therese was privileged to undergo such sufferings generally in connection with sins involving blasphemy or irreverence to sacred things. In reading Father Naber's notes in this respect we are surprised to discover that her sufferings were frequently a reparation for priests—a source of grace and help for those who occupied a position that was so close to our Lord. In this presumption, as in every other opinion expressed in the book, we must always understand the necessary proviso that the Church will eventually recognize the events that took place at Konnersreuth as really the work of God.

3. Knowledge of Relics, Consecrations, and Blessings (Hierognosis)

Therese Neumann, especially when she was in the state of "prepossession," enjoyed the faculty of recognizing relics, consecrations, and blessings. When she was in this state, if someone touched a relic against her finger (generally her eyes would be closed), she would react negatively, or not at all, if the relic was not genuine or only a facsimile. But if it was genuine, then she would react positively and enthusiastically and frequently also tell where it came from; sometimes adding that "it was only touched to the relic." The same was true of blessed objects.

With persons too, who would touch her finger, she could immediately tell whether they were priests or laymen. Whenever a priest gave her his blessing, even if he was not standing in her field of vision, she would register the experience and the impression it made on her with a friendly smile and say: "Something from our Savior." Even when the person happened to be standing right in front of her, when she was in this state, she still would not be aware of his presence, since her visual sense was not operative in this state of "prepossession." Only her sense of hearing and her "inner feeling" reacted on her surroundings.

4. Knowledge of Hearts - (Kardiognosis)

In describing the state of elevated calm we already pointed out that Therese, after her stigmata, was able to look into the inner heart of the person who was speaking with her. The person's thoughts and intentions were all known before being spoken, and even when they were not actually spoken at all. She also had a privileged knowledge of the individual's former life. But references to such knowledge, excepting for very exceptional cases, were made only when the individual was alone with Therese. Thus the only proof for the exercise of this faculty could come from personal experience, or from the strong emotional reactions of people who had experienced this knowledge, or from sharing such experiences in conversation afterwards. Even in the childlike state of prepossession Therese possessed this faculty, whenever a person touched her finger.

5. Appearance in other Places - (Bilocation)

Although she was still present in Konnersreuth, bodily, Therese was also present to other people at the same time, in other places. According to what she said in a state of elevated calm, it was her guardian angel that took her form and represented her in these cases (For examples, see p. 193).

6. Elevation

Cases have been reported in which Therese Neumann was no longer subjected to the law of gravity, and, in a visionary and ecstatic state, would hover free of the earth. In his book, Huber (p. 120) notes that "elevation" occurred "a few times" in Therese Neumann's life, but offers no verifiable evidence of any given occasion. Two cases, however, are related with full details of locale and personalities involved. The one case, described by Boniface (p. 126), is supposed to have taken place in the monastery church of St. Walburn in Eichstätt. The Abbess, Maria Benedicta von Spiegel, suddenly noticed that, at consecration time, Resl had fallen into a state of vision; she had been sitting lower than the Abbess at the beginning of her vision state but now she was about the same height. Later examinations proved that she had been elevated about one step from the floor. The second case was observed during a vision of the Assumption on August 15, 1938, in the Steyler monastery in Tirsehenreuth. See p. 177 for details.

7. Mystical Relationship with the Blessed Sacrament

a) In her normal state Therese was aware of the presence or nearness of the Holy Eucharist.

b) When she received Communion in her ecstatic state, the Sacred Host entered into her body without being swallowed first. The host was no longer visible after it had been placed on her tongue (Mystic Communion).

c) There were also verifiable instances of "tele-communion" (without the intermediary of a priest to bring the host).

d) The species of bread remained undissolved and undigested in her body until shortly before the next Communion (with the exception of Advent season and some particular instances).

8. Mystical Relationship with her Guardian Angel

Therese Neumann lived in close relationship with her guardian angel. According to her own report, she ascribed many of her special enlightenments, even in her normal state, to his direct insights into persons who spoke with her, warnings about some who were too curious, inspired advice to give her questioners, etc.

This contact would not be anything extraordinary in itself, even though it occurred in a very elevated state in Therese Neumann's case. Frequently enough even a person who is not privileged to partake in any mystical graces, can, to the degree that he believes in and honors his guardian angel, experience a sudden inspiration, a counsel, or consolation, which he realizes did not result from his own deliberations, but just "came to him."

In Therese Neumann's case this relationship with the guardian angel developed into mystical proportions: she actually saw her guardian angel. In her state of prepossession she saw him as a "luminous Man," as she expressed it, standing at her right side. In this same state she also "saw" other "luminous Men" standing at the right hand of each of her visitors, without seeing her visitors themselves, corporeal luminous bodies, which she occasionally described as "mightier than her own." This was not properly speaking an act of seeing with her bodily eyes—in the state of prepossession they were generally closed—but a perception with the inner eye, similar to the way one "sees" things in dreams, without the medium of bodily eyes.

According to her own account, as recorded in Father Naber's notes, in the second part of this book, her guardian angel used to do all kinds of things for her: he took over the task of representing her presence in the cases of bilocation described above, he helped her in the performance of projects she would never have been capable of herself, he defended her when she was being harassed by the devil. In the eyes of normal men like ourselves, much of this must seem improbable, but who is really in a position to measure and weigh the powers that lie behind the veil of our senses? In the history of mysticism there are many such cases.

Gerlich once reported that, when he was at Konnersreuth working on Therese Neumann's biography, he met a woman (she was visiting in Konnersreuth too) who used to foretell something every day that actually happened that same day, so that he almost no longer knew quite what to make of Therese Neumann. But he mustered his courage and presented his doubts to her when she was in a state of elevated calm. This was the answer he received: "You must know that Satan still has some strong mystical powers left too, which he uses to lead people astray, insofar as our Savior allows him to." After hearing this explanation, he began avoiding that woman (Oral account to the author).

9. Mystical Relationship with the Poor Souls

Therese Neumann's relationship with the "Church suffering" was not limited to what she experienced in her visions of particular judgments. Individual souls were sometimes allowed to appear to her and beg for help. Thus she once saw a priest whom she had known in her youth, Ebel, who asked her to "pray for me; I baptized you and gave you your First Communion. Later on I punished you without asking you, because

I thought you were in error: I didn't know that your behavior was based on your extraordinary visions." Therese accordingly began to pray especially for him and soon had the great joy of seeing him among the blessed.

It was in connection with this apparition that she first told Father Naber about the vision she had at her First Holy Communion: she had seen our Savior himself coming to her, and as a result, no longer able to contain herself, she had not followed all the prescribed ceremonies properly. Father Ebel, as she testified under oath on January 13, 1953, before a solemn ecclesiastical commission, also bound under oath, "took it [my behavior] as a sign of distraction on my part and reproached me for it the next day and punished me in front of all the other children."

Many other cases could be cited as well, in which the poor souls came to beg her to help them reach eternal happiness, and then, later on, appeared to her once more to thank her. Most of the time it was not for any particular soul that she prayed as such; the soul would be selected without her knowledge, but would then appear to her afterwards to thank her and tell her who he was. The persons involved had frequently been dead for some time, and thus Therese herself had never known them personally. In her state of prepossession, Therese referred to the poor souls as "little beggars." The Second Part of the book contains a few more examples of this relationship.

A Decade of Affliction - Medical Investigation and Observation

In 1927, when the desire for a positive proof of Therese Neumann's claim to be sustained without nourishment was expressed to her parents, the immediate reactions were very negative. The refusal was based on grounds of reverence for the phenomenon. Even Therese's spiritual director asked why it was that upright men of irreproachable honesty, possessed of a conscience that was deeply rooted in religion, should not be willing to believe the account, even without medical observation. Her parents felt that they might have been really thankful if the doctors had shown a little more interest in their daughter during her years of sickness, instead of showing all kinds of medical interest now that Therese no longer needed a doctor's help. Friends of the Neumann family, called in for advice, pointed out that it was a serious offense against the fundamental rights of human freedom for the doctors to try to force a free citizen to undergo a clinical observation, a person who "had never done any harm to anybody, and never asked to be either visited or looked at in any way" (Gerlich, I, VIII).

Despite all this deliberation, Therese Neumann herself, and later her father too, who throughout his entire life made it a very serious obligation for himself to watch over his daughter's welfare, both gave permission for a medical observation, which was to take place in their own home (the episcopal ordinary of Regensburg was instrumental in persuading them)—but only after they had been promised (it was only an *oral* promise) that this would be the only such demand made upon Therese.

This consent to a positive scientific proof of Therese's lack of nourishment intake involved a risk of death (cf. Mayr, p. 249) if her claim were a lie, or at least—since she would be forced to break her fast in order to survive—the risk of losing her reputation all over the world. This would have resulted in severe ecclesiastical and secular penalties. But considerations such as these were not even weighed in Konnersreuth; the people there had no doubts as to the outcome of such examinations. Therese's attitude was always the same: "Savior, you have started things here; you can also bring them to the conclusion you desire; we leave it all to you." The results of the medical observations of July 14 to 28 have already been described (cf. p. 28).

Due to a breach of professional medical discretion, the story of this clinical observation (it had not proved to be restricted, as things actually developed, to the single phenomenon of Therese's lack of nourishment intake) were published in the *Munich Medical Weekly* (No. 46, 1927) as a scientific report, by Professor Ewald. Even granting the claim that this publication was intended only for the instruction of the medical faculty, it is still an undeniable fact that it did involve a complete violation of professional medical secrecy and ethics, in that the whole report was published, without the patient's personal consent, as a special, general brochure, in an effort to call world-wide attention to the story of Konnersreuth.

It was advertized under the title "Die Stigmatisierte von Konnersreuth ... (The stigmatic of Konnersreuth, report and evaluation of clinical observations by Dr. G. Ewald, university lecturer in Psychiatry, etc...). The outcome: The stigmata is most probably genuine and qualified by psychic experience of an hysterical nature. But we have no explanation, nor can an explanation be found, for the month-long fasting, accompanied by a gain in weight. Science recognizes no miracles, no interruption in the network of causality. In this case only a medical observation in a neutral clinic can shed full light upon the facts."

It appeared to be necessary to recall the facts and content of this brochure, first in order to clarify the one-sidedness of the "evaluator's" point of view in making the presumptuous statement that "science recognizes no miracles, no interruption in the network of causality" (such a position, serving as the basis of a medical evaluation that was intended for the Catholic Bishop's office, involves a point of view that is sharply opposed to the Faith and teaching of the Catholic Church and furthermore presumes too heavily on the definition of a word like "neutral"), and secondly, by calling attention to the violation of professional secrecy involved in this unwarranted and unauthorized publication of the results of a medical observation, to explain why the Neumann home had to be more closely guarded than ever before against admitting a second attempt to establish strict medical proof for Therese's lack of nourishment.

The Bishop's office at Regensburg made the following statement on October 4, 1927: "The extensive and thorough report of the sanitarium director Dr. Seidl, together with the evaluation of the University Lecturer Dr. Ewald, combined with the two daily records kept by the four nurses involved, forces us to the conclusion that the originally desirable but unfeasable medical observation, to take place in a hospital or clinic, would not result in any greater success. Signed: Schlegmann, Vicar General. Wührl, Secretary." The above cited medical report was a powerful incitement and, constantly repeated, it quickly began to wear down resistance in certain circles which had originally been satisfied with the first medical observation.

The years that followed, accordingly, saw an increase in the demands for a second clinical observation—and, in like measure, an increasing show of opposition. The reasons behind this opposition, already mentioned above, were further strengthened by the fact that several bishops now strongly advised the Neumann family not to have Therese brought into the clinic a second time. People also felt that, if this observation were to take place in a clinic operated by Catholic doctors and with only Catholic Sisters on the nursing staff, even if all those concerned were bound by oath, as actually was the case, the results were not likely to be recognized by other secular clinics and thus the demands for clinical observation would never end.

Meantime, National Socialism had taken over the political world of Germany. The clear opposition between Konnersreuth and the "Third Reich" escaped no one. Not that Therese Neumann had ever taken an open or public stand against the Nazi Party. Nor did her private conversations, barring the possibility of some treachery on the part of her visitors, offer tangible grounds for any attack. The higher echelons of the party were opposed to any course of action that would stir up public notice, now that Konnersreuth was a word to be reckoned with throughout the world, and such action would certainly have alarmed the world press—although local Gestapo officials constantly tried to bring matters to a head (by house searches and official investigations).

The official party line found it a more logical objective to let Therese Neumann sink into oblivion as quietly as possible. Everything positive was left to the past, to be forgotten, and Konnersreuth came up only occasionally, for derogatory comment, in the columns of a few obliging newspapers. The demands for "consignment to a clinic" kept coming up. There was no further talk of "observation," or "examination," but always "consignment." Opposition to these demands (as in the case of Professor Aigner) could easily involve the "Schwarze Korps" for any public expression of dissenting opinions.

However, a new medical corroboration of Therese Neumann's lack of nourishment intake, and thus the confirmation of the miracle involved, with consequent profit to the Catholic Church, certainly did not correspond to the intentions of the new political powers. When the demands for "consignment in a neutral clinic" continued to be repeated so forcefully, people began to fear that the examination in such a clinic might easily be arranged to produce an "agreeable result" for the new political philosophy. The Neumann family was advised that "when we have succeeded in getting her into a clinic, then we will take care of the proper injections." [7] These statements needed to be taken very seriously. The "injections" used in the concentration camps show how feeble a concept of moral responsibility was entertained by the Nazi party.

In this extremely difficult situation, two representatives of the Regensburg Cathedral Chapter suddenly appeared, Döberl and Wührl, on December 10, 1936, and produced a decree of the Holy Office in Rome, stating that Therese Neumann was to submit to a second examination in a clinic, and that otherwise she would be officially declared *"inoboediens"* (disobedient). The background and the motivations and even the persons responsible for the initiative behind this decree appearing at such a turbulent moment, are too manifold and too personal to be treated in this book.

Regarding this important decision and the further development of the Konnersreuth - Regensburg relationship I was fortunate enough to get the following information during a visit to Konnersreuth after the Second World War (Sept. 20, 1949), in a conversation between Father Naber, Therese Neumann's father, and myself—Therese later joined the conversation herself.[8]

---

7. Cf. Radlo, pp. 160 ff.

8. The story behind the conversation was as follows: I had given Cardinal Faulhaber a copy of Aretin's recently published book: *Fritz Michael Gerlich, a Martyr of our Times.* Cardinal Faulhaber had personally administered the sacrament of confirmation to Gerlich in a private ceremony after his conversion, which resulted from his experiences in Konnersreuth — Professor Wutz was the sponsor — and on that occasion he had delighted Gerlich by saying: "The Apostle Paul once heard a voice that told him to walk the straight way; and so I say to you, Michael (the name Gerlich took in confirmation), walk the *Straight Way*" (*Geraden Weg*, in German — the title of Gerlich's newspaper).

Paging through the book, the Cardinal saw the chapter entitled "Gerlich and Konnersreuth." He mentioned that he often wondered if

"Just imagine my surprise and fright; me an insignificant country pastor, and here is a decree from the Holy Office!" said Father Naber. "I called Therese and she announced that she was perfectly prepared to follow the directions. Then I called on her father, but he was opposed to the idea." The objection might well be made that Therese was old enough (she was 38) to answer for herself without her father's consent. But her father always took the position—throughout his whole life, in fact—that "As long as Resl is living here in my house, she has to follow my orders; otherwise she can go somewhere else." Therese herself admitted the validity of this point of view and always obeyed her father's will. Her father also opposed the plans on the grounds that, as he put it, "The reverend Vicar General (Dr. Schlegmann) had promised him," after the 1927 investigation that there would be no further clinical observations. "I told the gentlemen there: When I promise someone something, I stick to it, and when the reverend Vicar General promises something, he's got to stick to it too."

This position was not widely accepted however, and there

---

history would not someday reproach the Bavarian Bishops for not having found a satisfactory way to arrive at a second positive proof of Therese Neumann's lack of nourishment intake. Therese herself was not to be blamed, he added, since she was perfectly willing to submit to authority. It was only her father that they could not come to terms with. When I asked him if I should discuss this matter in Konnersreuth, now that the tenor of the times had changed, he answered that he would not like to stir up this knotty problem once again, that it had been resting quietly for over a decade. It was just that he was somewhat concerned about his own responsibility to history. I was very much impressed by these words of the Cardinal's; they are evidence both of his good will towards Konnersreuth and also of the fact that his holding back in earlier years had been prompted by loyalty. I was confirmed in my own desire to perhaps be of some service in healing this breach, by speaking of our conversation at Konnersreuth and getting the most exact possible information on the events of the last years before the war, direct from the first-hand sources.

was a heated argument. They even reminded him of the Scripture passage: "But if he does not listen to the Church, then let him be as a heathen and a public sinner." After a rather lengthy discussion her father said he would give his consent, provided that a few stipulations would be strictly observed, particularly, that there would be no experimentation of any kind. He said he would have to think it over a good bit and inform the Ordinary of his stipulations. To me he said (in 1949): "I kept thinking that you've got to talk this over with some experienced friends and ask them for their advice and not just give right in."

Already in previous years there had been some discussion of investigations and some doctors who were friends of the family had expressed the fear that in an attempt to establish the authenticity of the stigmata they would make incisions, and if Therese appeared to be taking no nourishment orally, they would try to feed her through her stomach or by "injections" (that was her father's word for intravenous feeding), and use plaster of paris on her, etc. "and then," said her father, "when she has so many experiences and states that leave her all but unconscious, we were supposed to hand her over to a clinic! In the Third Reich, where no one knew what was ever really going in a clinic!"

When Professor Wutz heard about the whole affair, he was quite happy that those concerned had not given their unqualified assent; he advised Therese's father on the stipulations he should make. The principal conditions were (as her father tells it): 1. There was to be no experimentation; Therese was only to be observed. 2. Therese's mother or one of her sisters was to remain and be quartered in the same room with Resl throughout the whole course of the observation, in an effort to keep any experimentation from taking place on the stigmatic. 3. There had to be a strict guarantee that Resl would be allowed to receive Communion every day. These conditions were immediately forwarded to Regensburg. In answer, the Neumanns were quickly informed that no such qualifications would be admitted.

"Well," said Father Naber, "you can well imagine the embarrassment in which I now found myself. But then I got a letter from Archbishop Kaspar of Prague, saying that he had to go to Rome for a consistory and wanting to know if he could do anything for us. I thought: here is God's hand in the whole business, and I wrote him everything that had happened and begged him to see what he could do for us. He must have presented our case exceptionally well, because I soon got a reply that there was a further decree from the Sacred Congregation stating that Therese Neumann was to be *invited* to a new observation, without any formal order at all.

"In December, 1937, I received an unannounced visit from a University Professor from Rome acting on orders from the Holy Office; he questioned us all most urgently: Therese her father and mother, and me. Obviously I neither can nor will tell you anything about what was said or asked, or later written, in an official capacity, during this visit. But in a private conversation I asked him, 'Doctor, you surely realize, from your knowledge of the history of mysticism, that many people who have been favored with this special grace have been harshly handled by the Church, and later beatified.' He was apparently quite satisfied with his visit and, as he was leaving, and passing by the Neumann house, he gave it his blessing.[9]

"From that time on, we never heard another thing about Therese entering a clinic for further observation, either from Rome or from Regensburg. For a long time I always hesitated to ask her about this during her state of elevated calm. Particularly in this case I wanted to avoid every possible danger of giving rise to the impression that there had been any discussion of such orders. Because if a person did not believe in the extraordinary occurrences that were going on here, any statement

---

9. The Professor's name — I made a photographic copy of his calling card which Father Naber had kept — was Monsignor Giuseppe Graneris, Professor at the Ateneo Lateranense, in Rome — Author.

made by Therese in this state would not have served as an argument for, but rather against, whatever she was saying.

"But when her father's conditions had been refused, and I was left in this great embarrassment and doubt, I did once ask her what was to be hoped for from further investigation. This was her precise answer: 'If our Savior could have expected anything for his own glory or the help of my fellow men, he would have insisted on such an observation a long time ago.' I wrote this later to Bishop Michael." Thus far Father Naber.

Bishop Michael Rackl, of Eichstätt, once happened to hear, during these days, that Mr. Neumann was in the city. He sent word to him that he should visit the bishop's house: the Bishop himself was ill at the time and could not leave his bed. Therese's father was most reluctant to accept the invitation and protested that he could hardly go in to see the bishop while he was in bed. He had to be talked out of this attitude. When he finally did visit the bishop, the bishop assured him that there was no further question of trying to force a second clinical observation. (Account of Professor Mayr, Eichstätt.)

Cardinal Preysing of Berlin, formerly Bishop of Eichstätt, who was familiar with the whole story from this date, expressed the following opinion: "I am glad to see that her father had such a hard head. Because one doctor would never believe another, and neither would one clinic ever believe another."

Pope Pius XI was discussing the report of a Milanese Theologian (Dr. Gemelli)[10] with Cardinal Schuster, and when the

---

10. P. Agostino Gemelli, O.F.M., M.D., was in Konnersreuth in 1928 as the envoy of the Holy Father, Pope Pius XI. Formerly a doctor, he turned to theology and became professor and rector in the university of Milan. According to the report of a Dutch medical paper, he had thoroughly checked Therese Neumann, not only as a theologian, but also as a physician, and made the following statement: "I have completed my investigations with the greatest possible care and I now make the very definite statement that there is no trace of hysteria in the subject, and that her extraordinary states are unexplainable on the basis of any natural

conversation came around to the subject of Konnersreuth, he said, "Leave the child in peace." To another bishop, who told Father Naber about the conversation during a visit to Konnersreuth, he once said: "Konnersreuth we will leave in the hands of Divine Providence."

Father Joseph Lechner, S.T.D., canon law professor, in a public letter and official opinion, stated that in Church law there was no possible grounds under which a layman could be forced to undergo a lengthy period of observation in a hospital and declared as *inoboediens* (disobedient) in case he should refuse. Quite the contrary, the Code of Canon Law was a protection of the fundamental human rights of freedom and personal inviolability.

The above-mentioned professor of chemistry and biology, Franz X. Mayr, in a thorough evaluation (see page 226) explained, in very simple and fundamental terms that, for the formation of a competent medical opinion on any of the problems involved, the clinical observations of 1927 were already more than sufficient.

Her father—and I can vouch for the fact—always had the same answer throughout his whole life: "As far as I'm concerned, they can put Resl in a glass house somewhere and observe her all they want, but they're not going to experiment around with her."

Father Naber's opinion, as he expressed it in connection with the conversation of September 20, 1949, was as follows: "If one of the people from the Regensburg Cathedral chapter or one of the professors were to come here, we would certainly do everything we could to make his work easy and give him

---

scientific explanation." When Pius XI had seen the report, he gave his apostolic blessing both to the author and to Konnersreuth. Therese Neumann was able to feel the blessing, and told Father Naber about it. A few weeks later they received the printed notice from Rome that the Apostolic Blessing had indeed been conferred on them (under date of May 3, 1928).

every opportunity to conduct a clinical observation whenever he wished."

Now that the Third Reich has fallen, many things have changed. The conditions set by Resl's father no longer appear to have been so improper and inacceptable. But the initiative for such a visit could hardly be expected to come from Konnersreuth; such a move could easily be wrongly interpreted. Father Naber also expressed this genuine concern during our last visit together in 1963. The adverse reactions of many people who had visited Konnersreuth during the last 25 years had been the cause of much suffering. All the more reason, accordingly, for the intense joy that was felt at the words of Archbishop Michael Buchberger who happened to be passing through Konnersreuth on a confirmation tour. He said approximately the following: "Over the last 25 years our people have had a lot to suffer, and in their afflictions the people also came to Konnersreuth. Here they found either higher meaning to their sufferings or went away much comforted. Others found the Faith, and still others were strengthened in their faith." These words were the source of both surprise and great joy. "But still," said Father Naber, "when all is said and done, no one ever came to see us from Regensburg, and now our Therese has gone and died."

Appendix to this Chapter

By way of appendix to this chapter, that follows Therese Neumann's life from the beginning of her mystical experiences, we submit the following three letters. The first two letters, and the interval of time between them—between the first and second letters, there is an interval of ten years—show how much Therese had to suffer from misunderstanding and mistrust; the third letter explains why her father's opposition to a second medical observation had grown so much stiffer.[11] Therese's two letters are written to Professor Wutz, in whom she had the greatest confidence, second only to Father Naber. The letters were discovered in Professor Wutz's notes. The copy of the third letter, written by Therese's father to Archbishop Michael Buchberger, came into my hands only after Therese Neumann's death.

I

Konnersreuth, October 25, 1927

Dear Father Professor,

Since I am convinced that you have a clear picture and a good grasp of what our dear Savior has been working through me, his miserable servant, I will write you about what is closest to my heart and what causes me such pain since it does not please our dear Savior, not in the least. I am not going to cry about anything to you; no, because I know that I have no call to do that. You already know what I always say: "The dear Savior is with me and he makes everything turn out best." In fact, even if knowledge and science make every effort they can and try to be smarter than our dear Savior himself, you finally have got to admit that, of yourself, you don't know anything. You know very well that I never like to hear a whole lot about real smart people like that, who want to explain everything in terms of human reason and don't even stop to think that our dear Savior is superior to them. They look just like the proud old Pharisee to me—I see them almost every Friday and I am sick and disgusted whenever I see them. Often there are good and reasonable doctors—I saw one just yesterday—I always think that true science and knowledge are supposed to lead to our dear God, but the contrary is usually the case.

---

11. References to people who are still living are passed over by the following sign: . . . . . .

When I think of what I just recently experienced—and it is the reason why I am writing you—I can hardly bring myself to say it quietly. Such a dishonorable conduct and what arrogance besides! Dr. Seidel, from the sanitarium, has just finally come back to see me, and we talked about all kinds of things that let me understand how conscience-less some people are acting in regard to what our dear Savior is trying to accomplish. Even though I'm not so very smart, I can still understand how it's going right now. Professor Ewald I used to have a much better opinion of, otherwise I would never have given him my trust at all. Just think what Dr. Seidel told me. He said: "Ewald made a good impression on him and he was very much moved by what our Savior was accomplishing here. But when he got home and spoke about it with his superior, Professor Specht, he changed his opinion." I was very surprised to hear this, and he went on: "Yes, that's the way with these younger professors; they let themselves be overawed by their superiors; I didn't think that it would come to that either." "And that's what they call science?" I asked him. "An old peasant woman who doesn't even claim to know anything is smarter than that.... Even I myself—and I can't even help myself—I'm firmer than that and not so fickle. O you poor world." I mean, really, no matter how poor and wretched a person is if he only trusts our dear Savior, he won't have to fear a single thing, even if all hell and the evil world spirits storm up against him.

If you have such a true and trustworthy friend at your side as our dear Savior is, then nothing can ever go wrong. I told Dr. Seidel my opinion very openly and several times. I am not angry with him and I forgive him, but I want to have as little as possible to do with it, if it doesn't have to be direct, the way my Ordinary forced me to the last time. I know what I went through then, and is all that supposed to be in vain? I will follow punctually whatever my superiors order me, no matter how hard it is and no matter how much I have to force myself.... It's all the same with me; I'll go along with anything. Even if they told me today that I was supposed to go right into a clinic, that's all right with me. I really have nothing to fear and our dear Savior takes care of everything so that it will all be all right. But my father says that he won't let me go; he says that once before he gave in, at home, and the Ordinary was satisfied, but these people think one thing today and something else tomorrow. And you know my father; that was the way you had to meet him, just like our Father Naber.

But it will all be all right soon enough. What I really mean is that I know for sure that our dear Savior will not make me suffer from seeing these proud scientists making their forced interpretations and nag about everything they investigate, and still can't explain anything. Not a single soul ever comes to him that way, otherwise our Savior and the Apostles would have gathered a whole regiment of scientists around them. But he had no need for people like that and our dear Savior is the same today as he always was. Today too it is a question of God's grace and our own cooperation and good will. I don't know how these people who keep torturing me, like the doctors (who aren't accomplishing anything at all), can have such a poor grasp of the fact that God can do more things than they can understand. And then they pretend they are doing the Church a big service; I think it is just the opposite. But I don't bother a whole lot about it and I just leave it all to our dear Savior,—everything is subject to him and he guides everything for the best and we love him above everything else and want to put all our trust in him. In the end we'll always say: "The Lord has done everything well."

Well, now I seem to have given you a lot of opportunity to practice patience in reading this letter; I just keep writing and writing when I get started.... Let us pray and beg our Savior to forgive everyone whose arrogance makes them oppose whatever our dear Savior is trying to accomplish; they really don't know what they are doing.

With best wishes to your dear old mother, I remain

Your grateful — Therese Neumann

▲ Geographical position of Konnersreuth: politically in the area of Tirschenreuth (Oberpfalz), physically between the Fichtelgebirg and the Bohemian Forest.

▼ Landscape of Konnersreuth — cradled in a valley in the Fichtelgebirg spur.

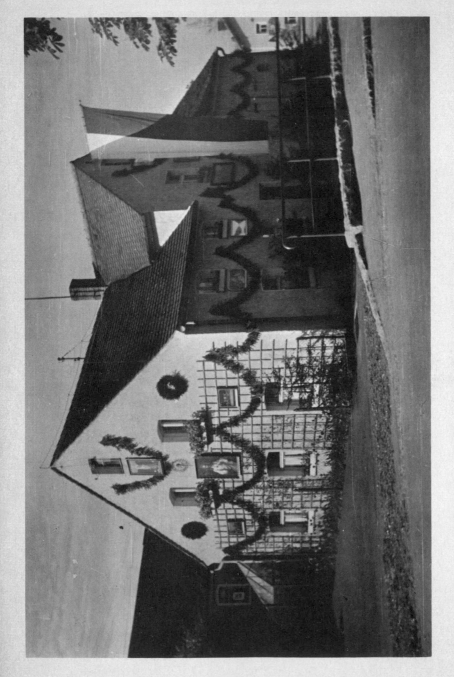

Schneiderixenhaus (Neumann family home) decorated for Corpus Christi.

Therese Neumann's father at work in the field.

▲ Mother Neumann and her
ten living children in 1916.
The picture was taken for her
husband who was in the service.
Left to right: Therese, Marie,
Anna, Ottilie, Engelbert, Kres-
zenz, Agnes, Hans, Mother,
August.

◄ Therese Neumann at the age
of three.

► Neumann's Mother at work
in the field.

Therese Neumann after her cure, end of 1925.

After receiving the stigmata.

▲ *The altar dedicated to St. Therese of Lisieux, the Little Flower, in the parish Church, May 17, 1928 (third anniversary of her canonization).*

Konnersreuth Parish Church — constructed in 1775-1782 (Late Roccoco).

Therese Neumann's spiritual director from 1909 up to her death: Father Joseph Naber.

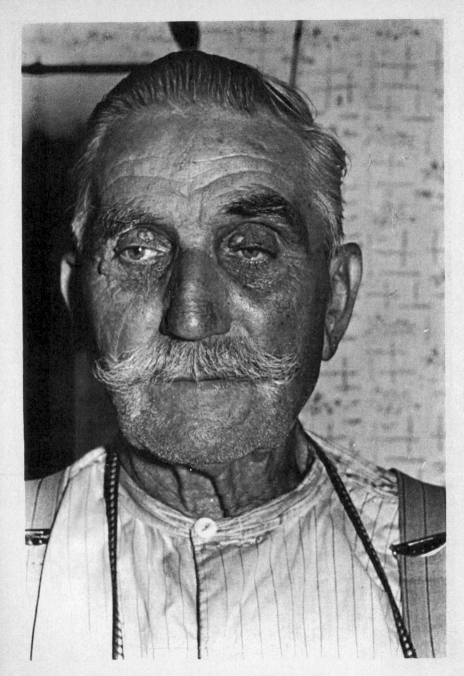

Ferdinand Neumann, Father, 1952

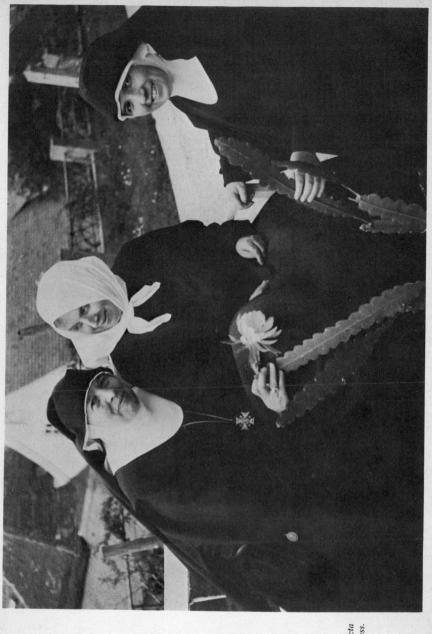

In Eichstätt with M. Benedicta von Spiegel, O.S.B., Abbess.

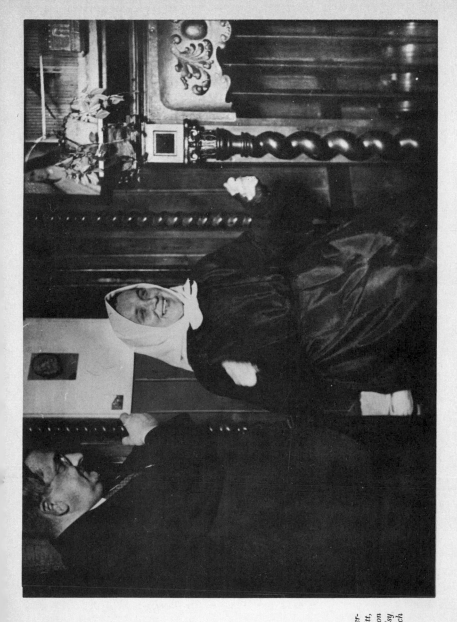

*On the occasion of Dr. Ger-
lich's conversion in Eichstätt,
Therese experiencing a vision
of the man with the palsy
(Sept. 27, 1931). Dr. Gerlich
on the left.*

Ordination of the Convert Bruno Rothschild, June 29, 1932. (Died December 24, 1932) Front row: Father Naber, Bruno Rothschild, Professor Wutz, Father Cosmas, OFM Cap. Back row: Therese Neumann, her sister Agnes, Marie, Ottilie, and her brother Ferdinand.

◄ *Mother Neumann (around 1945).*

▼ *Relaxation with her sisters in Eichstätt.*

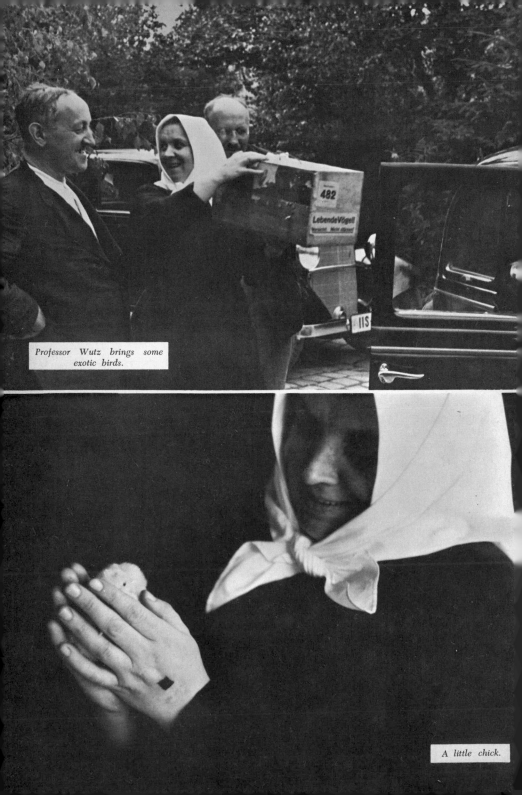

Professor Wutz brings some exotic birds.

A little chick.

II

Konnersreuth, February 22, 1937

Dear Father Professor,

I realize only too well that you have more important things to do than read my letters and their words of sorrow. But what can I do! You understand me best, because you are so devoted to everything that is good and you have a clear and calm judgment of things. Today I have had a very heavy heart. I am still crying in fact. I let them come, the tears, because when you are all cried out then things are easier. Lent is really terrible. But I am glad to put up with it, with God's help. But it surely is hard. My head is visibly whiter every day. If only I would always have the strength I need from our dear Savior, just to persevere. Recently we've got several different letters in which people are writing that some people who don't believe me are calling me a cheat and a fake, because they're not allowing anyone in to see me. But when you keep hearing that they are always making all kinds of derogatory comments in the Bishop's office, that makes you think. I keep telling myself: "What is it that you've done, that they are treating you like this?" Really, I haven't done anything, I have to answer. For our Savior and His Church I've been suffering and bleeding now for ten years. And my parents have had to make the same kind of sacrifice together with many other people. And now, as a reward for all this, we're being threatened with being shut out of the Church. It's really terrible, Dear Professor, when you're lying there in pain and can't sleep, and they keep making digs at you. You can't pray all the time, you know.... I just wish that my dear parents and I could be treated just like the poorest and most insignificant person in the diocese.... But all this continual torture for the last ten years—it makes you tired.

We're all suffering from it. Our only consolation is that it will all come to an end some day. And eternity is long enough to show everyone what the truth really is. Here on earth there's really no place for rejoicing any more. It's all the same! I keep saying: "Savior, I'm happy to suffer, for whomever you wish." It's all a part of the overall picture, but first you've got so much to learn. Our dear Savior has taught me a good many things. And everything always came out right. Just recently I've been dunked right back into pain and suffering; but you can also tell our Savior's power and strength. If only they don't try to take him away from me, they can threaten me with anything else they please. Everything else I'm glad to bear, as long as he permits it. Fridays are just like last year. Head, shoulders, heart, hands, feet, and knees all bleed. Besides that, I've got a good deal of pain from my weak heart, my rheumatism, and my kidney trouble. I sit in bed quite a bit, since it's hard to lie down at times, on account of my kidney trouble. But it will all pass in time. Maybe by the time Easter comes, we'll have an answer to the big question and can all start breathing again.

And then, in addition to everything else, there is our hard time with the dreadful school question and everything else. And there are so many pitfalls to a person's faith these days. When you stop to think about it, it's really not so hard to understand what our Savior is trying to do with all these heavy crosses he sends. If only he will keep giving me the strength I need, then I'll be glad to take everything he sends. Then if the Church people or some outsiders like to think that I'm nothing but a fake, well, that's all right too. It's all right, too, if you want to lock me in tight while I'm at Holy Mass or Benediction; so that I can feel it. You'll soon realize that a lot of prayers are being said for someone. Sometimes, when things are really hard, I like to think: If it didn't hurt, it wouldn't be a sacrifice. It would surely be a strange kind of sacrifice if you could be spared, wouldn't it now? You must destroy this letter immediately, so that no one else reads it.

There now, I had to go and talk myself out again; but I'm sure you won't take me to task for that. I won't forget you either. And your good superior, I think of him every day too, and all his problems. On his last visit I had a chance to see how fine and fatherly and upright a man he really is.

With best greetings,

Gratefully yours, Resl.

III

Konnersreuth, March 10, 1937

Your Excellency,

Today I received some news from my daughter Therese which radically alters my position on the subject of a second clinical observation.

On the occasion of the observation which was arranged for by your predecessor, Professor Ewald examined my daughter, without my knowledge and without her permission, in order to determine her virginity. My daughter had to put up with these indignities without being in a position to make any effective protest against it; Ewald really should have had her permission for such an examination, and all these years she has kept quiet about it out of shame. . . .

I find it both unheard of and shameful from any point of view for a doctor, and a Protestant doctor at that, under guise of a "clinical observation of lack of nourishment intake," ordered by the Catholic Bishop, to be allowed to treat an innocent young girl the way they examine a harlot at the police station. This information alone is enough to close, once and for all, any question and any dispute about the possibility of a new medical examination. . . . Stigmata and lack of nourishment intake are no grounds whatsoever for such an unheard of affrontery—you wouldn't dare offer such an insult to any normal person.

And finally, I shall no longer allow anyone to misuse the confidence of my family in such a shameful manner, since it now appears that even episcopal sponsoring of the examination provided no real protection for my daughter....

With all respect, Ferdinand Neumann

From a report of Father Naber, Sept. 8, 1937:

"... Therese Neumann suffers very much, terribly, and only the Day of Judgment will give us a clear picture of what she could and should have been together with her crucified Savior, in a world that wants to throw off the yoke of the cross; and the heaviest crosses she has to bear, crosses that come close to breaking her strength in suffering, are her constant difficulties with her ecclesiastical superiors. In April 29 of this year, the anniversary of her beatification, the Little Flower appeared to her and said: 'Dear child, go and accept every suffering and every trial willingly and joyfully. Souls are waiting for you. Do not lose your courage. Trust blindly. You have so many clear proofs of love. And you always have the calm assurance of our help. We will not ever forsake you. You have to fulfill your whole vocation, and be more like our despised and misjudged and persecuted Savior.' Misjudged and despised! I was frightened at these words and I prayed to our Savior: 'Please never let me be a tool of this suffering!'"

Weighing all these circumstances and events, that are now a quarter of a century behind us, it is impossible for an impartial witness to avoid the impression that a more prudent and careful handling of the situation would have managed to bridge over the gulf that separated official desire from parental objections.

The story of Catherine Emmerick is a case in point: acting on all the best intentions in the world, the Vicar General Droste-Vischering, on the doctors' repeated insistence, forced her to undergo one clinical observation after another. Only too late did the Vicar General realize that he had been deceiving himself, and that his intention "of meeting every possible objection and accusation" was being gradually lost sight of, and that the upper hand was passing rapidly from theology to medicine (cf. Radlo, pp. 176-179).

The first clinical observation made such heavy demands on Therese Neumann's psychic and physical strength, that it would have been no wonder if she had herself refused to undergo a second. But yet she was prepared for a further clinical observation, in obedience to the Church. She had discussed this explicitly in a letter to Bishop Michael Buchberger,[12] wondering if she should not perhaps secretly leave her home and go to a clinic. But she was not certain where she could then spend the rest of her life, since her father would certainly no longer take her back into the family home. In this respect the Bishop advised her [13] to be obedient to her father first of all, but to make an effort at securing his permission.

If all the pertinent documents could be published they would certainly set the whole question of a "second clinical observation" in the proper light. Only when the decisive documents are published and available, will a final judgment ever be possible.

---

12. Letter of November 21, 1937.
13. Letter of November 25, 1937.

Therese Neumann's
Sphere of Influence

Up to this point we have become familiar with Therese Neumann's most intimate circle of acquaintances — considering chiefly her own experiences, her activities and sufferings within her immediate surroundings. But she was also extraordinarily active far outside her immediate family circle.

We cannot measure the effects of her suffering and prayers in God's great plan of salvation. From the letters that have been preserved from the time of her sickness (cf. p. 110) we can come to appreciate the heroic spirit of willing resignation with which she placed these seven years of serious sickness as a sacrifice in the scales of Christ's own sufferings. Hers was a spirit modeled on that of St. Paul: "Now I rejoice in my sufferings for your sake, and in my flesh I complete what is lacking in Christ's afflictions for the sake of his body, that is, the Church" (Col. 1, 24).

We know that every year, provided her health permitted, Therese used to give a beautiful example of spending the whole night of All Saints Day and All Souls Day in the Church, praying the indulgenced prayers continuously, leaving only for the prescribed brief moment between each set of prayers and stepping into the sacristy. From her own visions of particular judgment, she had firsthand acquaintance with the terrible needs and feeling of abandonment that the Poor Souls suffered. Too many times she had seen a soul witness the glory and majesty of the Savior for one moment, at the time of particular judgment, and then remain behind waiting, sad and alone. Thus she made every possible effort to help the departed souls. Communion and Rosary indulgences she offered up for the poor souls, throughout her whole life.

But it was not only the dead who benefitted from Therese Neumann's attentions; she devoted even more time to the care of the living. The large amount of mail she received every day has already been mentioned; she spent many of her night hours reading her correspondence. Naturally enough, she managed to answer only a fraction of the letters. But she included every one of them in all her daily prayers.

To a much greater degree it was personal contacts that came to absorb much of her time. There is no way to even estimate the number of visitors who came to see her in the 36 years between 1926 and 1962. The most we can arrive at it, is an approximate statistical count. In the years prior to Hitler's regime, the throngs were so great, often several hundred in a single day, that her parents were happy when the Bishop's office decided to issue passes and control the visiting. From 1933 the number of visitors began to decline, but it swerved sharply upwards again at the end of the war. Counting only seven or eight visitors a day, with whom she could hold a more or less lengthy conversation, and only 200 per year, we still reach a grand total of well over 50,000 visitors to whom Therese spoke on an individual basis and gave both advice and encouragement, new hope and deeper faith. The good she thus accomplished is tremendous, as well as the number of people she inspired and encouraged in the good they were doing.

There are dozens of letters from cardinals and bishops addressed to her (among them one signed by Pacelli, Cardinal Secretary of State—1935), asking her to give an especially warm welcome to a particular friend of theirs, or recommending a particular problem or even their whole diocese, to her prayers.

The last of these letters—she was no longer able to answer it—
dates from September 15, 1962. It was from the Chinese Bishop
Vitus Chang, begging for a chance to visit her.

About 700 times in the course of her life she had her "Friday
sufferings." On many Fridays there were thousands—on Good
Friday there were sometimes more than ten thousand—who
came to see her on her bed of pain. There were at least hundreds
of thousands who thus witnessed the picture of her passion,
all of them seriously, and for the most part extremely moved.
Our pictures of the throngs of visitors she had on Good Fridays
are sufficient documentation for this statement. The pictures
show that the crowds stood there even during a steady down-
pour. Frequently prayers were offered in front of the house.
Many of the visitors were moved to tears when they saw the
blood streaming over Therese's face and the bleeding wounds
in her hands. And Father Naber's suggestion to go into the
Church after their visit and thank our Savior and pray the
Way of the Cross did not go unheeded.

These "smaller" fruits of her sufferings are, however, less
significant than some others, notably the many *conversions*. Already in the earliest years of the Konnersreuth story the young
Jewish druggist, Bruno Rothschild, found the way to the Catholic Church, and continued to build upon the graces of his
conversion by studying theology. In 1932 he was ordained, but
on a trip to Konnersreuth on Christmas Eve of 1932 he died
of a heart attack at the age of 33. Who can tell what fate he was
thus spared? He lies in the Konnersreuth cemetery, since he
was disowned by his family.

Dr. Gerlich's case we shall consider later.

A Berlin family, husband, wife and four children—on the
occasion of a visit to Konnersreuth in summer of 1930, all embraced the Catholic faith. Therese Neumann and the above
mentioned Bruno Rothschild were the official witnesses of their
declaration of intent to embrace the faith.

The conversion of the Mecklenburg Counsellor, Paul Schondorf, in 1933, is thus described by his son Heinz in answer to

a query under date of March 5, 1963: "My parents lived in a mixed marriage: Mother and my brother Hans, who died on the Russian front, were Catholics, while Father and I were Protestant. Naturally, it was Mother's wish to see us all united in the same true faith. Since she could not influence us, she turned to Resl with the request to have this intention included in all her prayers and sufferings. We then became personally acquainted with Resl in Konnersreuth and were thus in a position to witness the great supernatural events that were taking place there; we had only to draw the logical consequences and return to the One Holy Church. My conversion took place on May 17, 1933; my father's on December 30, 1933. I was 28 at the time and my father was 60."

At the time of his conversion, Paul Schondorf was active as a Counsellor for the Ministry. It took a lot of courage for a man in his position, and in a predominantly Protestant section of the country, and in the year 1933, to convert to Catholicism; it was a time in which other highly-placed officials were learning to stay away from church or break their ties, for official reasons. In 1934 Paul Schondorf wrote a statement which we record on page 243. This document gives a good picture of the difficulties this conversion necessarily involved, and it shows the unhesitating spirit with which he walked along the path to the truth he had discovered in his own inner soul and through the events he was privileged to witness at Konnersreuth.

The Jewish merchant from Vienna, Dr. Benno Karpeles, had heard Father Helmut Fahsel speaking about Konnersreuth. He asked him to arrange a visit for him, and the priest complied. Dr. Karpeles was privileged to see a great part of the Friday sufferings and was strongly influenced. The following Saturday he visited Therese again. His account, which dates from 1933,[14]

---

14. Father Odo Staudiger, O.S.B.: "Wie ich durch Konnersreuth den Heiland fand," Wels 1946, p. 22 ff. (*How I Found the Savior at Konnersreuth.*)

contains much that is characteristic and thus we reproduce it below, in extract form:

"On Saturday I found Therese with the priest. Yesterday she had been a terrifying picture of suffering, but today she was a fresh and healthy looking peasant girl and certainly gave no signs of having lived for seven years without taking any nourishment. During the course of a two hours' conversation she ran off three times into the nearby church to supervise the arrangement of the altar flowers for the Capuchin mission which was then in progress. She is just like a big overgrown child, with wonderful blue eyes, full of wit and sparkle, just like all the other peasant people. . . .

"From the very first moment I was absolutely convinced that this person was not lying. In my whole life I have never seen a person who had absolute truth written on her face the way Therese Neumann has. . . .

"What is happening in Konnersreuth cannot be explained in any natural way: It is supernatural. I saw Therese Neumann a second and third and fourth time—always with the Bishop's permission—visited with her for a few days and watched her in the most diverse conditions. . . .

"I was convinced that I should be a convert and wanted to be baptized at Konnersreuth. . . .

"When I got to Konnersreuth, I found Therese in her sufferings. . . . The next day at five in the morning, I was baptized in Konnersreuth, with Therese as my sponsor. In the Mass that followed I knelt on a hassock alongside Therese. At the moment in which the priest spoke the words of consecration, she passed into a state of exalted calm.[15] It is a touching thing to see how

---

15. Our observer, in his inexperience, has obviously confused these different states. This was almost certainly the state of visionary contemplation and the prayer of quiet, which, during the Christmas and Easter octaves lasted from consecration to communion, and only then passed over into the state of exalted calm. — Author

she starts up, how she tries to stand in order to go and meet the priest who is coming towards her with the host. Suddenly the host is no longer there.[16]

"To my utter embarrassment I must confess that I did not receive my First Holy Communion with the proper recollection, because I had my whole attention on Therese instead. I looked very closely and saw the host disappear. I saw it with my own eyes and I am quite prepared to assert this under oath. . . .

"I have found the path that led to the Church and to the Faith through the impressions of what I experienced and saw in Konnersreuth, not what I just read or heard, and not just what the people who were connected with Therese for several years had told me. I know I am not the only one; the three to five hundred letters that find their way to Konnersreuth every day are witness to that fact. Konnersreuth has meant a strengthening of faith or a rediscovery of faith for thousands of people. For me, Konnersreuth is an absolute proof of the fact that God has plans for us, that he has found us in time to remind us that there is something more to living than our daily bread, something more than our daily cares and amusements."

The number of conversions that took place in Konnersreuth is beyond counting; the number that were influenced by Konnersreuth in other parts of the world is beyond grasping.

But there were also setbacks, as there are in every human life. Witness the following statement of Father Naber: "May 12, 1932. This week Therese has been suffering for a young convert, until he died. . . ."

Therese devoted herself to the *sick* with great love. Until 1947 there was no doctor in Konnersreuth and no hospital nurses. She managed to get a little cart and a small horse—"Lottie"— and traveled around for several years, caring for the sick. At

---

16. This took place only in the mystical communions, when Therese Neumann would see our Savior himself coming to give her the host. — Author.

home she would bind the wounds of those who came to visit her. Dr. Seidel, a member of the board of health, was always glad to avail himself of Therese's help: he frequently advised his patients from her locality to let Resl care for them after he had treated them.

The *Church* at Konnersreuth was always kept *decorated* with great love and devotion and everyone was constantly amazed at the perfect taste with which she arranged everything. In the course of this work she managed to get hold of a small plot of ground just outside Konnersreuth and she used it as a flower garden to supply the Church with an abundance of fresh blossoms, for every season of the year.

Significant, if not in their sum total at least in their number, were the financial projects which she organized or set in motion during the course of her life, especially for the so-called deserving poor. Whenever any money came into her hands, to be used for some good purpose, she always used it primarily in the spirit of love of neighbor, and then in the service of the parish church. Whenever she begged for funds and took up collections for some specific project, for example, the rehabilitation of the church after the end of the war, for the church bell, etc., she always conscientiously used the money she got for that one single purpose. Since there was money in many of the letters she got, to be used for "some worthy purpose," she had frequent opportunity to send donations to the missions. She also liked to give financial support to various stations of the diaspora parishes in Sweden.

Our particular case deserves special mention: it goes far beyond her activities in the parish circle. Dr. Fritz Gerlich, who was at that time the chief editor of the Munich Newspaper (*Neueste Nachrichte*), a Calvinist in his religion, had come to Konnersreuth in 1927 in order to get his own personal firsthand impression of the events that were taking place there, as the chief editor of the biggest paper in South Germany. Moreover, since he was naturally gifted with extremely sharp powers of observation, a quality further heightened by his training as an historian, he had determined to unmask every fraud he encountered in Konnersreuth, if there were any to be found. Since he had always been in earnest search of truth, he was favored with a very special grace. He immediately recognized the events at Konnersreuth as unexplainable in the natural order of things and went back to Munich like a second St. Paul. He later gave up his position and wrote a two volume work on Konnersreuth—the present biography is largely dependent upon his precise dating.

In Konnersreuth he became acquainted with Prince Erich von Waldburg zu Zeil. He later discussed with him the foundation of a newspaper that would be independent of any control by financial powers, with himself as editor and the Prince as financial backer. The prince was moved by Gerlich's words that "Hundreds of souls are hanging in the balance" (as he later related to the Author), and in the course of the years 1930-1933 he sacrificed some half million marks for the newspaper that they then published: "The Straight Way." The publishers were known as the "Natural Law Publishing House," because their chief program was an expression of the fight for recognition of human right.

As publishing adviser to this paper I was once or twice directed by Gerlich to travel to Konnersreuth and ask Therese questions when she was in a state of ecstasy. Without making any attempt to thrust myself into the foreground in this enterprise, I must report the following facts as historical truth: The answers that Therese gave in her state of ecstasy always renewed his courage in his battle against National Socialism and also Bolshevism. There were never any definite orders. Free will and personal responsibility and knowledge were never in any case suspended. But there were insights and hints that put him in a better position to hit upon the correct decisions himself. Words like "Look, in the last analysis this is all directed against our Savior," were enough for him. There were also clear statements of the justice of the stand he was taking and demands for trust and confidence, such that judging from the cumulative effect of all these various visions, it was hard to avoid the impression that this trust and confidence was not meant to be limited to life on earth.

Dr. Gerlich had an uncommonly aggressive and choleric temperament—but he was also possessed of an almost childlike readiness to reconcile and forgive and ask forgiveness, whenever he recognized a mistake—a temperament that was evident not only in the political field, but also within his own circle of co-workers, whenever he felt that someone was being cautious or timid. One answer from Therese in her state of elevated calm: "Temperaments are certainly not all alike, but they have to work together for the success of any venture." This advice (he told me of it himself) made a profound change in his relationship with his inner circle of fellow workers. I mention this only as evidence of the fact that the circle was held together by a few, well chosen ecstatic responses from Therese.

Father Ingbert Naab, Gerlich's faithful fellow warrior in the "Straight Way," who rounded out Gerlich's predominantly political propositions by his own profound philosophical views of the world, became acquainted with Dr. Gerlich through Konnersreuth and he too was strengthened in the justice of his efforts and thus confirmed in his desperate defensive against National Socialism by answers from Therese in ecstasy. When Gerlich converted to Catholicism, Father Ingbert Naab was his catechist and Professor Wutz was his wise and understanding father confessor. On the occasion of a stormy outburst against "The Straight Way" on March 9, 1933, Gerlich was taken into "protective custody," and on June 30, 1934, he was murdered in Dachau.

In the summer of 1933 I had to deliver the following ecstatic reply to Father Ingbert Naab: "Tell Ingbert he must disappear. If nothing happens now, as long as it's only a question of politics, it doesn't make any difference, and if it's a question of religion later on...." At this point the ecstasy was interrupted. "What then?" I asked, but there was no further answer. Father Naab was able to make his escape out of the country,

smooth-shaven and dressed in civilian clothes—he had been
warned from other sources as well. He was not a day early,
either; he would have been arrested by the Gestapo. He died
in 1935, in exile. Both of these men will some day be counted
among the outstanding witnesses to the truth of the Konnersreuth story.

In 1937, when I was questioned for five hours by the Gestapo and asked to identify the source of the strength and courage that made Gerlich take such a persevering stand against
the advance of National Socialism ("A man couldn't do a thing
like that by himself," said my questioner—he was perfectly
right), I answered simply: "All I know is that he was a close
friend of Father Ingbert Naab." (Fr. Naab had died in the
meantime, of course.) The deposition of historical truth now
demands that I put my finger on the true historical background
in this question.

End of the War [17]

The end of the second world war was destined to be a
bitter experience for Konnersreuth. All around them, the pene-
tration of the defensive fronts went forward without any ap-
preciable resistance and consequently without any particular
harm to the population, but at Konnersreuth there was a short
but, for such a small place, really fateful battle. The last official
German war despatch issued from that area records that "There
is a fierce and bitter battle raging for world-famous Konnersreuth."

On April 20, 1945—Hitler's Birthday—Konnersreuth was occupied by the Americans. There was a division of the SS there
which had been established only a week before. A few months

---

17. Account according to Therese Neumann and her brother, Ferdinand Neumann.

previously, a convalescent company had been quartered there, out of Koblenz, and they had remained on good terms with the local population. Their commanding officer, a major, had even visited Therese Neumann on several occasions. During the last days of the war this SS unit began to assert itself. A short time before the American occupation, the leader of the unit came to the Neumanns and asked to speak with Resl. They told him she was not at home, and probably could be found at the church. He took some of his men to the parish church, to look for her. But she had hidden. Then the SS troops threatened a house search, in the church and rectory, and in the Neumann home. While the SS troops were on their way back to the Neumann home, there was suddenly a sharp argument between the major of the convalescent corps and the SS leader. The major was strictly forbidding them to bother Resl. The SS leader challenged him to a pistol duel which fortunately never came off.

On the morning of April 20, the SS unit began measuring distances in Konnersreuth with a long tape. The people could not fathom the reason behind the measurements. Early that afternoon the SS company withdrew from the town. Without informing the convalescent troop there, they suddenly began to shell the town with light artillery, about 4 o'clock. They had mounted their artillery in the direction of Froppenheim-Kappl, only about 1200 meters away, and their shooting was very accurate. The parish church was hit; about 30 shell fragments landed in the parish garden; the Neumann home was hit in the roof gable, and the parents' bedroom, alongside Therese's room, was destroyed. The shelling all came from the northeast whereas the Americans were approaching from the west. When the Americans heard the shelling, they sent a reconnaissance plane on an observation flight, but the SS gunnery shot it down. Then the Americans also opened fire. Incendiary shells were fired, too, and one of them set fire to the shed on the parish grounds. Beneath this shed Ferdinand Neumann had built a dugout, in which at that time, Resl and her numerous nieces and nephews, 30 people in all, were staying.

"I had not built the dugout as a bomb shelter against air raids," said Ferdinand Neumann, "but only as a temporary shelter for when the defensive fronts were penetrated and perhaps as a defense against plundering, and that's why I camouflaged the entrance too. I made the whole thing out of wood, and that turned out to be the dumbest thing I could have done. I hadn't reckoned with a fire. I had a second exit, of course, really little more than a hole to slip out of, reached by a ladder. But when the whole shack started to go up in smoke, the wood in the dugout started burning too. That made it impossible to use the main exit. Resl smelled the smoke and at the same time she saw everything outside burning lickety-split. She ran right back to pull all the children out through the emergency exit. The mouth of the exit was opened and Resl handed the children out. There was no time to spare; the draft that was created by opening the emergency exit drew the fire into contact with the combustible material in the dugout and Resl herself was lucky to come off with nothing more than badly singed clothing—they had to put out the fires in her clothes after she climbed up the ladder. It was a very dangerous situation for her. There was no time left to rescue the articles that had been placed in the dugout for safe keeping. Together with the furniture, benches and tables, whole cases of documents and letters went up in smoke, including some Mass vestments and even a monstrance. When the occupants had managed to find their way out, they saw the whole place in flames. About one fourth of the homes in Konnersreuth burned down as a result of the shelling, or were at least very severely damaged.

"Towards evening, the forest superintendent, who had a little house just outside Konnersreuth along Waldsassener Street, came and invited Father Naber, Resl, and the family to stay in his home for a while. They were happy to go with him. They stayed there for a few hours before they learned that the Americans had entered Konnersreuth, and then they went back to the town. Meantime the American advance troops had quartered in all the empty houses in Konnersreuth. Everything was in a state of confusion, even in the rectory. But at the very moment that Father Naber and Resl came along, the troops immediately relinquished their quarters and everything was back to order. "They were in my parents' home too, but they did not disturb anything. Our home was just as it had been before, excepting for the damage done by the shelling. The advance troops were followed almost immediately by the American war correspondent, named Jordan, who had visited Resl in Konnersreuth before the war, and the division commandant of the American troops. They expressed their sincere sorrow for what had just happened in the town. They had had strict orders from their military superiors to spare the whole neighborhood of Konnersreuth if at all possible, but there was nothing else they could do, since they had encountered heavy resistance and their reconnaissance plane had been shot down. This war correspondent, Jordan, later studied theology and joined the Benedictine Order (in Beuron) where he was ordained a priest in 1950. He maintained his close personal contact with Resl.

"There is no doubting the fact that the greatest part of the destruction was the work of the SS troops. There were also some casualties in Konnersreuth, including three or four dead in the convalescent company, which had not been warned of the impending artillery barrage. Late in the afternoon the barrage became sporadic and then ceased entirely. From deserters in the SS corps we later learned that they had begun to run out of ammunition. They tried to get more ammunition from other SS units who were camped in the neighborhood of Wernersreuth (behind Waldsassen, near the Czech border), but as it turned out, these groups had already evacuated towards the south, and when the troops from Konnersreuth learned of this development, they withdrew as quickly as possible.

"Resl had a lot to do in the following days and weeks, caring for the wounded and trying to ease the state of emergency in the village. Very soon the American soldiers began their mass visits to Konnersreuth—they always behaved most

properly and circumspectly, and in fact they did a lot to help
Resl over this most difficult time."

Significant Individual Experiences after the Second World War

A personal accomplishment of Therese Neumann was the
acquisition of the property at Fockenfeld near Konnersreuth as
a home for training priests (1951). She had learned from Doctor
Mittendorfer, who had treated the owners of the property, that
this piece of land, which had previously belonged to the Waldsassen monastery and had been in private hands, since its secu-
larization, was going to be sold. At first Resl was not particularly interested in the property; but when someone suggested
that it would make a fine location for a seminary, she was all
ears. Shortly afterwards Prince Erich von Waldburg-Zeil came
to Konnersreuth and asked Resl if there was anything she
wanted. She told him that there was nothing she wanted for
herself, but she did tell him about her plans for Fockenfeld.
Since the plans involved a rather high purchase price, the
prince was not in a position to give his consent at once. "Resl,"
he told her, "the French people have taken about a million
marks worth of wood out of my forest preserves; if you can
help get the settlement I'm after through the courts, then I'll
help you in Fockenfeld." Resl knew how many sacrifices the
prince had made for the "Straight Way," and also for other
charitable purposes, and she did not hesitate very long. After
the war many influential Americans had come to Konnersreuth
and she was encouraged to attempt a begging expedition for
the prince, and thus also for Fockenfeld. She and her brother
Ferdinand took a trip to visit the proper American personnel,
and the trip was a success; the prince's settlement was immediately expedited and the prince gave the Oblates of St. Francis
de Sales, in Eichstätt, the money for the purchase of Fockenfeld

on very favorable terms. This order later established a school for delayed vocations, and several priests have already been ordained from their school.

Within her own family circle, in the years that followed the war, Therese Neumann had to face heavy losses. On September 5, 1949, her brother Engelbert died after a long sickness, during which she had been caring for him and keeping him in good spirits at a great personal sacrifice—part of the time he was in Munich. A little later, on December 9, 1949, her mother Anna Neumann died. On the day of her funeral Father Naber, Resl and I were all three talking together about death and the life hereafter. I mentioned that I found it difficult to think of eternal bliss in the form of "eternal rest," and that I leaned rather towards the expression "eternal life." Then Father Naber said; "I think of eternal happiness as a perpetual sharing in the work of God. In God we contemplate everything that has been, is, and will ever be." And finally Resl said: "O no, Father, much more than that—everything that *can* even be."

Ten years later, in 1959, death struck the family circle once again. On May 1, 1959, Ottilie Neumann died in Eichstätt; she had been a president of the Third Order, and kept house for Professor Wutz. Resl, who spent the last days together with her sister, saw our Savior coming in shining glory at the moment of her death, with a smile on his face, to take the suddenly pure and radiant soul of her sister back to heaven with him. During the vision, Therese kept crying, "Take me along!" but afterwards she was in a state of great peace and joy, despite the loss of her sister.

She was struck a particularly heavy blow on November 26 of that same year, when death claimed her faithful and devoted father Ferdinand Neumann (in the 87th year of his life), after a brief illness. After that there was hardly anyone of her brothers and sisters left to share her life in their family home. Thus she was particularly happy when Father Naber decided to resign his post in 1960, at the age of 90, and, together with his housekeeper, Therese's sister Marie, moved into the family barn and stable buildings that had been made over into a living quarters for him.

Therese Neumann's last active project developed under the stimulus of the new diocesan Ordinary, Rudolf Graber, who was enthroned in 1962. He had written, shortly after being named bishop, that he would welcome the erection of a cloister of perpetual adoration in his diocese, in which there would be daily prayer for the intentions of the bishop and the whole diocese. This set Therese into an immediate flurry of activity. She and Father Naber made a trip, during the last weeks of her life, to a well-disposed benefactor in the Bodensee district, who promised his generous support. They spent about a week in the family circle there. It so happened that during this last journey Therese had a chance to meet Cardinal Augustine Bea, the president of the secretariate for Christian Unity, who was then presenting his very impressive account of the purposes and problems of the Council, in Germany. Like many other men, he spoke about his problems and ambitions with Therese, and begged her to pray constantly for them, especially for progress, and a happy outcome of the Council.

The plans for the monastery were not abandoned after Therese Neumann's death, which occurred shortly after this visit; they were quickly carried to completion through the energetic activity of the above mentioned benefactor. The amazing thing was the world-wide interest that spread over the widest circles in thousands of big and little gifts which all contributed to the success of the work. Within a few months the necessary sums for the construction and furnishing of the monastery and cloister and adoration chapel were all subscribed. On Sunday, April 28, 1963, the diocesan bishop presided over the laying of the corner stone. The event marked an unintentional coincidence, discovered only later, with the fortieth anniversary of the beatification of the Little Flower, after whom the institution was named "Theresianum" (The anniversary fell on the following day, Monday April 29.).

In his sermon at the Pontifical Mass, the bishop enumerated the motives that had led to the establishment of the cloister. He told how, on the occasion of his first visit to the Sacred Heart Basilica on Montmartre in Paris, he had been deeply impressed by the inscription: *"Gallia poenitens et grata et devota* —France, repentant, thankful, and dedicated to God." He had asked himself: are we in Germany any more innocent than our neighbors to the West? From that time on the idea of making official and public reparation through a cloister of perpetual adoration had never left his mind. And when he was named bishop, he had written about his ambition to Therese Neumann, at the same time expressing his opinion that it would certainly be a great blessing for the diocese if, in the fullest sense of the Mystical Body of Christ, there would be perpetual prayer for the intentions of the bishop and the diocese in a cloister of perpetual adoration. Therese, in her impulsive way, had quickly seized upon the idea and together with her dear friends, the Sisters of Mary of Carmel in Regensburg, and various benefactors, had taken the project upon herself and cleared away the obstacles; the whole project had appeared to be especially blessed by heaven in view of the fact that the land and property on which the cloister now stood had been donated at about this same time. Perhaps, he concluded, Therese had now been interred within the ground like the grain of wheat that was to die and thus produce a hundredfold yield. The result would be a new institution in which God would be constantly adored and the words of Scripture would be fulfilled: "The Father seeks worshippers who will adore him in spirit and in truth" (John 4, 23).

A half year after the laying of the cornerstone the cloister was ready to be occupied. Bishop Rudolf Graber had called for a day of prayer and reparation for the Council and for world peace, to be held in Konnersreuth on September 22, 1963—the occasion was to coincide with the consecration of the adoration chapel and the cloister. About 40 or 50 thousand faithful answered this call, a number that had not been seen in Konners-

reuth since the time of the mass visits in the twenties and on
Good Fridays. Seven bishops celebrated Pontifical Masses, and
Bishop Venacio from Leiria-Fatima gave a very impressive sermon which was simultaneously translated into German by his
secretary. Bishop Rudolf Graber consecrated the chapel and
cloister in the morning and kindled the undying light before the
tabernacle, destined to burn on forever, accompanying the un-
ceasing adoration.

In the consecration sermon he said that it bordered on a
miracle that today, precisely on the anniversary of Therese Neumann's burial, both the church and the cloister were completed
and could be occupied. In the main sermon, which took place
on the afternoon in the open air before thousands of worshippers,
he once again alluded to the meaning behind the cloister, and
drew a sharp picture of the dangers facing our modern world,
threats that were not only exhausting its strength in eastern
atheism, but in the west, with all the destructive cultural consequences of the rise of Bolshevism, the decline of religious and
moral life, the refinement of the taste for secular living, the
"eroticism" of modern living, the lack of a spirit of sacrifice,
the disappearance of all ideals.

He concluded: "In order to insure against the sudden out-
break of war, they've established a direct line of communications between Moscow and Washington, so that the leaders of
these two world powers can get together immediately by tele-
phone in the event of any emergency. Will this line be any help?
I do not know. But our Lord has given us another emergency
line, one that bridges not merely two continents, but goes all
the way from earth to heaven; this is the line that binds together
the pearls of the rosary. It is an infinitely stronger line than
the one from Moscow to Washington. Don't you believe that if
millions of people keep praying from the depth of their heart,
'Pray for us in this danger-filled hour of humanity,' that our
heavenly Father will hear them? That is why we have come
together. That is why this adoration chapel has been erected.
That is why this ever-burning fire has been kindled, so that

strength and fire will emanate from this holy place, for the renewal of the diocese, for the salvation of the world and all humanity."

We might well regard it as the special working of divine providence that precisely the final weeks of Therese Neumann's life were filled with activities that are easy to recognize as the climax of her spiritual work: prayer for the Council and the foundation of a cloister of perpetual adoration.

Death of Therese

Therese Neumann had long suffered from angina pectoris, that treacherous heart irregularity which sporadically results in spasms and serious cardiac disturbances and shortness of breath, and frequently results in sudden death by heart failure. Still no one of Therese's circle of acquaintances really believed that she was close to death, since they had often seen her in similar circumstances before.

For a year now she had not undertaken any very involved or lengthy journeys. But her determination to set to work at once on the plans for the adoration cloister made her forget every consideration of health. The trip was immediately planned and executed. Shortly after her return, on September 13, 1962, she decorated the mission cross in the church, and the Sorrowful Mother statue beneath it, for the last time, with great devotion. The next day, the feast of the Exaltation of the Holy Cross, after three hours' sufferings in her wounds, she had the same vision she always had on this feast day: She saw Emperor Heraclius, dressed in full imperial robes and accompanied by a great crowd of worshippers, trying to carry the cross up to Mt. Calvary. He was unable to proceed beyond the city gates. Only when he followed Bishop Zacharias' advice and put aside his crown and imperial robes and took off his shoes, was he able to carry the cross up to Golgotha, and plant it there before the awestruck crowd. This vision of the triumph of the cross was the last vision that Therese Neumann experienced.

On Saturday morning, the Feast of the Seven Sorrows of the Blessed Virgin Mary, when Therese Neumann rose and was dressing, she suffered the heart attack, accompanied by a very intense stab of pain, that was to lead to her sudden and lonely death. The doctor from Konnersreuth, Dr. Stuchlik, tried to alleviate her condition by injection and heart massage, but Therese then experienced such terrible pain that they had to sit her up in her bed and prop her up on a pile of cushions. In this very position, on Tuesday, September 18, she was taken into her sister Mary's arms (she had been called in at the last moment) and died there, without being able to say a single word of farewell.

At half past ten she had received Holy Communion for the last time. Here is Father Naber's account: "I think about Resl's last Communion. On Tuesday, the day she died, she begged me to bring Communion at noon. But at half past ten she sent word that she wanted to receive at once. I brought Communion at once. She was very weak. Then she told Marie to bring her some water, because her mouth was so dry. Since 1927 she had not been taking any water with Holy Communion. This was the only time she ever asked for it, on this Tuesday morning Communion. This seemed extraordinary, but neither Marie nor I thought anything about her dying, since we had often seen her suffering as much as now. I took a spoon with a few drops of water and put the host on the tip. I brought the host to her mouth and, without any effort at swallowing on her part, the host disappeared at the very moment that the spoon came to her mouth [mystical Communion, as described above—Author].

"Now, it regularly happened that the species of bread would not dissolve in her body, as it does in our case, in about an hour or so, but would regularly remain undissolved until shortly before her next Communion. Thus she always had the awareness that her Savior was within her. Naturally this was a great joy and strength for her. When I asked her, 'What do you live on?' She answered simply, 'On our Savior.' We cannot help having the impression that our Savior was to come to her one more time before her death.

"Right after her Communion I heard a confession, and then we were called to the table. We soon heard the bell ringing from Resl's room. Marie ran to answer, and a moment later she began to call 'Father! Father!' and I quickly ran into the room. When I got there it was already too late; her life was over. Marie said: That looks just like it does when she dies in her ecstasies of suffering. And for a long time, she could not believe that Therese was really dead. We had all experienced the same thing hundreds of times: in her Friday sufferings she would suffer death agony together with our Savior and would then simply collapse and lie there for a time like a dead person. Marie waited there a while for her to come back to life, but she never did. And thus Resl died in her arms." They sent to the Church for the holy oils, which Father Schuhmann immediately administered.

In Father Naber's notes there is a passage in 1932 that points to a sudden death for Therese Neumann. Under date of November 8, 1932, he reports that she received Communion without a priest. Father Naber was in Waldsassen and did not get back until eleven o'clock. When he brought Communion to her after his return, he noticed that Therese was already in a state of elevated calm, as she regularly was after receiving Communion. He reports as follows:

"When I asked what had happened, I learned that Therese had been seized by such mighty longing for our Savior that her heart had ceased beating and was only vibrating and in a few minutes would have stopped completely. In order to prevent this, our Savior had come from the tabernacle without the help of the priest. This gave me an insight into how suddenly Therese might well pass away. In her normal state, afterwards, Therese knew only that she had been more or less unconscious and that the Savior had suddenly come to her in visible form."

Thirty years had passed from that day, and the words had grown old in everyone's memory. Too many times they had seen Therese in a state like death, and now everyone was completely overcome by the sudden arrival of the actual experience itself.

After her death Therese Neumann was laid out in the downstairs room, which had been her parents—they installed a glass window in the door. From Tuesday until Saturday, the day of the funeral, from early morning until midnight, thousands of pilgrims passed by her body. They made their way in through the front door of the Neumann house and went out through the exit that leads towards the courtyard. The stream was a constant one, and everyone regretted that they had to keep urging the people to hurry along, so that everyone could see Resl for one last time. On Saturday the funeral Mass took place in the parish church and towards the end of the services the casket was closed. Before Therese was put into her casket, three doctors (Engelbert Ernst, M.D., chief physician of the hospital at Tirschenreuth, Eduard Stuchlik, M.D., Konnersreuth, and Elisabeth Stuchlik, M.D., Tirschenreuth) all substantiated the fact that despite the four days of lying in state there was no trace of decomposition and no perceptible odor, even though the closed room was low-ceilinged and the time of year was very warm and there were always four candles burning and adding their additional heat to the narrow room.

Therese Neumann's funeral attracted so many participants that the cemetery walls and the roofs of the surrounding buildings were in danger of breaking down because of the crowds. The number of people present is hard to estimate; the most we can honestly report is that ten thousand would be too low a figure. There were busses there, not only from Germany itself, points near and far, but also from the Saar, from the Rhineland, from Belgium, Holland, Switzerland, and Austria. From Alsace and Paris there were visitors. Telegrams and thousands of letters came from all parts of the world.

Immediately beside the great cemetery cross of massive granite that was modeled on the description she gave from her ecstatic vision, Therese found a resting place near her dear sister

Ottilie, who had preceded her in death. Her grave was cared for by the people who loved her and many confident visitors stormed her with prayers for help and intercession. Many of them also prayed that our Savior would continue the work begun in her lifetime even after her death, and contribute further to the glory of his handmaiden by subsequent beatification.

Very quickly, far too soon for her old spiritual director Father Naber, God took her sister Marie, in whose arms she had died, into eternity with her, on June 15, 1963. Marie had been Father Naber's housekeeper for 34 years in Konnersreuth, and she lies beside her other two unmarried sisters in the Konnersreuth cemetery. A few weeks before her death she had willed her parents' home to the "Theresianum" cloister to keep it up and have the use of it; since her brother August had left and her father had died, the home had become the property of the three unmarried sisters, Ottilie, Therese, and Marie, and since the first two had died it was her sole concern.

Part Two

Inner and Mystic Life
of Therese Neumann

Interior Life

Therese Neumann's interior life, into which we have already had some glimpses in the first part of the book, is mirrored most clearly in her own letters. Particularly those from the years 1923 to 1926 are the most enlightening. They date back to the time in which the highest degree of interior concentration was possible for Therese. On April 29, 1923, the day of the beatification of Therese of Lisieux, she was suddenly cured of her four-year blindness. She was once more able to write and give us an insight into her spiritual life, during her blindness and during the lameness that still persisted. It is a deep inner union with the Child Jesus and blessed Therese the Little Flower, but also the dark night of the soul that every mystic has to pass through, that we hear in the words of these letters.

Particularly striking is the passage in which she disagrees with her mother's advice about putting her bed near the window so that she could look out onto the street—her grounds for refusal being that it would be too much of a distraction, and the other passage in which she offers herself as a sacrificial soul, since sacrifice and suffering are her vocation and it is in this direction that she could still be useful as a member of Christ's Church. The letters are presented below, unabbreviated and uncorrected with respect to writing and grammatical errors, together with all the abbreviations used in the original, in order to avoid the danger of any subjective selection in editing the pertinent passages, and also in an effort to preserve the precious and childlike descriptions of her surroundings, her accounts of the little joys that, even as an invalid, she knew how to find in her daily life.

Account of Therese Neumann's Cure from her Blindness

Letter of Therese Neumann to Miss Simson, Pielenhofen, (formerly a teacher in Konnersreuth)

Konnersreuth, May 27, 1923

Dear Miss Simson,

God bless you and Hello! This is my greeting, full of joy. Just think; our dear Lord, through the intercession of blessed Theresia, has given my eye sight back to me. What joy! I will tell you about it very briefly. About three days before St. Nicholas, I got a small lameness in my neck, and I could take only fluids. I couldn't even swallow properly. Even Holy Communion I had to take with water, and only a real little piece of the host at that. This condition got so much worse that on Christmas Day I couldn't even take a single drop of water. This lasted all throughout the twelve days. I was so miserable and exhausted that I hardly was aware of the thirst any more. I thought I was going to die; but what a terrible sorrow that would be, to die without our Savior in your heart. This seemed utterly impossible. Our dear Savior didn't want it that way either and on the day before Three Kings he opened my throat for me again just enough to let me swallow a little bit of water. My condition gradually got better.

But I noticed that, since Christmas, a sore was building up in my stomach again. A little before Easter I could swallow pretty well again but on account of my stomach I couldn't take any food. When Holy Week came around, things were so bad and my stomach sores were so terrible that my heart and lungs no longer functioned, just on account of the swelling alone. I could hardly breathe any more. This condition lasted until April 25. I received the last sacraments in the evening; I was close to suffocation. Our priest felt that the sore would not go away any more; I was so miserable that I hardly knew what I was doing any more. Once, my mother told me later, I suddenly turned stiff and blue, and my breathing stopped, and everyone thought that I was going to die right then and there.

Then just as suddenly the abscess broke and the condition was much improved, but I was still very weak. I could swallow only ice, and the bleeding refused to stop. But it did finally start to be easier again, and things got better slowly; but of course I couldn't lift my eyes, I was so weak. It was April 25 that the abscess broke, the Wednesday evening before the beatification of the Little Flower. On Saturday everything was still night time and dark before my eyes, just like the last four years. Sunday morning, April 29, I opened my eyes again a little—they were still heavy from my last stomach problems.

I was really very weary, dear Miss Teacher, when I opened my eyes all of a sudden, and at first I thought I must be dreaming: everything was bright and clear before my eyes and I pounded for my mother. She came running up, thinking I had taken a turn for the worse with my bleeding. I could hardly express my joy and happiness. I said, "O mother, I can see!" She thought I was imagining it and held a small branch of flowers before my eyes, and I said: "My, but that's a beautiful white blossom. We'll have to take that to Church for May, for the Blessed Virgin Mary." Just think, dear Miss Teacher, what our joy must have been on that Sunday morning. Saturday everything was dark like always and Sunday, early in the morning, I could see everything clear and sharp.

A thousand thanks to God, and to the Little Flower! No one would ever have believed, and me least of all, that my eyesight would ever come back. Just a year ago Dr. Seidel had told my aunt that there was no more hope for my eyes. The optical nerves were dead and it would take a miracle to make them healthy again. On Saturday, April 28, he came to see me and my cramps had drawn my left foot all the way over to my right knee. Then he told me once more: "There's really nothing left to do." I got just a little bit impatient with him for that. Doctors can't see into the future any more than the rest of us can. The future is hidden by God, for our own best interests. We are happy to commit ourselves to his Divine Providence. Our dear Lord can do whatever he wants with us. If he lets me be well, that's fine with me, and if he lets me suffer another fifty years in my bed, that's all right too; if he takes my eyesight away again, that's his business, and if he lets me die, well that would be a great joy for me. Sometimes I get so homesick for heaven. But maybe I have too many steps to climb along my own steep way of the cross.

Dear Miss Teacher, I often asked my sisters to write to Dear Miss Teacher but they never had any time. Don't be angry with me, dear Miss Teacher, for not writing to you so long now. But write me as soon as you can and tell me how everything's going: I'd love a few lines from you. But what I'd really like is for you to come visit us during the holidays. My joy would be really indescribable then. Miss Teacher has a beautiful room, and you could stay there as long as you wanted to. She visits me regularly, and is really a very nice woman and also loves flowers, just as you and I do, dear Teacher. That would be a real joy!

I've got so many flowers that I hardly have room for them any more, 42 different kinds. You could pick out the prettiest ones and then take them back home with you. I also have a cheerful little bird, a siskin. Dear Miss Teacher, do not forget me, I beg you, in your Holy Communion and in your prayers. I have also included you in my prayers and in my sufferings. Blessed Theresia helped me get my eyesight back, and I always had the opinion that she will also beg our dear Lord for the light of grace, so that I can recognize her childlike and virtuous way of life, and understand it and imitate it and arrive at real Christian perfection.

This is my wish for you too, from the bottom of my heart.

Gratefully, Theresia Neumann

Letters to a Cloistered Nun in Tutzing

This nun was a schoolmate and childhood friend of Therese Neumann and both girls had intended to join the missions. Father Naber, since he did not know where to turn, wrote to St. Ottilia's and explained the intentions of the two young ladies, and they in turn referred him to the missionary sisters of St. Benedict in Tutzing. There the other girl was received; Therese Neumann had meantime suffered her crippling accident.

Konnersreuth, May 27, 1923

Hello and God bless you! That is what I'd like to shout out to you from so far away. But above all else I'd say over and over again, "God reward you" for the dear letters which you kept sending me in my blindness and sickness. They always gave me a lot of joy and I had them read over several times. But your last lines, dear Sister, thanks be to God I was able to read all by myself. Your beautiful night prayer I especially like. I read it every evening. And I really think that my dear little canary understands it too. I always read it out loud and when the little fellow hears that I'm reading or reciting something, then he starts singing, and I can hardly understand my own words. Your dear mother once read me a letter from you, and when my bird started singing along, she said he must be happy, just like me. Dear Sister, I never keep him locked up, excepting at night. Every morning my little brother gives me the bird food and I feed him right on my bed, and now he trusts me so much that he eats the food right out of my hand and that makes me real happy and I sometimes tease him too. You know that when I have two or three good days in a row, which doesn't happen very often, then I'm likely to be in real high spirits for a while. Then when he's had his breakfast and some fresh water I let him go back to the window, and later when the little door is opened up he's right back on the top of his little house, and sometimes he sings so much that when

I've got a bad headache I can hardly listen to him. When he gets hungry he hops back into his little house, but he never stays there very long; where he really likes to be is on the little roof.

Dear Sister, my little bird often gives me occasion for many a half hour of meditation. It is true, when we think of it, that our dear Lord made the little birds for our pleasure and when they praise and worship our dear Lord the whole day long, they also encourage us to do the same, and we'd have to have a heart of stone not to have any feelings at all when we hear them sing. Dear sister, since I can see again I've been convinced that I'm in a different world. Everything is new all over again. My mother always wants to put my bed alongside the window, so that I can look out on the street, but I keep protesting, because I'm afraid I'd be too distracted that way. I can already see the beautiful sky and the green trees from my bed, and I've got so many flowers already that I haven't got any room for any more. But I'll tell you about the flowers some other time, if God so wills.

I'm also very happy that I can read things by myself again and don't have to bother other people. But I can't read a whole lot; my eyes will take it but my head gives me a lot of trouble and always starts to hurt. Dear Sister, since I couldn't read any more, I started loaning out all my books, and I had a really beautiful little book about the Sacred Heart, and I lent that one too and now I haven't ever got them back. My dear father wants to buy me another one, but I don't know what would be good for me. I asked our good priest here, and he said he knows the book, but not too well. Dear Sister, so I'm asking you to give me some advice as to what book I should get for myself now, you know, a book I could learn something out of and meditate on. I'm sure you know a suitable one. Then I beg you to be so good as to write me, when you can, where I can get it and what the title is and who wrote it. Dear Sister, I say "God reward you" once again for the Sacred Heart scapular which you took care of getting for me and the sister who gave it to me. I have also included this sister in my prayer and suffering. All the other venerable sisters have also been included in my miserable prayer and suffering. Every day I recommend them to the Sacred Heart of Jesus. You too, dear Sister K., I never forget you in prayer. We were always very close to each other and we want to stay that way. Even though I probably cannot ever come to see you again in this world, dear Sister, we are together in spirit every day. And then in heaven we can always be together again. I too am a Bride of Christ, and I have my own cross to bear. Even though I cannot come to the cloister any more, my bed is just like a cloister cell, where I can offer sacrifices, and our dear Lord will be satisfied with me. I have to do a lot of suffering, but that makes no difference; our dear Savior always gives me the strength and endurance I need to bear up under it, until I reach my goal, where there is no more suffering, in heaven.

Dear Sister, pray to our dear Savior that he will keep sending me patience and strength in my suffering. I can feel another swelling starting in my neck.

With a promise of mutual prayers, I remain

Your friend, Therese Neumann

Konnersreuth, November 21, 1923

Dear Sister,

Last night your dear Sister Anna brought me your joyous news about the approaching feast day. I could hardly contain myself, I had to cry for sheer joy. When I think that my very best friend is going to be able to consecrate herself forever to our dear Savior at the end of this very year, then I cannot keep from crying. You know that I had the same intentions as you did about going into the cloister, but our dear Lord did not want me to go there. I could almost envy you. But no, I will be content with my bed for now; that is the will of God for me. If he wanted to have me in the cloister, he certainly wouldn't have let me get so terribly sick. What our Lord does is always best. At times, of course, I couldn't always see it that way. But now I am happy with my calling. As you well know, dear Sister, I have made a complete sacrifice of myself to our dear Savior. Everyday I renew my act of oblation and sacrifice and unite my sacrifices and prayers with those of our dear Savior. I am also very happy that I am attached to the daughters of the Sacred Heart of Jesus.

I feel that even if I cannot be active, still our Savior will take my life as my activity. I have so many prayer intentions that I'd like to pray for everyone. I feel that our Lord will accept all this graciously. I am a Daughter of St. Theresia and thus I have many intentions. This association is almost the same as the Pious Union for the Poor Souls. The main work is sacrifice for priests and the conversion of sinners, and I have a part in that too. I have an extra reception formula card and I'm sending it along, so that you can get a better idea of the aims and purposes, in case you do not understand them too well right now.

Dear Sister, I congratulate you from the bottom of my heart on your coming feast day. I am so happy about it. Since you've written that you are preparing for the big day, I've been offering many sacrifices for you. In the month of December, in which I will prepare a little crib for the Child Jesus in my heart, I will not allow even the least opportunity for making sacrifices to slip by me. If our dear Savior does not send me enough of them, which is not likely to be the case, then I'll make some of my own. And if our dear Savior gives me the grace, I plan right here and now and solemnly promise you that everyone of them will be offered up to our dear Savior for your intentions. On First Friday and on Christmas Eve when I receive Communion I will present it all to you, dear Sister.

Every year at Christmas I've always kept a novena to the Little Flower so that she will teach me more about the way of spiritual childhood. If it is God's will, I will plan to make another one this year with the help of God's grace, and during those days I will have not myself in mind, but rather my dear friend K. May our dear St. Theresia pray to God to keep Sister K. a most worthy bride of Christ. And then on the day of our eternal espousals I will think especially of you and dwell on this beautiful day with you, in spirit.

Dear Sister, I have a request to make of you, too. Pray for me; especially keep telling our Divine Bridegroom every day not to forsake or abandon your poor sick friend. You don't need to pray for health for me, because our Lord knows better than I do what is good for me. Only tell him that I want to be his bride and remain his bride, even though, as long as I live in this place of exile, I have to keep lying on the cross; because there I am a little more like our Bridegroom, who dies for us on the cross.

Even though my human nature sometimes revolts against it all, there is always great peace in the higher part of my soul. I have only one more wish, and that is to be the cause of nothing but joy for our Savior and never hurt him. But that is precisely where I fail him so very often. And so, dear friend, do not ever forget me. Many greetings to all your dear sisters, I will also make a special memento for your dear Mother Superior on her name's day. On that day I wish her everything of the best.

Once again many many greetings and good wishes from my dear parents and family and especially from myself. I remain, your dear friend, always praying for you.

Theresia Neumann

Konnersreuth, November 7, 1924

Dear Sister,

Finally, after almost a whole year, I can write to you once again. You will be willing to forgive me, I know, because I had too much pain in my head all that time. First of all, "May God reward you" for the dear letter you sent me last year. The letter made me happy at a time when I didn't know what to do with myself any more. Do you mind if I cry on your shoulder a while? Apart from that I really don't have much to say. But I can tell you a good deal about what my dear family told me about my sickness during the early spring and summer.

I don't know a whole lot about it myself. But the girls who visit me tease me a lot. Just recently your dear sister told me again that I got rid of the girls and then was happy that I could be all alone with the Child Jesus to chat with him. But the girls only pretended. Actually they stayed and listened to everything I said. You know, dear Sister, that I spoke my mind and said what I was thinking. And I couldn't see anything either, because I could hardly lift my eyes I was so weak, and besides they were all shut with blood. Our parish priest told me just recently that it was a very precious thing to listen to me then. In my weakness I seemed to feel that the Child Jesus was standing along side my bed and I carried on a real conversation with him. I asked him all sorts of questions and told him all sorts of little things.

Once our parish priest told me the story of St. Lawrence, the Roman martyr, because my back was hurting me. But I couldn't remember it. Whenever anyone asked me if it really hurt a lot, I would just simply say, "Well, the Roman got completely roasted. I'd like to hold out a little bit longer for my dear Jesus." And when they read me your dear letter, I said, "Oh, that's all Latin, I can't understand a single word of it. It's a good thing, Jesus, that you speak German with me."

I used the familiar "thou" in talking to everyone, whether it was my father or mother or the parish priest. And I used to have a lot of arguments with the priest about heaven. He kept insisting that I'd have a gold crown to wear there and the streets would all be gold. But I don't think he really had it right. I said that if it was only gold, I wasn't interested. I had it all figured out with dear Jesus that I would pick only the most beautiful flowers and lay them at his feet and at the feet of the Blessed Virgin. And so I'd like to have some place

in heaven where there was ground to grow flowers in. Just
think!

But there's something else I've got to tell you; we had a
real good laugh about it the other day. I was arguing about
heaven with the priest and I happened to say: "You're getting
just a little bit arrogant, aren't you?" Then he started telling
me that in the Church the saints would also have golden
clothing, and that was enough for me: "That's a little too proud
for me," I told him. Yes, dear Sister, go ahead and laugh.
I have to laugh about it myself now. I used to keep on talking
with our dear Savior until I was so tired that I couldn't say
another word. They tell me all sorts of things that I did and
said. Father said that it was this that made my terrible pains
at least bearable. Just think, dear Sister, a swelling in my head,
and what a torture it was. My loved ones were afraid that I
would never come to my senses again. But, thanks be to God,
I'm back in good shape again.

After Christmas I kept saying: "Really, I haven't been very
brave this year, because my dear Jesus hasn't sent me anything
new to suffer." You know, dear Sister, that every year I get
something new for Christmas. But this year our dear Christ
Child was two weeks late. But then it finally did come, and all
the more for the delay. Two weeks after Christmas I got an
unbearable headache, that kept getting worse. My mind got like
a little child's. "Thanks be to God" I didn't go unconscious.
I could really feel all the pain very well. Even today you can
see the scars on my hands where I scratched my flesh out of
sheer pain. I also pulled a lot of hair out. In Holy Week it was
the worst. I almost bit my tongue clear off, and the swelling
was so bad that I couldn't say a single word. The parish priest
told me that his fingers were always full of blood when he
gave me Communion.

On Easter Sunday I was once again able to take our dear
Savior into my poor heart. An hour later, my swelling went
down and I was a bit better afterwards. My dear mother said
that about a half a pint of pus came out. You can well imagine

how that must have made my head pound, dear Sister. But there was no way to clean out the infection in my head and so it built up again until Corpus Christi. This time the discharge wasn't so big. My eyes were constantly burning, from all the blood, and the lids were open because the wound wasn't quite healed. My eyes kept on bleeding a little, especially when I moved my head even just a bit.

Since Christmas I haven't been able to lie on my right side, and on my left side I can't breathe. So I have to lie there as if I'm tied up all the time. I let them change my bed every Thursday only, because then I always have to be carried to another bed on account of the bleeding. Recently the doctor has noticed that my heart is beginning to fail a little; he says it comes from lack of blood. I'm bothered a good bit by heart cramps: I can't get my breath and I get real stiff. I experienced this seven or eight times during confession. But now it's better again.

So now I've really cried on your shoulder, and you really have a belly full of it. But, dear Sister, now I want to tell you something that will make you happy. Just think, *every Friday* I can receive Communion now. Just think how happy I am. That makes it easy to bear up under everything else. And when I was worse this last year, then I got to receive it even oftener. You'll be perfectly amazed at how I got to receive our Lord. Our dear parish priest always says that I never had any awareness of what was going on around me, but when he came and said who he was then I'd ask him right away if he had my dear Jesus with him in the Sacred Host. If he said no and asked me when he should come with my dear Jesus, then I'd be ready right away and say: "Right now!" Then he'd come next morning.

But my mother would have her cross that night! She couldn't ever leave my bedside, day and night, on account of the bleeding and because they were afraid that every breath would be my last. Our priest came every morning, and evening. Whenever he'd promised to bring our dear Savior in the morning, I'd keep asking my mother all night long if it wasn't morning yet. Then I'd have to laugh and break out in smiles, even though I always had to grit my teeth in pain. We talk about those times a lot!

Dear Sister, thank our Lord with me for giving me so much strength to have all this happiness. I could have almost despaired. But I always managed to hold out, in patience, with God's grace. In fact, once our priest asked me if I wouldn't be willing to give up a little of my suffering, and I answered him right away: "No, our dear Savior only gives me just as much as I need." I pointed to my finger tip and told him: "See, you won't even get that much away from me!" Oh dear Sister, I only wish that you could be here once when our dear priest visits me. Then you could laugh with us, the way he makes everything so highfalutin' when he tells it. I often say: "Oh, Father, we'd better stop right now, my head hurts me when I have to laugh so much! Yes, he said, yes we laughed a lot together, but then we cried a lot whenever we heard you sigh." You see, dear Sister, that there are always some new sufferings to face, but our dear Savior always helps us bear them and he never sends us more than we can bear up under. And I realize that many dear souls are remembering me in their prayers, and that you, dear Sister, are at the head of the line, I have no doubt of that.

"May God reward you" many times for your prayers. I haven't done anything to deserve so much grace from our dear Lord, and so much strength to persevere; all I can claim for my own are sins and weaknesses and negligence. I beg you, dear Sister, and all the Sisters with you, to send a little thought my way, every now and then. Oh Lord, if you really knew how much suffering I have when I write to you you'd be afraid. I can't say exactly how it is, much less write about it. You know I have so much interior suffering too, and that's what's hard. I have such strong temptations against my faith, and against patience, etc. I often feel I'm on the brink of hell. Then I don't even know my own self any more, I'm so abandoned by our dear Savior, and everything is black and dark. And then I have so much anxiety that I'm close to despair. Ah, that's really hard— to really want to have our dear Savior and only other thoughts keep coming into your mind.

I can't write directly how I feel right now. I just can't find the right words. Dear Sister, you'll understand me soon enough. Just think of me from time to time during Holy Communion. I'll never forget you and all the other sisters there who have been included in my poor prayers and suffering. Whether it does any good for them I really doubt, because my present state of soul is really not the best, despite the fact that I receive our dear Savior into my miserable heart every Friday. Every Thursday night all these thoughts keep coming into my mind, and they try to rob me of all my inner peace. But with God's grace I just don't let them take away my peace, no matter what it costs. I keep thinking only that this is the holy will of our Heavenly Father. He knows exactly what such a useless thing as me really needs. And so I abandon myself entirely to his Holy Will. If he hides from me, that's all right, and if he sends me consolation, that's all right too. But it is really hard, when you see all hell gaping open in front of you. Yes, it really scares you some, dear Sister.

Now I've got a cough again. I caught a cold in bed from drinking cold water. I was perspiring from my pain and where I had my rheumatism and I drank too much cold water. But this is really nothing much. Well now, I've cried on your shoulder enough. Next time, if it's God's will, I'll have something different to tell you. How are you and all the other sisters? How did everything go on your Reverend Mother's trip? I think of her a lot. Tell her I send my greetings. How is dear Mother Prioress? Is she still in Ireland? Tell her I send many greetings too. And how is dear Sister Bonita? I've got the beautiful book she sent once more. I had the new one bound and now I've traded it with Father. Tell her hello from me. And how are all the other sisters, Sister Salaberga, Edeltraud—the dear Sister I got the scapular from? Is she still in Bulgaria? Hello to her

and all the other sisters. What is Sister Imelda doing now?
Is she still sick? Hello to her too. But I have a sort of pre-
monition that she's no longer living. And how is Mother Bir-
gitta? Hello to her, too. My thoughts are with you all very often.
If it were God's will for me to be well again, I'd surely come
to see you if I could. Yes, dear Sister, I'm afraid I'm a little bit
curious.

I include myself in your prayers and all the other Sisters'
prayers, especially during these times when I have so much
inner suffering. I need a special supply of grace right now. I
also pray and sacrifice a lot for your intentions. But right now,
my prayers haven't got much value. But I do have another way
to help you. I offer our Heavenly Father the sufferings of Jesus
Christ and the merits of his dear saints and all the pious and
just souls on earth. Neither do I forget the departed members
of your community, and especially Father Hildebrand. Today
I received Holy Communion again which I offered just for him.

And now dear Sister, I'll have to tell you about my two
little birds; they're both so cute and dear. The canary keeps
flying down onto my bed table and pecks little seeds and pieces
of apple right out of my hand. If I have any drinking water
there and he sees the glass, he hops right onto it, swoosh!, and
takes himself a bath so quickly that I'm not even safe from the
flying water in my bed. Now and then he hops onto my pillow;
then he hops from one flower to another. He stays in his little
cage only during the night time. When he sings, he perches on
top of the little roof. That is really precious. But what is truly
beautiful is that such a dainty little creature can be so trusting.
And the other little bird, the goldfinch, sits in his little cage all
day long. But he does sing a lot. And he is so beautiful, so
many different colors. It makes you wonder at God's great
power. Right now they both look sort of depressed and they
aren't singing very much because they're moulting.

Now I've got to close. Just look at the date that I started
this letter. You know, dear Sister, you can't believe that it was
meant to be all one letter. It's long enough for five letters. You

know that often I can't write and when everything is going well enough with me the first thing I do is write to Tutzing. I don't really understand myself what it is that draws me to you this way. Just as if I'd already been there. If I'm getting to be too much of a burden for you, because I really do know that you have many more important things to do than try to puzzle out my handwriting; then you'll have to forgive me again.

You know, dear Sister, I write exactly what comes into my mind, and I can't say any nicer words, not even while I'm talking to our Heavenly Father. I talk to him just like a little child too. And he probably gets a lot of little chuckles out of what I tell him. For the beautiful books I've received I want to say "God reward" you many times to dear Reverend Mother. The Imitation of the Sacred Heart of Jesus is so beautiful that I could almost get by without any other books at all. I'm sending along a few of my old books. I've also got a few marks, from my dear father, and I'll send them off to you whenever I write a shorter letter.

Once again, many greetings to all the sisters there. And especially to you yourself. From your poor friend.

Therese Neumann

Konnersreuth, February 14, 1927

Dear Sister,

Once again I've got far enough along to chat with you, dear soul. In spirit I'm with you a good deal, especially in my poor prayers and sufferings I have not forgotten Tutzing. You'll have to forgive me for being so silent for so long; I had good intentions but never managed to get a letter started. I've been occupied so much with all sorts of people lately and then I was suffering too much again to write—it's always hard to write on account of the wounds in my hands. Maria and Resl have probably already told you that I've taken a change for the better; and you know, dear Sister, things really aren't going so badly for me, although my suffering does take up a lot of my time. But that's my vocation after all. Not in the foreign missions, I can't work there and lead souls to our dear Savior; that is a calling that has been withheld from me here at home.

But it's all the same, no matter where you are; we can be at home anywhere, as they say, until we finally arrive at our true home for which we long so terribly. Ah, that will really be beautiful, some day. Just think, dear Sister, always to be with our dear Savior, never be able to hurt him again, but only to please him, and to live with all the other souls who have the same intention. "Ah, dear Savior, how good you are!" I keep saying. Often I can't even pray any more, just cry. I can't write at all how I often feel; I feel at home and still so strange; you know what I mean.

You know, dear Sister, maybe it is God's Holy Will for you to be able to come and see us, so that we could talk only about our dear Savior. You know hardly a week goes by that you don't see some foreign sisters here, some of them really far away from their homes, and then I keep thinking, maybe I'll be able to see my dear Sister friend again some time. You know that it is not for our own sakes, but we always understood each other so well and liked to chat about our Savior, and I like to do that even more now. Ah, yes, our good Savior. How he has suffered for us. So unspeakably much. And with what resignation and patience and submission he suffered everything. Indeed, we should try to suffer with joy in our turn. You know, dear Sister, our dear parish priest says that my former life was only a preparation for what I am to suffer now. Even if it is hard, it is still easy to suffer and suffer joyfully because you know how good our dear Savior is and how much he is being hurt and insulted even today, and you can do a little bit of reparation this way.

Ah, our dear good Savior. That is all I want to keep on saying now, and crying. Ah, if only we could cause him all sorts of joy. We must use every opportunity we have, whether it is joy or suffering. He wants only what is good for us. Everything tells us the story of his goodness and beauty and love. Yes, nature is an open book in which we can read about God's love and goodness; but we can recognize this love even clearer in the suffering of our good Savior. We must give him all our heart and suffer everything he sends, for his own dear sake. Ah, dear Sister, from the bottom of my heart I beg you and all the other sisters there who are included in my poor prayers and suffering, do not forget me in your prayers and sacrifices, so that we will always recognize God's holy will and act in accordance with it and thus please him and give him joy, and persevere in all our sufferings and all the storms and battles of life. Ah, I beg this with tears in my eyes. Ah, dear Sister, I am almost forced to empty out my heart to you, but I can tell it all to our dear Savior and he understands me.

At present my dear ones and I have another hard battle ahead of us. Don't ever forget us. It's two a.m. right now and I'll close. Please give my very best regards to Reverend Mother, your Superior, and all the other sisters there with you.

In the love of Jesus I greet you too, dear Sister.

Your poor sister and comrade in the Lord.

Therese Neumann

Letters from Therese Neumann of Konnersreuth to a Carmelite Priest

This priest asked her for an account of her sudden cure from her appendicitis through the intercession of the Little Flower. The letter is not dated, but must have been written about the end of 1925 or the beginning of 1926.

On November 1 had a few days of intense stomach pain and fever, which grew so much worse on November 13 that my family called the doctor, who came that same evening. When he had examined me, he said that I had acute appendicitis and it was high time to operate. By next morning even it would be too late. My parents were really frightened; especially my mother who carried on something terrible because I was so weak, she thought, and could never survive the operation. And now I'd have to die in a stranger's hands, after my own loved ones had suffered with me for seven long years. That was really hard for my mother. It was all right with me; with the help of God's grace I was afraid of neither operation nor dying; and where it happened made no difference to me either. In my weakness I told the doctor: "You know, you can cut my head off, if that's what our dear Savior really wants."

My mother composed herself and got everything ready for my departure; we were a good hour's trip away from the hospital. The doctor wanted to take me along in his car, but he was afraid that I was already too weak to sit up. So my father arranged, on doctor's orders, for a carriage in which I would have been able to lie down. I told the doctor: "If I were to tell the Little Flower about this, she'd help me right now." And he said, "Do you think that the Little Flower always works miracles?" He himself telephoned to Waldsassen, to have everything ready for the operation. My mother had the priest called, thinking that he might talk the doctor out of the operation. He spoke with the doctor because he felt that in a case of this kind it was the doctor that should be listened to, and that's right. So everything was just about ready for me to leave.

But the Little Flower proved that she had spoken the truth that year in May—when she said: "No doctor can help you." After the doctor had left, I said to the priest: "I feel that if I were able to tell the Little Flower, she would help me right now; but I don't know if I should do that, whether it would be pleasing to God or not; not for my own sake, because it's all the same to me, but for Mother's sake." And he said it would be all right. Then they put the relics of St. Therese, which I always carry about my neck, over the source of the pain and we prayed to the saint. During this prayer I experienced an almost unbearable pain.

All of the sudden I was in the same state I had been in

on May 17. I saw the same light again, the same right hand and the sweet voice that said this time: "Your perfect resignation and joy in suffering pleases us. And so that the world will know that there is a higher plan at work, you will not need to be cut open now—but right now praise and thank the Lord. But you will still have a lot to suffer and you do not need to be afraid even of the suffering within, that is the only way you can cooperate in saving many souls. Your own self you will have to constantly keep dying to, more and more. And keep your child-like simplicity, always."

When the light had gone away again, I sat up in my bed, after I was convinced that I had been cured, then I got dressed and the priest opened the church for me, after I had told him that St. Therese wanted me to go to church right away. And we all went to church together. I was in perfect health. The doctor was informed immediately, by phone. The poor man simply didn't know quite what to make of the whole business. That night a lot of infection passed out through the bowel. And on Saturday morning I went to Mass and Communion as usual; Saturday afternoon the priest took me to see the doctor who was just amazed when he examined me and couldn't find a trace of sickness left; I was completely cured. Only my lips and gums were so completely burned from the fever that they stayed sore for quite some while. Help me to thank our dear Lord and the Little Flower for this great and undeserved grace!"

Letters of Therese Neumann to a cloistered Sister, a former schoolmate, in Oberschönenfeld

Konnersreuth, June 16, 1925

Dear Friend,

I want to tell you about the great and undeserved grace that I received on May 17. Just think, dear friend, I can now sit up and walk around. I just can't tell you how I feel. The whole world looks new to me again. Yes, every day I go out

walking with my teacher in God's beautiful nature; most of
the time I'm in the parish garden. Sometimes I go with Sister
Xaveria from Altötting. She is here for three weeks recuperation.
We visit the church every afternoon. It's too cold in the morning,
and I don't like to go out among the people too much. On
Sundays I go to Mass, of course, but behind the altar. I always
receive Communion at home, because I can't swallow without
water, in fact I can never swallow the whole host, only a half.

You know, dear Therese, I'm not completely well yet; that
I know for sure, because the voice said that I still have a lot
to suffer. And this makes me happy, because I can't picture a
life without suffering and sorrow. But the worst of the suffering,
in my spinal column, is completely gone now. The bad spot,
thanks be to God, is all cleared up and the vertebrae are all
straightened out once again. I'll tell you briefly how it all came
about, dear Therese.

On May 17, the day the Little Flower was canonized, I was
all alone in my room, making a May meditation. At the moment
I happened to be praying the rosary. All of a sudden it was
so bright and there was a beautiful light in front of me. It was
so bright I can't describe it. At first I was so frightened that
I uttered two loud cries, and even my family heard me from
downstairs. But when they came running upstairs, I neither saw
nor heard my parents at all. My family could see at once that
I was in an entirely different state. Then the Arzberg nurse
came, and my sister Anna; then they went to get the priest.
He said that when he came in the door he saw what state I
was in right away; I didn't look like myself at all. I didn't see
or hear a single thing of what was going on outside me, or
who was there.

But what was going on inside me I do know and remember,
just as clearly as if it were all yesterday. When I saw this light,
I also heard a calm voice begin to speak, and ask me if I wanted
to be made well. I said: "It's all right with me, live or die,
sickness or health, whatever our dear Lord does with me is all
right with me. He knows best." Then the voice said: "Wouldn't

you like to be able to take care of yourself again?" And I answered: "I want anything and everything that comes from God." Then the voice said: "Since you are so resigned, this pleases our dear Savior, and now you shall have another little joy. But you must still suffer long and hard; I have always stood at your side, and I will continue to be your helper; no doctor can help you. Yes, now you can sit up; try it once; I'll help you." Then something took my right hand and I sat up.

At the same moment I felt a terrible pain in my back, on the bad spot. Then I lay down and the voice started talking again. But now the voice spoke only about my inner life. It had a lot of serious things to say about suffering. I won't make any of this public; I only told it to my confessor, out of obedience. There was one more sentence she did add about suffering; "I've already written it." That was the sentence that made the confessor realize that the voice was the voice of St. Theresia, because he was able to find it in her writings, on the following Monday. When the voice had spoken a lot about spiritual things, it went on to say: "Yes, you can sit up now; you can also walk." Then something took me by the hand and I got up once more. Then the voice said a few more things. And all at once the beautiful light disappeared. I started to cry bitterly.

It was only then that I saw and heard my family. I recognized the priest at once, he was sitting beside my bed. He said: "Resl, where have you been just now?" I said: "Yes Father, I can sit up and even walk now, and I want to go out." They took the bed away, I put on a coat, and the priest took one hand while the nurse from Arzberg took the other hand and I walked around in the room for a while: it had been seven years since I could do that. My dear mother looked like a corpse. I lay back down in bed. Then the priest said: "Resl, you've experienced quite a bit now, you'll have to tell us about it." And I answered: "I'll tell you sometime, all alone." He had everyone else leave and then I told him all about it. Then he said that it was a miracle. The next day he came back and wrote it all down.

Yes, dear Therese, the vertebrae in my back are all straight again; my leg is straight again, too, although it is a little bit shorter. How it managed to stretch back out I never really did notice happening. But my dear mother and my dear sisters saw how it was stretching out gradually; at first it was still way up in the air. You can easily recall what it looked like before; and now I can actually walk on it. A few days later Dr. Seidel came and was simply amazed. He examined me thoroughly and discovered that my rheumatism was completely cured. But I'm still not entirely well, you know, because the other suffering that comes from the bleeding is still there. If it were God's holy will for me to be well again, then the voice would have told me that. But the voice only said that I would experience a little bit of joy, and that I could take care of myself again. Now I'm content; without suffering I wouldn't even be able to live. But my family doesn't have all that work to do for me any more. Just think! the cramps and the lameness have all disappeared, thanks be to God.

Dear Therese, be so good as to help me thank God for the great and undeserved graces he has showered on me. I believe you can well imagine my joy. You were very familiar with my suffering. You will remember, too, that I had no hope of ever getting well again; and now, unexpectedly, I am in such high spirits again. At very least, my dear family will not have so much trouble taking care of me any more. Now I can do the washing and I always tidy up the room myself. You see, I can do little jobs like that. Then I go out walking in God's beautiful nature. Everything is so new for me now. How good our dear good God really is towards us sinful people! Oh the many joys of nature! I enjoyed it so very much whenever you would bring me some flowers; and just think, now I can pick them for myself.

Therese, there is something more; pray for me constantly; you know I have so much suffering inside, that I will be persevering and have patience. Then too my longing for death, for the eternal home of heaven, is even greater than it was before. You know what I mean. Say a Hail Mary now and then for the young people, too. Oh it hurts my heart to see how thoughtlessly and foolishly they act. How it must all hurt our dear Savior. The world seems to be a lot different now than during the war. Dear Friend, I know you'll fulfill my poor little wishes. I always pray for you, for your intentions. Every position has its own difficulties. But with God's grace we can overcome everything.

So now I've told you the whole story. I know that you are interested in it. I'd like to write longer, but I've already been at this letter for quite a while—just look at the date I began it: there was always something else. You know I have so many strangers coming to visit me. [There follows a series of personal observations about acquaintances — Author.]

Let's just be content; our dear Lord will make everything come out right. On earth nothing is ever perfect, least of all we ourselves. Often we decide to do everything right and then it never works out that way. And our Lord has got to be satisfied with us, too. He knows we have good will, but he also knows our misery and weakness. With many greetings to your dear sisters in religion I close this letter and remain, in the love of the Most Sacred Heart of Jesus,

Your poor friend, Therese Neumann

P.S. Write me a few lines if you can.

Konnersreuth, October 13, 1926

Dear Friend,

Yes, I've let you wait a long time, but you'll forgive me, I'm sure. You'd hardly believe how busy I've been. I'll be happy when it turns cold again and then most of the strangers will stay away; you know how I've always liked to be alone a little bit; and especially now. Last Saturday a theology professor took me and the parish priest and my father to Waldsassen, where I had a chance to visit with Sr. Emerentiana. She was very happy to see me, and sends you her best regards.

Dear Friend, on your coming name's day I wish you every blessing in soul and body so that we will be able to love our dear Savior with all our strength. We must pray diligently for each other, so that we will always recognize God's holy will and act accordingly. In the coming days I beg you for your own prayers and those of your dear sisters in religion—I never forget them. You know, something very special is in the offing. I'm really quite upset about it, too. Just think, in a short time I'm supposed to leave my little room and go into a hospital for a thorough examination and observation. You know it really does hurt a lot: among doctors that are nothing but strangers and all the examination through and through—it's just terrible. I really beg you, from the bottom of my heart: you and your sisters there pray for me—It's so hard. Oh if only we could recognize God's will even in a case like this.

But don't write anything about this to your father, so that the people here in Konnersreuth won't know anything about it in advance—I don't want any kind of an uproar, because I know they will try to keep me from going. I don't want the people to be stirred up on my account and I don't want to be pitied either, no matter how hard things are. Things weren't any better for our dear Savior. Out of love for him we ought to be able to hold out a little longer. He'll take care of everything and it'll turn out right.

As for my health and general condition otherwise, you can hear about that from your dear father. Every Friday I am privileged to suffer with our dear Savior. Let's both pray for each other so that we'll have the grace to persevere in patience and make our dear Savior happy. In this hope I now close this letter and greet you in the love of Jesus.

Your poor Therese.[18]

---

18. (Author's note on the Letters Quoted Above:)
From a large number of available letters it was possible to select only a very few. The remaining letters are largely a matter of repetition,

Another Letter

The following is a letter written by someone else, a report that Father Kunz, S.J., wrote for the then cathedral pastor, Joseph Kumpfmüller, later Bishop of Augsburg, in 1927. His notes only serve to deepen the impression of Therese's interior life that the reader can already form from her letters.

Feldkirch, August 20, 1927

The Rev. Dr. Joseph Kumpfmüller
Regensburg Cathedral Pastor

I find very satisfactory news to report to you, etc.... In addition there are the impressions that Therese Neumann made on me, which I count among the "great" external graces of my life. Through the kindness of the pastor there I had the opportunity to speak to her and listen to her in her extraordinary states and in her normal state, and especially to get a good picture of her interior life — a golden soul! In the language of the *Exercises,* I might characterize her interior life as the heroic practice of the third degree of humility — the climax of St. Ignatius' *Exercises.* This is joined in her makeup by a burning zeal for souls, an apostolic element ("If only everyone loved you—that would be fine!"), together with her prayer for priestly

———

and this would only prove tiresome to the reader. The repetition is understandable enough: Therese Neumann, in her great joy, had to tell all her various friends and acquaintances about her cures, and in slightly different words. In other cases she had been asked for reports, and in the years before 1926, until publicity and a wider circle of interested public suggested more reserve, she generally answered such requests. She had not counted, at least before 1926, on the prospect of her letters being preserved, and even less that they might be published some day. Thus we can still enjoy the originality behind every sentence. But when her stigmata gained a world-wide reputation for her, in 1926, her letters became more sparse and reserved.

vocations, which are a source of joy for our Savior—and furthermore a sense of reparation in keeping with St. Paul's "I compensate for...." Only she expressed it this way: "I add my suffering to yours, and can distribute it to others, so that everyone will come to love you." Her strength is the Blessed Sacrament, whose nearness she can feel—at least sometimes—with a burning sense of longing. In my opinion this child is highly favored by God and is a living example of the truths of the *Exercises*, all practiced in a very high degree: full understanding, love, and an imitation of the Savior that delights in sacrifice!—And now I recommend myself to your Reverence in the Holy Sacrifice, and remain, in gratitude, etc., J. Kunz, S.J.

Twenty-five years later the following article about Therese Neumann's interior life appeared. It was occasioned by the book of Hilda Graef, the Berlin emigrant: *The Case of Therese Neumann* (see p. 46). The authoress had managed to gather all the opposing voices with great diligence, and without any personal contact in Konnersreuth had managed to construct a book that occasioned much scientific discussion. The false conclusions to which it necessarily led, by reason of its extreme onesidedness, soon quickly provoked a spirited defense by those who were familiar at first hand with the events in Konnersreuth. Thus, already during Therese Neumann's lifetime, we have official statements about her interior life that might otherwise have never come down to us. Father Leo P. Ort [19] died before Therese Neumann.

The Interior Life of Therese Neumann

Character and Religious Life

Therese Neumann's interior life can be judged only by a person who is familiar with her spiritual life and her character

---

19. Leo Ort, O.F.M. Cap., Cathedral preacher, Regensburg.

and temperament. You have to spend a good bit of time with Therese Neumann first and get to know her fairly well, before she lets you see what is going on in her spiritual life. She is not one of those people who like to open up their inner life and experiences before just anyone, in an effort to make themselves interesting. A person who does not know Therese Neumann on her spiritual and characterial side, really has nothing to write about her.

In her book, *The Case of Therese Neumann*, Hilda Graef has, despite all her lack of qualification, undertaken to devote two chapters to Therese's interior life. She admits openly that she has a poor array of material for undertaking this objective, and that she has no personal knowledge in this area. Even though these absolutely necessary sources are closed to her, she still writes and judges about the interior life of Therese Neumann and comes to the conclusion that Therese is a presumptuous and vain person, without any spirit of penance and without any love for our suffering and crucified Savior. In fact, she goes so far as to claim that Therese Neumann is an hysteric and that Konnersreuth could hardly be genuine.

Can this judgment of Hilda Graef's be considered as scientific? Can it hope to stand up under real investigation in such a decisive question? Therese Neumann's character and interior life are precisely the one fundamental basis upon which all the other external phenomena are to be explained. Her characteristic temperament is a decisive factor in determining the genuinity or non-genuinity of these extraordinary external phenomena. If H. Graef is proceeding on the basis of faulty premises, then she must necessarily come to false conclusions.

The purpose of the following paragraphs is to portray a picture of Therese Neumann as she really is. The author of these lines has known Therese Neumann since the year 1940 and had many many opportunities to observe her in connection with his work as a priest and on other visits. Most of the time I spent a part of my vacation there. I believe that I am not being presumptuous when I claim close familiarity with Therese Neumann's character, temperament, and interior life. It does go against the grain some to lift the veil already from many well kept secrets, since it might look like a kind of canonization. But Hilda Graef's book demands a correct statement of truth, a defense of Therese Neumann's honor. May the following exposition offer some small service to this noble purpose.

It makes no pretense to completeness; now is not the time, while Therese Neumann is still alive, to make all these details public. Besides, the interior life of the soul, something that takes place between God and the soul, is something so delicate and mysterious, that even the most thorough description will necessarily be very poor and insufficient.

Father Naber, obviously best acquainted with Therese Neumann's character, described her in the following words:

"Therese Neumann is a big child. She is simply endowed, and has nothing artificial or superstitious nor anything of the devotee about her. She is a simple, natural child, the most simple child in the whole parish, a genuine child in the purest meaning of the word, innocent and deeply religious. Thanks to her sufferings she remains simple and cheerful despite all the extraordinary things that have happened to her; she is a child in her predilection for everything that is small and insignificant."

Childishness is a characteristic trait of Therese Neumann. She is *natural* like a child. Anyone who comes into even momentary contact with her necessarily gets the impression of a natural and normal human being, much like any other. There is nothing extraordinary about her, she is a child of her country with its hardy climate and often bitter poverty. It takes real prejudice, an already solidly formed and final judgment, for the visitor to Konnersreuth to diagnose Therese Neumann as an hysteric. Such a position is a strong echo of the position the Pharisees took towards our Lord. The Gospel said of them: "So they watched him, and sent spies, who pretended to be sincere, that they might take hold of what he said, so as to

deliver him up to authority and jurisdiction of the governor"
(Luke 20, 20).

It is the universal impression and the universal judgment
of all people I have ever met in Konnersreuth, be they priest
or doctors or laymen, that Therese is only natural; there is no
trace of hysteria to be found in her, no desire to make herself
important or interesting. She could hardly be more natural than
she already is. Every complication is contrary to her nature.
She is simple, the way that children are simple, and keeps right
on living her external life even though all these extraordinary
events have given it quite a different stamp. Therese Neumann
has thus remained the same natural person that she always was
and always will be. Therese Neumann cannot be considered
as a stranger to the world or a stranger to life, or filled with a
great "Weltschmerz." She is open to everything good and noble,
and delights in the majesty of God's nature, in flowers and
birds, and also in the accomplishments of technology: automo-
biles and radio. Who could blame her for that?

Therese Neumann is naturally cheerful in her dealings with
people and never loses her sense of humor, even when she is
being teased a little. Her sense of humor is a good one and she
has a lively wit. Dr. Gerlich once saw her decorating the church
and noticed that none of the decorations seemed to satisfy her.
"Therese," he told her, "if you had to earn your bread this way,
you wouldn't get very far." Therese answered him: "The bread
I need I can always earn." (She doesn't require food and needs
only to receive Holy Communion every day.)

Therese Neumann is completely untouched by all suggestive
influence, her own as well as other people's. She is neither
"suggestive or suggestible." It is impossible to suggest a vision
to her or to prolong a vision by the process of suggestion.
Therese Neumann is far too sober and unimaginative for that.
Her visions and extraordinary experiences are quite beyond her
own power and sphere of influence. She does not create these
conditions; she merely suffers them. Every attempt to influence
her through hypnosis comes to no account.

As far as the extraordinary experiences in her life are concerned, Therese Neumann has never looked for them. She finds it uncomfortable to realize that these extraordinary experiences have brought her into the very focus of world wide interest. What she would like most of all is to remain an unknown peasant girl, just like before. But she puts up with the situation because it is our Savior's doing. Of herself, she does not ever want to see anything from other people's point of view. What she likes best is to be alone with her work and with her God and not to be bothered by anyone. I often had a chance to observe how she tried to avoid people. Even when she was watering the flowers in her window box, she would draw back whenever she saw someone watching her, and look for something else to do. "When people pester me," she told me, "I don't like that." She means the curious and importunate people; these are the ones who really get on her nerves. Another time she put it this way: "There's nothing I fear more than these big cars with lots of people who come only out of curiosity and otherwise would never look for the road to Konnersreuth."

When someone suggested to Therese that they ought to lock her up because it was all a fake anyhow, she said: "I wouldn't be opposed to that at all. I'd still have our Savior with me and a lot more rest from people besides." It is impossible to make the honest assertion, as H. Graef does in her book, that Therese Neumann loves "the limelight, being famous."

Therese Neumann is *honest and humble like a child.* Honesty and love of truth are an outstanding trait in her character. There is no trace of pretense about her. It is inconceivable for her that anyone should say something other than what he thinks, and pretend that he is something other than what he is. "I always speak what is inside. I always want to be just what I am, nothing better, and nothing worse either. Everything that is not true is hypocrisy and I don't want to have anything to do with it."

Her love of truth seems to be innate. She stands on the truth, without any other considerations. She always speaks the truth, even when it will cause embarrassment. To deny the truth or conceal it is equivalent to treason and cowardice in her eyes. Even when speaking to highly placed persons, professors and clergy, she always stands up for the truth and, for instance, she won't allow them to strike out one single letter of what she hears in her visions, whenever her recorder understands a word wrong or incorrectly tries to set her straight. Many a time she has done this to Professor Wutz, not because she is stubborn, but because she loves the truth. When Therese Neumann was still a school child and the teacher was telling them stories in school, Therese got up and asked her: "Is that really true?" Even as a child she was the perfect opposite of what Hilda Graef presents in her book.

Since she is honest and stands up for the truth, Therese *openly admits her mistakes.* "I'm so hasty," she admits of herself, that is, easily provoked. Therese does have a lively temperament, but never lets herself get carried away; she always gets hold of herself right away. I had frequent occasion to witness this trait, whenever her brothers' or sisters' many children were visiting her or when she was assigned to help with the servers while she was decorating the church and they often really tried her patience. It is really moving to hear her pray to our Savior and admit her faults: "When a word like that escapes me, [a thoughtless word or a deliberate expression of pain], Savior, pay no attention to it."

Therese's temperament makes it quite possible for her to be unfriendly towards people now and then. She openly admits this about herself: "I certainly can be unfriendly whenever they press me too hard or get too inquisitive; because they've really got nothing important to talk about. . . ." Actually a lot of people do regularly come to Konnersreuth who can be very inquisitive and even tactless. They think they are the only ones who ever make the pilgrimage to Konnersreuth and that Therese has nothing more to do than satisfy their curiosity. . . . It might be that Hilda Graef provoked an unfriendly response from Therese Neumann on one or the other occasion.

But what really counts is the innumerable other cases in which Therese is happy to receive people and listen to their problems and needs, comforting and encouraging them and promising to pray and sacrifice for them. Doesn't Hilda Graef know anything about these cases, or doesn't she want to know? At any rate she might be certain that Therese herself suffers from her temperament. In her honesty and humility Therese herself reckons with the prospect of having to spend some time in Purgatory on account of her "hastiness." Therese Neumann's somewhat rough nature, together with her rather sharp temperament, makes every purely external expression of etiquette as unwelcome as every form of sentimentality. It is a mistake to look for the over-refined ways of a finishing-school girl in the manners of a simple country girl who has gone through a life of bitter poverty and hard work.

Nor must we forget that even in the Gospels we find many strong expressions of dislike in the mouth of the saints, in fact, even in the mouth of our Lord himself, expressions which can cause scandal to oversensitive souls. When, for example, our Savior calls Peter a Satan (Matt. 17, 23). Or let us recall his sharp expressions against the Pharisees. Then there were judgments about our Savior too: People speak a lot about him; some say he is good, others say, no, he is seducing the people (John 7, 12). How could it be any other way in the case of Therese Neumann, or, necessarily, with anyone who wants to take Christianity seriously?

Therese Neumann knows her own mistakes, but she does not, on that account, consider herself as the worst person in the world: "I am not the worst sinner, Savior, that is not true. Nor is that arrogance on my part. You know what a poor wretch I am, but I cannot make myself out worse than I am." Therese could never stand the kind of people who pretend they are worse than they are—we call this "hunchbacked humility"—because it is a veneer over so much dishonesty and secret pride.

There is something infinitely conciliatory about the fact that people who are highly favored by God have their faults too

9 *Therese Neumann*

and often have a serious struggle with their temperamental weaknesses. Sinlessness and holiness were only for our Savior and his Blessed Mother. All other men, even the saints, have to pay their bitter tribute to original sin.

Therese openly admits she is a "dumb girl." "Oh yes, I really mean it. I know that I'm stupid." She knows how to put this weakness to good advantage, by abandoning herself more and more completely to the will of our Savior; because "the Savior does nothing wrong, but I could always get things all mixed up." "After all, what have I really got to be proud about? I'm not very clever, and even if I were, that would be a gift from our Savior anyhow." Whatever is extraordinary in her she ascribes to our Savior from whom all things emanate. "It would be pretty stupid to imagine you are really something; it's all our Savior's work; he can do whatever he wants." This is Therese's way, for instance when she tells our Savior: "Savior, we weren't the ones who started all this, that was your work. And you have to bring it all to a happy end, too."

Therese Neumann is *pious like a child*. The essential quality of Therese's soul is her *restless, unconditional, and childlike-trusting resignation to our Savior and his divine will*. "I want everything that our Savior wants. It's all right with me: being sick or well, living or dying, whatever our Savior wants. If our Savior wants me to suffer, then I suffer. If our Savior sends me some joy, then I accept the joy. I don't want to have any other will than our Savior's." This is why Therese is happy when feast days come, when the suffering diminishes; but she is just as happy on the days that her suffering increases. She seeks our Savior and his love. This is why she does not look for deliberate or personal extraordinary sufferings and sacrifices.

This attitude is the *key to her spiritual life*, to her piety, to her whole way of looking at life. Anyone who considers Therese Neumann from any other point of view and tries to understand her, cannot possibly be correct, even with the best of good will. This piety holds up under every criticism. Is such resignation to our Savior and his divine will merely the beginning of perfection or is it perhaps already a rather high degree of moral maturity? Isn't this the very same attitude that our divine Savior, according to St. Paul, first expressed at the very beginning of his life on earth; "Behold I have come to do your will, O God"? (Heb. 10, 9). And that is also the attitude of the Blessed Virgin when she spoke to the angel: "Behold the handmaid of the Lord; be it done according to your word" (Luke 1, 38); holy conformity to the will of God in accordance with the teaching of the Gospel, the Church, and all the saints, is the touchstone of perfection. Such a spiritual attitude harmonizes perfectly with the demands of Christ, the teaching of the Church, and all the basic principles of the saints and theologians.

Hilda Graef is scandalized at Therese Neumann's lack of piety. She finds so much vanity in every conversation with the Little Flower, because Therese "lets herself be praised" for her equanimity towards sickness and health. But we must briefly recall Therese Neumann's position. She was already in bed for more than six years; what is more, she had been blind for four years, and as helpless as a child, dependent on the help of her parents and sisters. Who would not like to be well? Besides, Therese Neumann was used to work from her childhood and had a will and zeal for work that few other people have. Idleness was and is something fearful to her. Work is second nature for her, a heritage from her parents. You can hardly think of Therese without anything at all to keep her busy. And now this mysterious voice holds out the prospect of health; and still Therese says: "It's all right with me, being sick or well, living or dying. . . ."

What would we have said? Without a single exception we would have accepted the very first time it was offered and said: yes, then I could work again and be with people and not need to bother people with my sickness any more. But Therese said: "It's all right with me, being sick or well. I am happy with everything that our Savior wants. And my greatest joy is in our Savior himself." Surely such an attitude is pleasing to our Savior. And surely such resignation must draw down the choicest of God's blessings. It takes a completely false concept of perfection to pass over such unqualified resignation to the divine will and look for any other explanation.

Hilda Graef objects to the fact that Therese Neumann has no love of suffering. She is right insofar as it is repugnant to the natural man to say yes to suffering. But what Therese Neumann really says is, "Suffering is something you cannot want." Is there any more natural conception than this? No person can possibly look for suffering for suffering's sake. That would be against human nature. Even our Savior in Gethsemane prayed: "Father if it is possible, let this chalice pass me by" (Luke 22, 42). Was this imperfection on his part? According to H. Graef this is the only explanation.

But Therese Neumann says: "Suffering can be desired only out of love for our Savior." From this point of view, Therese Neumann does have an explicit love for suffering, because she has an explicit love for our Savior. "It would be terrible," she once told me, "if our Savior were to spare me all my Friday sufferings." When I asked "Why, after all, are you in this world?" She answered me: "So that I can work, and speak with our Savior and endure suffering." Another time I asked her: "What does religious life really consist in?" and I got a really splendid answer: "In really loving our Savior, putting great trust in him, and being glad to endure suffering so that our Savior can distribute the merits from it." These words are the expression of a true love for our Savior and a love for suffering at the same time, and also a great apostolic love for souls and the awareness of what Paul describes in his letter to the Colossians (1, 24), "In my own flesh I make up for the body of Christ, the Church, whatever is still lacking in the sufferings of Christ." Therese says the same thing in her own clear simple way: "I add my little bit to the very much that our Savior has done." On another occasion she was speaking of her intentions: "That other people also learn to know and love our Savior." She likes to write this on the little holy picture she distributes: "Savior, every sacrifice willingly for love of you." She herself would have dearly loved to be a missionary sister and have gone to work among the pagans, to win souls for our Savior.

H. Graef can establish no tangible fruits of this suffering and prayer in Konnersreuth, especially no mass conversions. But are we to expect that the workings of God's grace would register such precise results in a soul? Surely the words of our Savior are true, "By their fruits you will know them" (Matt. 7, 20), even for Konnersreuth. But it takes a bit of insight to see these fruits; they are not wanting. I have been personally acquainted with the parish of Konnersreuth since 1940—I worked there as a priest—and I must admit that as far as religious and moral life are concerned, Konnersreuth stands in the very first place with respect to other parishes.

On the mission in October, 1947, in which I worked myself, my superior, Father Expedit, an old and experienced Capuchin missioner, admitted in the very first days of the mission: "You cannot miss the undeniable influence of Therese Neumann." And another of the Fathers said: "This is a prime example of a real parish; one you don't often run into."

H. Graef is scandalized by the fact that Therese performs no extraordinary works of penance, never wears a hair shirt, has her own "luxurious" bench in Church, and sleeps in a soft bed at home. She portrays Therese Neumann as a person who is afraid of sacrifice, prudish and affected, and unwilling to suffer. And yet Therese's life is filled to the brim with suffering and sorrow; she certainly does not need to go out looking for any more. Suffering is her own personal vocation in life. Her life consists of one suffering after another. She suffers constant pain in her stigmata and from the wounds of the thorns in her head. Even the least movement causes her pain. You have to have experienced it yourself, the way she softly moans in her sufferings and then keeps saying: "Gladly, Savior, gladly!"

It is characteristic of her Friday sufferings that she not only sees our Savior, not only follows him on the way to the cross, but suffers along with him, in body and soul, everything he suffers in his body and soul, and with the immediacy of a person who was right there with him, all the way from his agony in the garden and sweating of blood in Gethsemane, to his crucifixion and death on Golgotha, until she sinks down all but lifeless on her pillow.

It is impossible for this suffering to have a psychogenic origin in an hysterical imagination. "I could always do without my suffering" she said just recently. "I'm always glad when a day with a feast comes along. I'm happy when our Savior wills that I don't have to suffer. And when the day of suffering comes, I say: "Savior, it's all right with me." Therese never looks for suffering, the way many saints have done. She accepts everything, just the way it comes, with a brave and positive resignation. This is precisely what is so natural and attractive about her attitude. This also excludes every danger of self-satisfaction and self-seeking, as so easily occurs in the case of a self-conquest that is self-imposed. It takes a lot more self-denial to accept every sacrifice that comes along with life and which God imposes upon us, than it does to look for sacrifices of our own choosing. If Therese were vain or hysterical, then she certainly would have undertaken external and extraordinary works of penance and would have delighted in speaking about her mystic experiences; but this she always carefully avoided.

Because of her physical constitution Therese suffers a lot from colds, which often result in inflammation of the lungs, glands, and nerves. It is impossible to understand how anyone could take exception to the "luxurious" chair behind the high altar in the parish church. Why shouldn't Therese have a cushion and an upholstered chair, to spare herself, after she has hardly been a single moment without suffering and is cold from loss of blood. The chair was given to her as a present, to keep her hidden from curious eyes. I can recall the occasion of one visit during which she suffered the entire time from a severe toothache, with the nerve exposed. When I advised her to see her brother or his wife, both of whom were dentists, she said: "I won't die of a toothache; you've got to be able to put up with it. I've already made a present of the suffering to our Savior. I'd be ashamed to take back the sacrifice now." Is that avoiding suffering and being afraid of sacrifices? Anyone who describes Therese Neumann as afraid of pain and suffering and sacrifice, simply does not know her. Therese is never concerned about herself. She works until she can do no more and she suffers until she is unconscious. She leaves herself out of the picture with an energy and intensity that are seldom equalled.

Therese Neumann is familiar with the worst kind of sufferings and is glad to accept them. But she also knows the *beauties of suffering*, because she accepts it all willingly; "Suffering is hard, all right," she once told me, "but it is beautiful too. Then I'm away from the world; then I'm in Jerusalem, walking with my Savior." This state of affairs makes it possible and bearable for so many people to be admitted to Therese Neumann's suffering. That is also why all these visits present no temptations for Therese; in her spirit she is no longer present. Our Savior has carried her off and brought her to the place he wants her to be.

Once again it is always the *Savior* about whom the thoughts of her mind, the feelings of her heart, the decisions of her will all revolve. It is a really passionate love that she has for her Savior; working and suffering for him, taking his side and fighting for him, that is her deepest and most heartfelt joy. This is the precise area in which she applies the whole energy of her strong and lively temperament and its inclination to sacrifice. This is why Joan of Arc is such a favorite saint for her:— In her love for our Savior nothing is too much, either time or money, in her effort to decorate God's house, the Church. Anyone who comes to visit the Konnersreuth Church on a great feast day is astonished at the magnificent decorations that adorn not only the altar, but the whole church. Therese puts each individual flower in the vase with great patience and love, and prays while she is doing it: "Savior, I love you and when I am no longer here, then this little flower will still be here to tell you that I love you."

Her whole *prayer life* is built up upon her love for the Savior H. Graef also criticizes Therese Neumann for not meditating on sufferings, making the way of the cross, and praying the sorrowful mysteries of the rosary. The reason for all this is to be found in the fact that when Therese meditates on Christ's sufferings—in the way of the cross or the rosary,—the pictures and experience from her visions of Christ's sufferings all come to life again and she becomes unconscious. "That's bad," she says; "that really gets to me." Therese never deliberately offends anyone, quite unlike the usual hysterical type of person. Hilda Graef need not be disturbed to learn that Therese accuses herself of distraction in prayer, because she is so deeply absorbed in one religious thought that she cannot pray with other people. Actually, she prays more intensively than any of us do. Her prayer is an active prayer and not a quietistic one.

Therese also prays and meditates much more intensively than we do. She has arranged her own form of the rosary. At every bead she prays: "Savior, I love you, you are so good." Most of all she loves the "exultation" as she calls it—prayers of praise. "Savior, you are good. Savior, you are wise. Savior, you are mighty. Savior, you are the Most High, etc." She has great wonder before God, and she is deeply moved by the prospect of God's grandeur and power, whether she experiences this in prayer or in the contemplation of nature and its glory. Her prayers of petition are almost exclusively apostolic. "I have to pray for the other people now; I don't have any time for myself."

In other respects Therese's prayer is much like our own, sometimes out of prayer books. She especially loves to pray the Mass prayers along with the priest, as well as the psalms and breviary. She has a special devotion to the Holy Spirit, the Eucharistic Heart of Jesus, and the Blessed Virgin Mary. And she values personal prayer, the kind that rises from her own heart much more highly than mere oral prayer. Hilda Graef must be suffering from a serious misunderstanding if she believes that Therese wants to do away with oral prayer or the priest's breviary prayers and put the prayers of her own heart in their place. Therese would like to say simply, in her conversation with every priest, that we must praise God not only externally with our lips, but even more so in our hearts. This is in perfect harmony with the words of our Savior: "The people honor me with their lips, but their heart is far from me" (Matt. 15, 8). Even in her prayer life, Therese's inner truthfulness comes out strongly. She never prays any prayers that do not suit her and correspond to her own frame of mind.

It is always one of the most moving experiences for any visitor to Konnersreuth to hear Therese, if possible, when she is talking about the events of the Passion or making her thanksgiving after Communion. She speaks with our Savior in such a childlike way that everyone is deeply moved. In these moments we can see deep into her soul and being, and realize that she is nothing but a child.

Therese's spiritual life can be described in the words of our Savior: "Unless you become like children, you cannot enter into the kingdom of heaven" (Matt. 18, 3), and "Father, I praise you, because you have hidden these things from the wise and clever, but have revealed them to your little ones" (Matt. 11, 25). Perhaps our Savior means to illustrate these words anew in the case of Therese Neumann. As long as Therese Neumann still lives in our midst, there can be no definitive conclusions about her interior life; final judgment belongs to the Church. But this much can be said with certainty, right here and now: Therese Neumann is completely free from all hysterical traits. She could not possibly be any more natural than she is and act any more naturally than she does. She has both feet firmly planted in the reality of life, full of understanding and capable of sharing in the joys and sorrows that countless people are always bringing to her door. She is constantly and unreservedly devoted to our divine Savior and his holy will, and filled with a childlike and loving confidence in him. Therese Neumann can be well described in the words that begin the Book of Wisdom, and serve as admonition to all of us: "Think of the Lord with goodness, and seek him with sincerity of heart. For he is found by those who do not try him, and is manifested to those who do not disbelieve him" (Wis. 1, 1).[20]

---

20. This statement, never published by the author, was made available to me in a carbon copy. Meantime it was published in July of 1963, in the journal: *Ewige Anbetung* (*Perpetual Adoration*) 56th year, Volume 7 — Author.

Mystical Life

The mystic and charismatic life of Therese Neumann was many-sided and in a constant state of development. In the first part of this book, in the chapter on charisms, we presented a schematic survey. The following accounts of Therese Neumann's experiences are arranged in the same outline, to facilitate comparison. In many examples there are traits that are common to several distinct charisms. The individual accounts in the following pages are not broken down, in an effort to keep this outline intact, but reproduced in the same form as they are noted in Father Naber's journals, or recounted by eyewitnesses. This procedure avoids the inconvenience of distorting the plastic composite view of an individual report or breaking individual sections out of their context and continuity.

Therese's Visions

It seems almost mandatory to preface the account of Therese's visions with a few general remarks. Visions, in the history of mysticism, belong to the rarer mystic experiences. In the Scriptures of Old and New Testament there are accounts of visions, and the history of the Church has never known a single century that has not been enhanced by the visions of one or several mystics. When we begin to examine into the phenomenon more closely, we are surprised to discover that visions on the same theme do not correspond in every detail in the account of every mystic. As a result, we are too easily inclined either to reject visions entirely as historical facts, or else to give credence to one visionary on some subjective grounds that seem to vindicate his claim, and deny it to others. Neither of these approaches is the right one. As we delve deeper into the study of visions, we learn to distinguish different factors in a comparison of visions on the same theme; comparison suggests prudence, but never prejudice in our observations.

The first and most important is this: God is not bound to an exact and precise reproduction of history in the vision. Most of the time he grants visions only for the personal edification of the visionary, although he might also intend them to stir up or deepen the faith of the visionary's milieu. Also he never lets the vision run very far beyond the grasp of the individual favored by this special grace. Thus the mere fact that unhistorical or legendary facts are often included in the vision, must not lead us to conclude immediately that the vision is not divine in origin.[21]

Secondly, we must not lose sight of the scholastic principle that everything that comes from God is received by the visionary or the recipient of an inspiration, *"per modum recipientis"* (that is, in the manner proper to the receiver), and then reproduced in keeping with his nature and natural abilities of expression. It is also conceivable for the contents of an individual's consciousness, already embedded in the memory, to blend together with what is perceived in the vision. The vision contents thus pass through a sort of subjective sieve. We can perhaps best understand this circumstance by thinking of the often immense discrepancies in eyewitness reports of one and the same event: for instance, a car accident. The individual accounts are often

---

21. Cf. Herman Lais, *"Eusebius Amort, and his Doctrine on Private Revelations,"* Freiburg, *Theol. Studien,* No. 58, (Freiburg, 1941) pp. 52-55. On the same grounds, stigmata, insofar as they apply to the case in question, show marked variations, both in form and in the part of the body affected.

quite disparate, not only on the basis of where the witness was located, but also according to his individual abilities of perception and expression, even though the genuine desire to tell the truth is quite beyond doubt.

A third factor, and one which frequently needs to be given far more weight, is the fact that the one who reports the vision or mystical experience is not always able to hold perfectly to the objective statement of the facts, either out of frivolity, or incapacity, or else the fact that they cannot write down the things they have seen or heard until some time after they took place, relying on their memory, and thus introduce slight variations of facts into their reports.

For Dr. Gerlich, for example, the fact that the visions of Anna Katharina Emmerich, as reported by Brentano, did not correspond with those of Therese Neumann in some points presented a serious problem. Brentano was a poet and we can easily get the feeling from his language and expression that much of what he reports is presented subjectively and elaborated for the edification of his readers. Even before he was taken into protective custody, Gerlich was working on a concordance of Emmerich and Neumann, and he was always faced by the basic question of whether a given vision was the vision as seen by Emmerich, or, in the best and honorable sense of the question, something added and interpreted by Brentano. This preoccupation of his proved to sharpen the historical judgment of those who were working together with him.

Taking all these facts and considerations into account, I have made every effort to preserve as far as possible the authenticity and love of truth that stands out in the original, in presenting the following visions, and also in reproducing any of the other reports and documents, and thus, to the best of my ability, excluding the third of the above-mentioned factors.

There is a further consideration in the special case of Therese Neumann: Therese was a simple peasant girl, and had not read very much up to the time that her first vision occurred. From the stations in the parish church she had formed a conception of the surroundings, clothing, and conduct of the people involved, that was completely different from what she experienced in her visionary accounts.

Gerlich once mentioned, when he was with Therese in the church, that she must see the passion in approximately the same way as it was presented on the stations there, but she answered: "Oh no, Doctor Gerlich, it's nothing like that at all, especially the soldiers" (Gerlich 1, 170).

Insofar as they could be controlled, these details were so striking and suitable (for example, the location of Jerusalem, the clothing of those times, articles of home furnishing, etc.) that the vision of the whole course of the event seems to gain in probability. Then, too, Therese had these various visions not only once, but year after year, as we have already explained, and the visions of the passion were repeated almost every weekend, throughout her whole life, always following precisely the same course of events. These facts, now that we have already called attention to the factors that make for uncertainty in the vision, might well serve to underscore a particular qualification in this special case, for the acceptance of the historical truth of many visions.

Historical and Tableaux Visions

Visions of the Passion

The most impressive of Therese Neumann's visions (and, since for decades visitors came from far and wide to see it, also the most famous of her visions), was the vision of Christ's passion, the so called "Friday sufferings." In contrast to the other visions which were repeated in the course of the church year in strict liturgical sequence, Therese Neumann had these visions more than 700 times over the course of her life: the Passion and the evening preceding the Passion were presented in from 35 to 50 partial series of individual visions, with different beginnings and endings. Every Thursday night and Friday they would be repeated, but they never occurred in the joyous liturgical seasons (from Christmas to Septuagesima and from Easter to the Friday after the Octave of Corpus Christi) and throughout the rest of the liturgical year on those Fridays on which a feast day fell (as well as on Fridays in the octave of feasts), for example, feasts of the Blessed Virgin and the Apostles, St. Joseph, and also the Feast of the patron of the church at Konnersreuth, St. Lawrence (August 10), or on the diocesan patron St. Wolfgang.

The liturgical connection was so strict, that in these last two cases the Friday sufferings were interrupted only if Therese happened to be in Konnersreuth for the Feast of St. Lawrence, and somewhere in the diocese for the Feast of St. Wolfgang. Since she had no experience or awareness of this fact, twice in her life she was "surprised" by the Friday suffering, because she had counted on having the next Friday "free" and had thus planned a trip or visit. The one case took place in the Castle of Zeil and the other in Eichstätt (see p. 193).

The Friday visions are distinct from all the other visions also in the fact that they left their mark on the body of the visionary. From the vision of the Garden of Olives, the blood would begin to flow from within her eyes and flow down over her cheeks, and the stigmata would also begin to bleed. The blood from the scourging, on Good Friday, would soak through her shirt and bed-jacket. The crown of thorns would bleed through her white head cloth in nine big areas and several smaller ones. At the Crucifixion, during Lent, her shoulder would swell up and then a large blood stain would appear on her bed-jacket. The witness to these visions always saw a complete and very moving image of a martyr, but always noble and edifying, never unesthetic. Her hands would move towards her head in an effort to tear out the thorns. In her visions of the nailing to the cross, the fingers of her outstretched hands would jerk violently in pain, and her tongue would run over her parched lips.

The bleeding phenomena were not the same on every Friday; they always increased in intensity during the Fridays of Lent, reaching a climax on Good Friday. On Holy Thursday and Good Friday the visions were also prolonged beyond their usual duration. They generally began with the vision of the passage to Mt. Olivet, shortly before midnight, and ended with Jesus' death on Friday about one in the afternoon. But on Holy Thursday they would begin with the preparations for the Last Supper and end on Good Friday with the vision of the burial. The hour of death, one o'clock in the afternoon, coincided with the death hour as marked in Jerusalem. There the clock is two hours ahead of German time at that season of the year; it is three o'clock in Jerusalem. Thus according to the system of reckoning used in the Roman Empire, in which the hours were counted from six in the morning, it was the ninth hour. These last visions, of Jesus' death, she sometimes used to have on the Friday before Palm Sunday, the so called "Sorrowful Friday" (in the former liturgy, the Commemoration of the Seven Sorrows of the Blessed Virgin) while the washing of the feet and the institution of the Blessed Sacrament occurred not only on Holy Thursday, but sometimes also on the morning of Corpus Christi.

As Therese grew older, her Friday sufferings also began to decrease in Advent and other times outside the feast days and festal seasons mentioned above, or at least they were shortened whenever Therese Neumann was sick or too exhausted from her sufferings of reparation. In the last years of her life she had visions of the Passion outside Lent only on the feast of the Sacred Heart.

Only once did these Friday sufferings have a very special character, entirely different from their usual form, and that was on Good Friday of 1951 (I was at Konnersreuth myself on this day, as I was on many other Fridays—Author). On this date Therese saw the whole Passion as usual, but she did not have to suffer along with it. As a result there was no bleeding either from her eyes or from her wounds, or any of the other

Therese Neumann, the bird-lover.

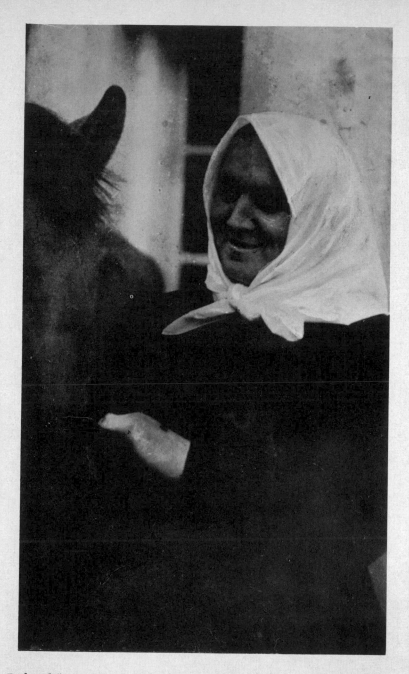

Resl and "Lotte" the horse she bought for her visits to care for the sick (around 1946).

Pilgrimage to St. Nickolaus von der Flue (1938). Therese was always well-covered and well-wrapped whenever she went out publicly.

The Trinity - Pilgrimage Chapel, 4 km. from Konnersreuth: note the strong symbolism in the three towers, three cupolas, and clover-leaf ground plan.

The tabernacle in the parish church at Konnersreuth, decorated by Therese Neumann in honor of the Church Patron (St. Lawrence). Several thousands of flowers have been arranged with great love and care.

Konnersreuth after the shelling in 1945.

Therese Neumann standing near the spot where she was later buried.

Therese Neumann in 1952. Therese asked the author to take this photo for the then obligatory identification card.

In October of 1957 the rusted weathervane was taken down from the Konnersreuth church tower and a great gilded metal cross was put in its place. An American helicopter flew the heavy cross to the tower. Left: Therese helping protect the top of the cross from the cable. Right: The pilot does a masterful job.

Visitors in Konnersreuth, Good Friday, 1950. The crowds are so thick that the Neumann home is not yet in sight. American soldiers in the foreground.

Good Friday, 1959. Visitors
stream to the Neumann home
despite the pouring rain.

Good Friday, 1957, in front of
the Neumann home.

Therese Neumann during her Pentecost visions (taken in her room).

The stigmata shines through Therese's gloves in her vision of light, May 17, 1927.

Therese is sitting in her place behind the main altar. In the background, the sacristy door.

▼ Therese Neumann during her Pentecost visions (taken in her room).

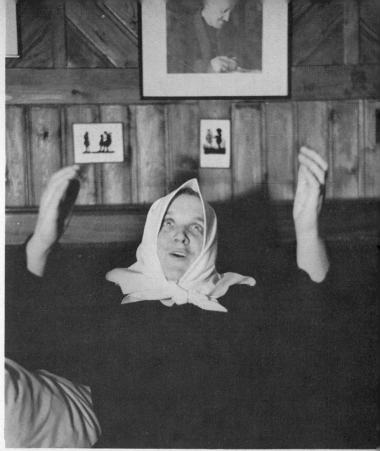

The vision of the Ascension, Easter, 1936. above: Christ hovering above the ground. below: Disappointed at our Savior's disappearance, Therese attempts to seize him and cries out: "Take me along!"

Early that Easter morning Therese had an ecstatic communion, after her visions of the Resurrection. Sitting in her place behind the altar during Mass, she is swept into a vision at the words of consecration; with an expression of great joy she sees the risen Savior coming down onto the altar.

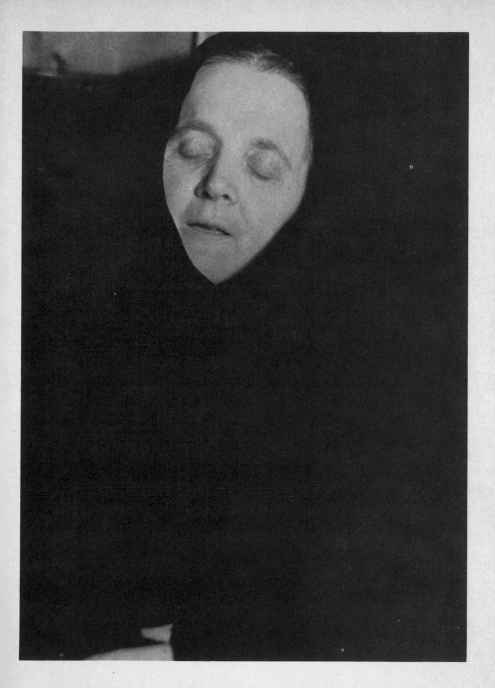

This was followed, up until the priest's communion, by the ecstatic state known as the "prayer of calm."

Ecstatic Communion: (Easter morning, 1936) In place of the priest, Therese sees our Savior coming with the Sacred Host. Taken in Therese's room.

usual places on her body. The thousands of serious and curious visitors were informed that today they would not be able to see Therese Neumann. The next day the sensationalistic press was already announcing that Therese Neumann's special graces had apparently ceased, and her adversaries were rejoicing in their sudden triumph.[22]

What had happened? Father Naber made an announcement

---

22. Excerpt of a letter to a teacher in West Germany:

Regensburg, at Mt. Olivet
March 27, 1951.

"Dear and Honorable Madam......

All Good Friday I was on edge to see what this day would bring to pass in Konnersreuth.... On March 23, 1928, Konnersreuth experienced its first fiasco,... and now 23 years later, on March 23 again, and this time Good Friday, the whole thing fell to pieces right in front of everybody. In 1928 the mother of this "bleeding wonder" had called her to everyone's attention, now she is no longer here and can't be of any help. Her daughter will be 53 on April 9; where is she going to get the blood she needs?.... Konnersreuth is finished now; it's dead. Hilda Graef's book, *The Case of Therese Neumann* (Mercier Press, Cork, Ireland), came out at just the right time, in 1950 — I helped work on it. Do you understand English? If you do, then I'll send you one of my five complimentary copies. Greetings from M. Waldmann."

I refrain from expressing any judgment at all on this letter, which pretty well speaks for itself — the claims it makes have been pretty well repudiated by the facts over the course of the eleven years that followed. One thing should perhaps be noted: the author of the letter is a theology professor who was very active as a moulder of public opinion for many people and served as the fountainhead for many projects that were directed against Konnersreuth. The addressee asked Father V. in M. for his opinion; he sent directly to Konnersreuth for an answer and included a "verbatim" copy of the above letter.

Professor Waldmann, who wrote against Konnersreuth under the pseudonymn of Michael Silvanus, abbreviated as M.S., refers, in his mention of the date March 23, 1928, to the commission which was actually in Konnersreuth on that date, but had *missed the* beginning of the passion and the active bleeding.

to the waiting crowds and quieted them by telling them, all of them who had come from any real religious motivation (the explanation was suggested to him by Therese in her state of elevated calm), that that day marked the 25th anniversary of Therese Neumann's stigmata and that was why she did not have to suffer. As a result no one would be able to see her today. The visitors all urged to go to the church and pray and offer up their disappointment to our Savior; they would then receive greater merit than if they had been allowed to see Therese Neumann. Happily we can note that the dissatisfaction of a few of the visitors never came to any open expression; it was surpressed by the understanding and ready acceptance of the majority. After the end of Paschaltide of that year, on the Feast of the Sacred Heart of Jesus, 1951, the Friday visions and sufferings started again as before.

Below we present a catalogue of the visions as they used to occur on Holy Thursday and Good Friday. Essentially I am following the notes of Father Naber and Cardinal Kaspar, as enlarged and completed by Therese Neumann's own notes and descriptions of her visions. Another source of real significance were the recordings that Ferdinand Neumann made of her conversations (in a state of prepossession) with Father Naber during and after her visions. They made it possible to achieve a very special control and amplification of the material already on hand.

Course and Content of the Passion Visions

Holy Thursday, about 11:30 p.m.: 1. *Vision:* Our Savior on the street with ten apostles; Peter and John are missing (they had been sent ahead).

2. *Vision:* A hall (she called it "a beautiful big room") into which our Savior is being led by a "good man"; it is furnished. The number of men was more than had been on the street by "one and one more"—that is how she counted in her

state of prepossession between the visions. Peter and John were present this time.

3. *Vision:* Further description of the room: there were no chairs, but only seats with slanting backs to lean on, dark brown plates, not completely round, knives but no forks, only hook-shaped "little scrapers." A big knife in front of our Savior. There is a fire burning. There are three lights set up in a triangle, with "little beaks" from which the flame burns. A man with a "pointed cap" brings a lot of greenery and the Paschal Lamb on a spit. Our Savior paints some of the blood on the doors and sprinkles some into the fire.

4. *Short Vision:* Beginning of the supper.

5. *Vision:* Our Savior walks around with the men. They are singing; our Savior begins the song [Therese made a sign of the cross during this vision] and the others all join in. "Our Savior led the song beautifully." Then they all go out of the door. Asked whether she heard any of the words, she said yes, *"Halleluia, Elohim, Adonai."*

6. *Vision:* Our Savior washes the men's feet. One of them doesn't want his feet washed, but he gives in after being asked to (Peter).

7. *Vision:* Therese looks reverently upwards, then against her will and very sadly, to her side, then with a happy expression, upwards once again. (Before the words of consecration in the Mass the priest says the words . . . *et elevatis oculis in caelum.* . . . Jesus looked up to heaven before transforming bread and wine into body and blood. (Therese was following his gaze). Content of the vision: our Savior says "something big" (the words of consecration) and gives everyone a piece. He says something else and one of them, "the one with the red hair," hurries out. Then the Savior speaks again and gives the men something to drink.

8. *Vision:* The men are talking together. Our Savior gets up and prays (the "high-priestly prayer"). "It's hard for him." When he sits down again, the "young man (John) rests his face on our Savior's left side. Some of the other men are stand-

ing and some are sitting." After this our Savior goes out the door with all the men.

The group of visions recounted above were experienced only on Holy Thursday and partially on Corpus Christi. The next vision begins the regular weekly occurrences, about a quarter to twelve on Thursday and on Friday.

9. *Vision:* (normally no. 1): Therese searches all around her. It is dark, and she is following the others in their way to Mt. Olivet.

10. *Vision:* Our Savior goes over a little bridge (across the Brook of Cedron) with the men, up the mountain to his left, and into a garden. First he comes to a little house, then a big one. Here part of the men remain. Asked how many were left behind, Therese counted them in her usual manner, looking over the group, "one and one more and one more, etc." to the number of eight. Our Savior goes on ahead with three of them.

11. *Vision:* Our Savior is praying in the garden, on his knees; then he goes back to the three (first prayer). Therese begins to shed big tears.

12. *Vision:* Our Savior's second prayer. Once again he comes back and then leaves again, after he finds the apostles sleeping. Therese's eyes begin to bleed, the first drops of blood coming from behind her eyes.

13. *Vision:* Our Savior prays for the third time. He is sweating blood. An angel ("luminous man") comes and comforts him. He goes back to the three and wakes them. They were the "younger man and an older one and a still older one."—Therese already has streams of blood on her cheeks, drops of blood on her bed-jacket, and the wounds in her heart begin to bleed.

14. *Vision:* The crowds come with "burning boughs" (torches, that is) from the street. One of them is leading the way, the one that "ran out after our Savior gave him the bread."

15. *Vision:* Clash between the Apostles and Judas. The Apostles keep crying: *"Machada, machada* (What's wrong?)" Then they recognize Judas and start shouting: *"Ganapa, magera"*

(You villain, a sword!). Peter draws his sword and starts to fight (later, in her state of prepossession, Therese calls him the "earlobe-cutter"). They ask the policemen whom they want and they answer: *"Jeshua Nazarea"* (Jesus of Nazareth). Jesus answers: *"Ana* (I am he). All the policemen fall down, but not the "good men" (Roman soldiers). When Jesus says *"Kume"* (Get up), they all get back up.

16. *Vision:* Therese smiles. She takes Judas' kiss for a sign of friendship. But her expression takes on a note of horror. She complains of pain in her hands: they tied up our Savior's hands, after he had just "put the wounded man's (Malchus') ear back on." The stigma on the back of her left hand is inflamed and begins to bleed.

17. *Vision:* They lead our Savior away. They took hold of the smock of a "young man" (cf. Mark 14, 50 ff). When they tried to seize him, too, he undid the clasp on the right side and ran away.

18. *Vision:* "They pushed our Savior into the water" (crossing the Brook of Cedron). The stigma in the right hand and in the feet begins to bleed.

19. *Vision:* "One of them slapped our Savior for no reason at all. Our Savior didn't say anything sharp at all." Bright red blood flows out of the left hand stigma onto the back of her hand. Therese groans from the pains in the place of her heartwounds.

20. *Vision:* Our Savior is led into a house (Annas').

21. *Vision:* Our Savior is brought before Annas.

22. *Vision:* Our Savior is standing before a man with a big beard (probably Annas). He is mocked. The hand stigma bleeds once again. It is to be noted that the surface of the hands sinks somewhat when the blood streams out (Gerlich).

23. *Vision:* Our Savior is standing before another man, "with a brilliant robe, with something like little horns on his head and something special on his breast"; Therese traces a pattern with her hand, down and across on her breast: What she means

is the Ephod of the high priest, divided into twelve plates with the names of twelve tribes of Israel engraved on them. Our Savior is struck in the face.

24. *Vision:* Fire in the outer courtyard. "The earlobe-cutter is being talked to." He denies that he knows our Savior. She hears the rooster crowing, and refers to it later in her state of prepossession with the words: "The animal made his noise (using a dialect expression which can be applied to all animal noises and which occurs again in her vision of the three kings, when the camels and horses make frightening noises after the star goes down over the place where the Holy Family is staying).

25. *Vision:* "The man with the little horns has ripped his robe." The high priest Caiphas tears his garments as a gesture of condemnation. Peter is spoken to by an old woman and once again denies that he knows Jesus. Once more the rooster crows. In the same moment, "our Savior looks around and sees the man (Peter), who then goes out and cries."

26. *Vision:* Our Savior is led into a "dark, cold hole," along such a narrow and low passageway that you have to duck down in order to walk along it. The prison is a narrow cell in which at the most two persons can stand up together. Our Savior remains locked up there until morning.

Here, about two in the morning, the visions are interrupted. From the time of the approach to Mt. Olivet the visions had lasted a good two hours, from two to five minutes for each individual vision, and were always interrupted by a state of prepossession, in which Therese, in response to questioning, would express what she had just seen in her childlike way. During the visions she sat upright in her bed, her hands raised and held up somewhat in front of her. In the state of prepossession she would sink back weak and exhausted onto her pillows and her hands would drop to the bedclothes. After this last vision the state of elevated calm would generally come upon her, during which she would tell, in her usual restored vigor, how the Savior was now restoring her strength.

Next morning the streams of blood that had run down her cheeks would all be dried, her eyes caked shut, her bedjacket drenched in blood above her heart, even though, before the suffering and visions began, Therese had bandaged special compresses over the heart wound. Her wrists, too, showed evidence of dried blood which had come from the stigmata in her hands.

27., 28., 29. *Visions:* Jesus comes before Pilate, is sent away to Herod and then back to Pilate. Therese also sees Pilate's wife. She sends some word to her husband that makes him very uneasy ("Have nothing to do with this just man...." Matt. 27, 19).

30. *Vision:* Therese looks on in horror and turns her head from one side to the other. She is seeing the scourging. Our Savior is stripped completely naked, and he looks around very much disturbed. His hands are bound once again, and then, with his face towards a pillar, he is raised up with his arms stretched upwards by the same thong that binds his hands, until he is standing on his toes. Then three groups of men (two men in each) of drunken policemen start beating on him with different kinds of scourges, as hard as they can and with undisguised pleasure. When they see the exposed parts of his body are already all swollen and would be torn to shreds by further scourging, they turn our Savior around and scourge him the same way in the front. When they have finished, our Savior is so swollen and sore then that he can hardly bend to pick up his clothing which is lying on the floor. Then one of the servants gives them a kick with his foot so that they fly off a few feet further. While Therese is having this vision of the scourging, wounds break out on her breast and back, bleeding through her bedjacket. She gets particularly angry with the servant and speaks some rather sharp words to him. "If I'd have caught him, I'd have taken him down a peg or two."

31. *Vision:* Crowning with thorns. The crown of thorns is not made up of one single crown of thorn branches, as it is so frequently depicted, but it looks like oriental crowns, that are not open on the top, as in the Western countries, but closed

and round (compare the present-day head covering of the Eastern Church patriarchs), like a sort of a basket, with many long pointed thorns, which is placed on Jesus' head, and, in order to keep the soldiers' hands from being wounded, pounded into place with a stick. Now the wounds from the crown of thorns begin to bleed through her head cloth, in which nine particularly big patches of dried blood appear after every Friday suffering.

32. *Vision:* Jesus' condemnation. "The bald-headed man" (Pilate—he is often referred to as the "Idrauminet"—dialect German for *Ich trau' mich nicht:* "I don't trust myself." is washing his hands. Our Savior is delivered over to the Jews.

33. *Vision:* Therese thinks that they are loading building beams on our Savior's shoulder. The cross that she sees does not look like the way we picture a cross, but consists of three pieces of rough-finished wood, bound together with cords, one long unfinished stem piece and two shorter rough-hewn beams (these seem to have been hewn some time before; Therese noted that they are weathered). His already sore and swollen shoulder begins to bleed afresh under the weight of the load. A great spot of blood wells up over her right shoulder and stains her bedjacket.

34. *Vision:* Jesus walks along the way to Mt. Calvary. He stumbles under the cross and is roughly dragged back to his feet.

35. *Vision:* On the way of the cross Jesus sees his Mother accompanied by John and some of the women. Therese hears him call *"Immi"* (My mother!). One of the "good-for-nothings" who are carrying the tools that will be needed, notices that it is Jesus' mother standing there and he takes two of the nails out of the box and shows them to her; the Blessed Mother faints when she sees them and John catches her as she begins to fall.

36. *Vision:* They tell a stranger that he is supposed to carry Jesus' cross. Therese keeps beckoning with her left hand. She

wants to help get the stranger's attention and have him help our Savior.

37. *Vision:* The man is recognizable as a foreigner by his strange clothing and the way he wore his hair and beard (a Greek, Simon from Cyrene); he comes up with a cane under his arm, and two boys, a big one and a smaller one. They want to see what is going on there. The man is ordered to help carry the cross. He is adamant in his refusal. One of the prison people forces him. He is very angry to be treated and talked to this way, and he keeps complaining loudly and his lack of cooperation causes Jesus' second fall. Then our Savior turns to him as he gets back to his feet and looks at him with a "divine look" (Therese's expression in her normal state.) This "divine look" comes up from time to time in other visions as well. For example, when the Three Kings came and saw the poverty and misery of the Holy Family, they doubted whether they were in the right place. Then the child, who was now a year and a half old looks at them with a "divine look" and their eyes are immediately opened; they cast themselves on the ground and adore the child, touching the earth with their forehead. When he sees this look in our Savior's eyes, not only does Simon give up any further resistance, but he seizes the cross so powerfully in the very middle that our Savior hardly has any weight to support at all. Resl continues to walk the way of the cross behind our Savior. She hears a loud clatter in the group behind her. It is the two thieves who are in chains and have to drag their crosses after them over the uneven road.

39. (sic) *Vision:* A woman comes up with a young girl, who is carrying a jug of water. Resl knows the woman; she is the same one who secretly approached our Savior in the crowd and touched his garments, and he cured her of her hemorrhage (Veronica). Now she is very upset as she sees our Savior's disfigured face, all caked with blood; she takes off her shoulder veil and hands it to him. He wipes his face with the veil and gives it back to her: the imprint of his face is visible on it.

40. *Vision:* The procession has arrived at the city gates.

41. *Vision:* Women with children are standing along the way. They are crying. Resl hears the Savior call them *"Benat Jerusalem"* (Daughters of Jerusalem). The "upright men" (soldiers) force the women out of the way.

42. *Vision:* Our Savior's feet get tangled in one of the ropes that they are leading him by and he falls flat on the ground.

43. *Vision:* The policemen yell *"Kum"* (Get up), and seize our Savior by the shoulder, in order to raise him to his feet. They are afraid he will die before they have crucified him.

44. *Vision:* The procession has arrived at the place of the crucifixion, on the not too high mount of Calvary. It comes to a halt. Our Savior is led into an old and partially collapsed grave.

45. *Vision:* The three beams of the cross are nailed together. The pinned ends of the two hewn side beams are driven into corresponding holes in the long unfinished stem piece, and fastened there with wooden wedges and pegs.

46. *Vision:* Our Savior is laid out on the cross to see how everything fits. The place for the head and hands and heels and the middle of his body are all marked out. Then he is led back to the grave. Resl sees him sitting there, still clothed, but shivering in the cold. "You've got to remember," she once told me in her normal state, "that it was still early in the year and besides he certainly had a high fever by now from all the wounds."

After this vision—it was generally about 11 o'clock in the morning—there was another long respite of about an hour, during which Therese was once again strengthened by the state of elevated calm. During this same time, as Resl recounted in her normal state in the summer of 1947, the cross was being prepared in the following manner (she sees it lying there later at the beginning of the crucifixion vision): the unhewn stem piece is barked and planed down from the top down to the spot marked for the heels. Three hollows are hewn out, one for the crown of thorns, one for the middle of the body, and one for the heels. In the places marked out for the hands two holes are bored in advance, and a third hole is bored in the place hewn for the feet. Finally another piece of wood is nailed to the hollow hewn out for the feet, as a support. On the top of the main piece there is an inscription nailed on. In the rocky ground—Golgotha is made largely of limestone—a vertical hole has been bored out, to receive the cross when it is erected.

About twelve o'clock, Therese quickly rises out of her exhausted position on the bed and sits up again, holding both hands out before her. This is the beginning of the great crucifixion vision, which lasts until a quarter to one.

Our Savior is brought up and they rip his clothing from his body, even though it sticks to his flesh with the dried blood. All his wounds are torn open anew. Our Savior stands there naked, deeply troubled by the shameful treatment, and looks around in search of sympathy. A brave woman there takes off her shoulder veil and hands it to him. With a grateful look, he takes it and wraps it around himself. Then the policemen throw our Savior down on the cross, and tie him tight by the hips.[23]

Then they tie his right hand to the cross beam in the neigborhood of the wrist and drive the nail through the right hand in the hole that was bored there beforehand. When they come to the left hand, they see that the hole has been bored

---

23. Author's note: As a result of the hollowing out beneath heels and seat and the several bindings that hold him to the cross, there is considerably less weight on the hands than if the body had merely been fastened with only three nails to a smooth surface. This also does away with anatomical problems, such as that the surface of the hand must have been torn if the nails had been driven in through the middle of the hands, etc. Dr. Hynek, M.D., from Prague, was originally led by such considerations to postulate a nailing through the wrists, but when he heard of the Konnersreuth visions, he abandoned this view and revised his position — he was a champion of Therese Neumann and an ardent follower of her progress.

too far outside. They tie a cord to his wrist and pull it out until it fits the position of the hole. In so doing they tear the arm out of the shoulder socket. Then this arm is also bound tight and the nail is driven through the hand. Therese hears the individual hammer strokes. She jerks up her knee under the blanket as each hand is nailed in place. From the wounds and stigma fresh blood begins to flow. Her fingers are bent inwards and keep jerking back and forth in pain.

The nailing of the feet appeared in the following manner: first the knees were tight together. Then the prison people held the right foot tight against the footrest and drove the nail through it, the same size nail as in the hands. This nail is later pulled out and thrown away (later it is gathered up by Jesus' followers and kept as a cherished momento, together with the other nails). It serves only as a preliminary fastening, to keep the foot from pulling free when the other foot is nailed in place. Then the right foot is lifted into place over the left foot, and a longer nail is pushed through the already pierced right foot and with one powerful blow, followed by several other blows, it is also driven through the left foot into the pre-arranged hole in the wood.

The policemen put the title in place, lift the cross with the aid of a few beams, and let it fall into the hole bored out in the stone. Resl's violent shuddering and the expression on her face clearly portray the terrible pain that our Savior's body must have experienced in this sudden shock. Therese sees our Savior go unconscious for a few moments; his head falls forward. The cross does not extend deep enough into the ground; it doesn't hold well enough. The policemen lift it out again, deepen the hole a little and pile rocks around it. Then they set the cross back into place, a little bit more carefully than the first time. Then it refuses to stand up vertical; it hangs a little forward, weighted down by our Savior's body. It seems that the people have counted on this, or had the same experience with other crucifixions: on both sides of the cross, near the smoothed surface of the main stem, there were two rings already in place, a little towards the back and rather high up on the stem—so say the recordings—with cords hanging from them. With these cords the cross is drawn backwards and then braced into place against two pegs that are sunk off to the side. Then more stones are piled against the foot of the cross and wooden wedges are driven into place. When she was asked in which direction the Savior was looking, Therese said that she was facing the Temple herself while she stood directly in front of our Savior; thus our Savior was crucified with his back to the Holy City. The crosses of the two thieves were somewhat forwards and off to the side so that our Savior "had them both in view." The whole arrangement must have corresponded somewhat to three points of an octagon.

From now on Therese's gaze is upwards. She hears the mockers and the words of Jesus, praying for the soldiers and forgiving them. She turns her head to the two thieves who have meanwhile been crucified, too, smiling towards them right and left. Meantime, streams of blood have been flowing from the inside and the outside of the stigmata on her hands, joining in the neighborhood of her wrists and drying there. Once again she hears our Savior's words addressed to those below. John and the Blessed Mother have meantime come up and taken their stand beneath the cross. Therese looks back and forth between Jesus and Mary a few times, tenderly and full of compassion. At Jesus' words, John goes over to the Blessed Mother and supports her. She also sees Mary Magdalene: "The girl is standing real close to the cross and she's all covered with blood in the front.

Darkness falls. It falls also on the soul of our Savior as he writhes in his final agony and wrenches the final words from his lips: *Eloi, Eloi, lama sabaktani*—My God, why have you forsaken me! The hardest, the most desperate moment in his whole life has come. Darkness and gloom prevail in the world of nature, there is a pale and unnatural light. It is "uncanny." Therese hears the birds uttering frightened cries.

She says—according to the recording—"Our Savior felt as

if his Father no longer wanted to have anything to do with him, and I felt myself as if our Savior didn't want anything more to do with me." His fever makes him say: *"Aes-che"*— I'm thirsty.[24]

They give him the sponge with vinegar. Our Savior sucks at it, gets new strength, and cries *"Salem kulechi*—it is consummated." And a short time later: *"Abba, beyadach afkedh ruchi*— Father, into your hands I commend my spirit." Resl also observes that rocks are splitting open. Our Savior bows his head and gives up the ghost. At the same moment Resl also falls back onto her pillows as if dead. Her lower jaw falls slightly open, as in a corpse, her mouth comes open a little, her face turns ash grey, her nose becomes pointed and she looks just like a dead person.

This was, generally speaking, the end of her passion visions. On Passion Friday and on Good Friday, however, these visions were followed, after some little time, by still others.

1. The thieves have their legs broken. Therese turns away with a shudder and hardly dares to look at our Savior, because she fears a similar fate for him. But then a soldier comes along with a lance and pierces the dead Savior's side.

2. The Blessed Mother is standing under the cross. They are pulling out the nails and untying our Savior and letting his dead body down to the ground. Therese already knows the people who are helping with the work. They were with our Savior that night (Joseph of Arimathea and Nicodemus). The

---

24. When these words were heard for the first time, Professor Wutz refused to believe them. He had expected something different — *sachena* — and he pronounced the word for Resl. But she would not change her story: she had heard the word *Aesche*. Then Wutz consulted specialized works and discovered that there was such a word for "I'm thirsty." According to his investigation it is a neo-Hebrew word. Neo-Hebrew seems to stand somewhere between Hebrew and Aramaic. This example, like many others of a similar kind, effectively counters any attempt to explain the *phenomena* of Therese's visions in terms of suggestion.

ladder does not look like the kind of ladders we are used to: it was a strong shaft or pole with rather steep steps alternating on right and left.

3. The Blessed Mother is sitting on a carpet and leaning against a stone. They are laying her dead son on her lap. Resl sits very quietly and watches with deep emotion.

4. Resl breathes with distended nostrils. She smells a sweet aroma, the scent of the ointments with which Mary Magdalene, her dress still spattered with blood, is anointing the winding clothes which are to enclose our Savior. Therese puts one hand over the other and shows how Jesus' hands are arranged. She moves her hand in a gesture of wrapping. Then she sees them carrying the dead body away and laying it in the grave, not far from the hill of the crucifixion. In a further vision she sees the priests and Pharisees very ceremoniously sealing the grave. Then she falls into a deep and deathlike sleep.

This is the normal course of the Friday visions. They are not always divided so exactly from one vision to the other, as recorded above. But as far as the content is concerned, they were always the same, that is, Therese never saw anything different, anything she had not seen on some other Friday before, even though the extent of the vision varied during the course of her life, sometimes expanded and sometimes abbreviated.

In a conversation with Therese Neumann in her normal state, in 1947, I had occasion to record the following words about her visions of the passion, which are added here as an appendix: "As our Savior hung on the cross, you could see something between his arms and the cross beams, but not the way you see space between his arms and the horizontal crossbeams in our pictures, with the beams on top and the arms underneath, but just the reverse of that. The one cross arm was set in somewhat deeper than the other." I completed the following sketch under her supervision [p. 181].

She also made the following observation: "Longinus was not the captain that cried out: 'Truly this was the son of God.' This captain jumped down from his horse when our Savior died and passed on his superior's command to his subordinate officer. *That* was Longinus, and he then pierced Jesus' side with the lance. Both men were at the mass baptism on Pentecost. Pilate's wife was there too. From the time of the Ascension she had already joined the group of those who were privileged to be there."

The following interesting explanation appears in the recordings: When the soldiers had divided up his clothes and cast dice for his robe (not with our kind of dice, but with pieces of wood), the "old man who was with our Savior at night" (Nicodemus) went up to them and asked them for the clothes and robe. They were happy to sell them. "They were glad to be able to get something for the bloody garments; and the other man was even happier, but he didn't show it."

On Saturday Therese was generally fully recovered again. Only on Holy Saturday she had to sleep all day until Easter Sunday morning; she could not be talked to and it was only with difficulty that they could wake her up to wash herself.

In conclusion, since it is not Jesus' death but rather his resurrection, his triumph over death, that is the central mystery of our faith, we must report one more section of Father Naber's journals that lets us share their Easter joy.

Easter Sunday April 8, 1928. "About five in the morning Therese Neumann arose from the deep sleep which had lasted since Good Friday and had a vision, in five sections, of our Savior's resurrection and the related events in the garden where he was buried.... All the suffering had disappeared. Therese's heart was ready to burst for joy. Say in your sermon (these words were spoken in her state of prepossession) merely this: "The Savior is good, the Savior is good—even if everyone thinks you are a fool for repeating it."

According to Therese Neumann's visions, Jesus appeared to his mother first before anyone else. She had gone with the other ladies on Easter Sunday morning but, deeply moved, she had stopped at the place of the crucifixion, while the other women went on to the grave nearby. There our Savior appeared to her, just for a moment, without saying a word, just looking tenderly at her and radiating the indescribable and more than earthly glory of his resurrection. Immediately after this the events that are recorded in Scripture took place.

* * *

The material limits of this book, as we have already pointed out, are not broad enough to present the beautiful visions of Easter Week, the Christmas visions, the Three Kings visions and the more than a hundred other visions that spread over the liturgical year. They must be reserved for a later book. Here we have room for only one more important vision, that of the Assumption.

Visions on the Day of the Assumption

Preliminary Note:

The following notes are based on observation and questioning of Therese Neumann in her room in her parents' home at Konnersreuth, during and after the visions on August 15, 1947. The notes were read to Father Naber and Therese Neumann in September of 1950 and amplified and corrected by both of them on many points. The following presentation is based, as a preliminary report, on other visions for other feasts of the liturgical year and on statements made in the state of exalted calm, and also draws heavily on the notes of Dr. Fritz Gerlich, August 15, 1928 (I, 262-3). It must be expressly noted from the outset, that these visions do not begin with the promulgation of the dogma "Mary, bodily assumed into heaven," which took place in 1950, but already occur at the very beginning of Therese Neumann's visions, more than 20 years earlier.

Ephesus and Jerusalem

Mary, the mother of Jesus, had spent a few years with St. John in Jerusalem after Jesus' Ascension: John was working in and around the city. Then they both moved to Ephesus. A few years later, during which time the primitive Church kept spreading, they were given a beautiful house, a few hundred yards southwest of the city, and they lived there for several years.[25]

Mary's death

First Vision: Therese sees Mary and the Apostles gathered together in a large hall, which she recognizes from her earlier visions: it is the room outside the Last Supper room, the room in which the holy women were waiting during the Last Supper and preparing for the Passover by prayer and meditation. The Apostles have grown much older, but Therese still recognizes all of them. She does miss James (he had already been beheaded by Herod around the year 44—Author) and Thomas. But then the number is increased by the presence of the temperamental Paul, whom Therese also knows from her other visions, and another man, whom all the Apostles all treat as an

---

25. This presentation obviously contradicts the account of St. Epiphanius (403), and the Church tradition which has always maintained, since that time, that Mary did not leave Palestine after Jesus' death. But then she had been committed to St. John's care by her dying son, and given to him as a mother in turn, received and acknowledged with great love and respect, and why should she have any reason to part from him? Nor is there any grounds, on the basis of contemporary historical research, for putting off St. John's apostolic work in Ephesus until after the Blessed Mother's death. At any rate, it is our duty here merely to report Therese Neumann's visions, as they are presented to us by observation and inquiry, as precisely as possible, and leave everything else to subsequent judgment of the Church.

equal, but whom she does not recognize and has never seen in any other visions. In Father Naber's opinion this must have been St. Barnabas (cf. Acts, 9, 27; 11, 22-30; 13:1-2; 15). The Apostles are seated, or rather reclining, as was the custom in those days, all around the Blessed Mother. They are resting on upholstered couches that have an arm to lean on rising up at an angle on one end, but no backs. Therese also notices some other earlier disciples and some men she doesn't know, "but they were sitting farther to the outside." None of the women were known to her. And there were no women sitting among the Apostles.

They are talking about Jesus, and while the Blessed Mother is moved with great longing and love for him, she suddenly grows very weak and pale and sinks back. John catches her and she dies with her head resting on the breast of her "second son" lying in his arms. At the same moment Therese sees her soul rising up from her body, a living but incorporeal luminous shape. Our Savior appears with a tender smile on his face, radiating in the bright light, and takes her soul, then the luminous shape disappears from view. The Apostles stand sorrowfully around the dead body. John closes the Blessed Mother's eyes and mouth and kisses her on the forehead, the right cheek, and the mouth. Then all of the Apostles and women do the same. Therese takes a lively part in their grief, and during the vision tears stream down her cheeks. When she tells the story later in a state of prepossession, she goes back into the state of contemplation and the second vision follows, the laying out of the body.

Her Burial

Second Vision: The body is prepared for burial by the women, anointed and wrapped in winding clothes, with pungent herbs bound into the bandages. Peter and James (the Younger) go out into the valley of the Cedron and look after the grave for the Blessed Mother's body. It is hewn out of the rock that rises up from the valley floor, in such a way that the entrance is not vertical (as in Christ's grave) nor horizontal (as in Lazarus' grave) but rises at an angle. First you go up a few stairs (there were more stairs in Lazarus' grave, none in Christ's) and then the burial chamber narrows into a horizontal tunnel. There is no antechamber to the grave, as in the Savior's grave, only an oblique gate lying right before the entrance. On that same day, a Saturday, the body was laid to rest and the sepulchre was sealed. The fact that it was a Saturday does not come from Therese's first telling of the story: it was a note she added upon being questioned in a state of elevated calm. The other indications of the day of the week involved in each vision all originate from a like source. The Blessed Mother's death occurred on the same day, but rather early in the morning. Therese recognized that it was morning by the position of the sun and the angle of the shadow, because she had seen this same hall at other times of the day as well (dinner time).

The Assumption

The following, third, vision is the most beautiful and moving, the principal vision of the Assumption. Therese sees herself transported before the Blessed Mother's grave. It is early morning (Sunday); no one is to be seen far and wide. Suddenly there comes a light from heaven. Two angels come hovering down with the luminous substance of Mary's soul. Therese recognizes one of them: it is the angel of the Annunciation, Gabriel; the other she does not recognize (later, in a state of elevated calm she mentions that it was the Blessed Mother's guardian angel). The three luminous shapes make their way into the sepulchre without being hindered by the closed door. They come back out immediately, but Mary is no longer a transparent luminous form; she comes out with her living and transfigured body, radiant, and wearing a garment of light. It is indescribable; the closest description would be to say that it was as radiant as fresh new snow in the sunlight. But even that is not enough. Her head and hands are free, and only a little of her feet can be seen. The glory and joy of the apparition is shared by the visionary, and even those present can share something of it, since they are privileged to see a radiant human countenance, more brilliant than ever before.

The angels are escorting the Blessed Mother, supporting her with one hand under her arm and the other on her back; they are carrying her up into the air. This carrying is to be considered as an honor rather than a necessity; there is no longer anything material or heavy in the glorified body of the Blessed Mother (it had passed through the closed door of the grave). Therese's eyes follow the figures and the expression of joy in her face suddenly mounts to its fullest possible measure. Christ appears from above, radiant in unspeakable glory, together with all the heavenly court: countless angels and saints. The Savior moves towards the Blessed Mother, St. Joseph at his side, incorporeal but still recognizable. When they meet in heaven, St. Joseph and our Savior take the place of the angels who were escorting the Blessed Mother, in order to lead her solemnly into heaven as Queen of heaven and earth, amid the jubilation of the blessed choirs of angels—since it was she who first joined heaven and earth together.

With a genuine enthusiasm that far surpassed anything observable on the occasion of any other visions, Therese was able to share this glorious and joyful event. She cried "Take me along!" and raised her hand out towards the luminous figures hovering overhead, standing on the very tips of her toes. so that you had to look to see whether she was still standing on the floor or not. Actually, a group of absolutely trustworthy witnesses, among them priests, declared that on the occasion of the same vision in 1938 at the cloister in Steyler in Tirschenreuth, she was actually raised a little bit from the floor and hovering in the air for a while. On September 24, 1950, in Konnersreuth, I met an eyewitness to this event, Mr. Dost from Hildesheim, who vouched for its truth. Therese was lifted about a foot off the floor and stayed for a while in this position, hovering freely in the air. In 1947 I myself was unable to observe any such elevation.

Another experience must be recounted in connection with this vision: On July 7, 1940, when Therese was on her way back from the First Mass celebration of her convert priest friend Paul Lutten—formerly Evangelical, a high-school teacher in Hamburg—she had suffered a stroke. It attacked the left side of her brain in three distinct seizures (on July 7, 10 and 13) and made the whole right side of her body lame—testimony of the attendant physician, Dr. Josef Mittenforfer of Munich. Her right leg was lame, the arm hung down; her right eye could not coordinate with the left but stared straight ahead, resulting in squinting and great difficulty in seeing; the right side of her mouth was paralyzed, her tongue was impeded so that she could make herself understood only with difficulty. For nine days she lay in a sort of coma, her consciousness more or less impaired. On the occasion of the vision of the Assumption in 1940 the following occurred, in Therese's own words:

"When the Blessed Mother was taken away from the grave by the angels, she smiled at me, then moved slowly towards me and held her right hand over my head. Then, although I otherwise never feel anything from without in the course of my visions, I suddenly felt a very strong electric shock in the right side of my body. I raised my hand to grasp our Blessed Mother's hand." Father Naber adds: "For all of us it was a very moving sight to behold, Therese suddenly shuddered during the vision and then with joy in her face she raised her formerly lame right arm towards the left side of her head. Her eye also straightened out at once and she could speak normally once more. Her eye kept moving throughout the rest of the vision and she could stand up and walk. We all experienced great joy." After the vision Therese was able to go into Church without any help.

This event was also substantiated (in personal conversation) by the doctor who had been standing there attending Therese immediately after the stroke for eleven days, with great dedication but without much hope of alleviating her lameness. He was also present for the sudden cure. There were other witnesses there, too, religious among them, including the Cathedral Preacher from Regensburg, Father Leo Ort, who had already narrated the whole experience to the author.

The visions did not close with this third apparition. In the midst of her joyous announcement of the cure she had just experienced Therese suddenly sits up again. Her hands rise to shoulder height and she witnesses the following fourth vision:

The Apostles at the Empty Grave

Thomas, who was missing at the Blessed Mother's death,[26] has meantime arrived in Jerusalem (Monday). He is much disturbed at his having come too late, but he does want to see the Blessed Mother once more, even in her grave. So all the Apostles agree to go to the grave again, together. Therese sees them coming to the grave and testing the unbroken seal (early Tuesday morning). They unseal and open the door to the grave and look around in astonishment. They cannot find the body anywhere. The wrapping cloths which had been used to prepare the Blessed Mother for burial are still in their place, and just as if they were still wrapped around a body. Therese smilingly took her index finger and tapped it down twice. Later, when she recounted the story of the vision in her state of pre-possession, she said that she was imitating one of the Apostles who tapped on the winding cloths with his fingers in two places, in order to convince himself and the others that they were empty.

The wrappings had probably been stuck together by the ointments and propped up by the herbs that were wrapped in

---

26. In the recording she called him the "Netglaumwollerer" — "the man who wouldn't believe."

together with the dead body of the Blessed Mother: this kept them from collapsing, apart from any outside influence. The departure of the Blessed Mother's body cannot be regarded as such an outside influence: her body was no longer subject to the laws of matter and thus would not be impeded by the wrapping cloths any more than by the rock walls and the door.

The Apostles all remark the presence of an unearthly fragrance in the burial chamber. Therese shows that she can smell the same aroma by the way she draws in her breath strongly and gently dilates her nostrils. Her hand gestures and her expressions keep pointing upwards, where the Apostles are also looking intently.

After some time spent in lively discussion, the Apostles leave the burial chamber, obviously convinced that under the circumstances (sealed grave, undisturbed wrapping cloths, unearthly aroma), the Blessed Mother's body must have been taken up into heaven, even though they did not witness the event themselves.[27]

Even outside her visions, Therese Neumann sometimes gave information about events in Jesus' life, in a state of elevated calm, thus completing or correcting the information gained by inquiring into her visions. Sometimes there were completely unknown particulars, not seen in the visions themselves, that are all noted by Father Naber. When Therese was giving information in this state, persons and places were all described by their correct names, in complete opposition to the childish way she described things in the state of prepossession, as we have already seen. An example of this is selected from one of Father Naber's journals:

"January 19, 1931. Today Therese said the following in a state of elevated calm:

---

27. The description of this event appeared as a special edition in 1950, with ecclesiastical approbation (Munich, September 29, 1950, G.V. No. 8906 Buchwieser, Vicar General).

"Our Savior liked to come, both alone and with the Apostles, to see Lazarus, who was a very rich but very good man. They were always welcome to generous support and the best of hospitality, so that unfriendly people who got reports from the servants at Lazarus' house used to speak of revelry taking place when our Savior visited there. Our Savior particularly liked to go visit Lazarus whenever he had suffered any misunderstanding or ingratitude or something similar.

"Our Savior once visited Bethany, together with the Apostles, ate dinner there sitting between John and Lazarus and stayed up late into the night talking about what was closest to their hearts. But since Lazarus was expecting visitors, our Savior did not want to spend the night there; he planned to return to Jerusalem. The Apostles were to go on ahead, and he would come later. John especially felt disappointed at not being able to go at his Master's side, and kept looking back longingly at our Savior. The Apostles went up to Mt. Sion to the inn which contained the room where they had eaten the Last Supper. (Both belonged to Nicodemus, and our Savior and his Apostles always used to quarter there).

"Our Savior took leave of Lazarus at the city gates, and Lazarus returned to Bethany. Then our Savior walked along the wall and over the Cedron Brook, into the garden of Gethsemane to pray. John could not sleep in the inn; his longing for our Savior drove him out to Gethsemane, where he expected to find him in prayer. He soon found his dearly beloved Savior there. It was not hard; the moon was bright that night, and our Savior was wearing his white wool robe (with the four tassels hanging down from it), and his blue grey cloak. Even though John knew that his Master did not want to be disturbed when he was praying—he had been reproved for this once or twice before—he could not keep from rushing up to him, embracing him, and kissing him on the forehead, cheek, and mouth.

"What was our Savior to do in the face of such an impulsive manifestation of love? He responded in like manner and then went with John through the outskirts of the city to the inn on

Mt. Sion, talking about divine things. (The city gates were open that night because of the crowds of pilgrims, but there was a guard). Our Savior had a small room of his own there. John helped the Master get ready for bed, and then began to wash his feet. Our Savior had gone barefoot and had hurt his feet. Full of love, John tried to kiss the blood away. But our Savior drew John to his breast and tears flowed from the beloved Master's eyes onto the head of the loving disciple. After washing his feet, John got the bed ready and carefully covered the Savior and then retired to his own room.

"January 20, 1931. When Therese recounted the above vision in her normal state, her joy and inspiration was so intense that she became unconscious. The approach of the state of elevated calm restored her."

Visionary Participation in Divine Services

"Father Naber's Journal: December 14, 1930. Today Therese has a vision of the story that was related in the Sunday Gospel. Last week I was in Berlin on pressing business. I really didn't want to go at all. In a state of ecstasy Therese told me that I would come back satisfied and relaxed, and this really did happen, more than I had ever expected. Twice Therese attended my Mass in Berlin, in her ecstatic state. She told me about it right after my return. Even though she had never seen the church in which I celebrated Mass (St. Ansgar's), not even a picture, and had never heard anyone talking about it or even read anything about it, she gave me a very good description of it, size and furnishings and especially the altar. She told me that I had been unable to open the tabernacle and the server had to come up and tell me how to do it. The second time, the pastor was serving for me.

"Actually the first time I said Mass, there was a little purse on the altar with the key I needed to open the tabernacle. When Communion time came, I used it to open the tabernacle door. But there was an inner door, made of metal, behind the outer wooden door, and I was trying to use the same key for both of them. After I'd spent a few minutes in this vain attempt, the server stepped up and told me there was a special key for the second door, in the same little sack as the first. For the second Mass that Therese was privileged to witness my server was actually the Pastor of St. Ansgar's."

April 19, 1931. "Today, Sunday, Therese, according to the letter she sent me, was a visionary participant in the Parish Mass I celebrated here in Eichstätt about nine o'clock. She saw and experienced everything that went on, including the sermon, which she later repeated to me. From the Communion onwards, she was photographed several times."

Father Naber's Journal: "January 20, 1931. Today shortly after noon, F____ dies. Since Therese had been suffering before this, and thus could not come any earlier, it was almost noon before she received Communion, then escorted the Blessed Sacrament to the dying F____ who wanted to receive once more, and attended the Communion in the sick room. Then, since death did not seem particulary near, we both went back to the church. Shortly afterwards I was called back to F____, who died about one o'clock. When I got back to the church, I saw Therese's coat, but she was nowhere to be found; I looked for her and finally did find her in the dining room, sitting on a chair, facing F____'s house and in a state of ecstasy (elevated calm). She spoke of the deceased, saying that he had been committed to Purgatory. . . .

"In her normal state which soon followed, she immediately began to tell, without a single question on my part, how she had seen F____'s death: he was standing before our Savior, his guardian angel at his side, together with two young men, an older man and an elderly woman, and some three children, all of them in a glorified state. (Apparently these were the deceased's parents, his two sons killed in the war, and the children who had died in infancy). Since the deceased soul was not entirely pure, however, it had to remain behind while our Savior and the other souls went back to heaven: he watched them with a look of intense pain on his face."

Vicarious and Reparatory Suffering

Archbishop Teodorowicz has this to say on the possibility and actual occurrence of such sufferings (p. 367): "The religious idea of sacrificial suffering is something that lies deep in the human heart. All the religions in the world have molded this conception into a religious event that is sometimes so gruesome that even human blood is offered on the altars of their gods, in an effort to conciliate the offended divinity.

"There have been many attempts to vitiate this conception of things, which is a magnificent one despite its aberrations and imperfections, and to soil it with an impure and infection-ridden atmosphere.

"This concept of sacrificial suffering, stamped deep onto the human heart, passes on from century to century, from people to people, from one era to another, and despite its manifold character, it can be summed up in a very few words: the consciousness of guilt and the longing for reparation.

"It was not until Calvary that this concept of vicarious suffering came to its fullest and most perfect expression. Only the purest blood could buy back the impure, and the cross of Christ becomes the symbol and pledge of redemption, through the terrible but perfect suffering of the God-Man, mankind is once again set free. Since the time of the crucifixion, this reparatory suffering, by specially selected men, has all been directed along an upright and salutary direction. It is, as the Apostle so beautifully expresses it, the fulfillment of what is still lacking in the suffering of Christ, namely, the joyous cooperative suffering of humanity, which is to apply its own free will towards appropriating the fruits of the cross.

"The old concept of reparation is now cleansed and illuminated; man is to offer up his own sufferings no longer with horror, but rather with a love of sacrifice and reparation, in connection with the exemplary sufferings and redemptive role of the God Man.

"But the problem which occupies us in this respect is the reparatory suffering that one human undertakes for another. Can such a suffering have any genuine role when compared with the sufferings of Christ on Calvary, and if it can, then what character or meaning can such sufferings hope to have in view of the fact that Christ alone is the Redeemer and he alone can make reparation for the sins of all mankind?

"In this reparatory work of Christ's, it is also possible for one man to work for another, but how? Certainly not in the very essence of the sacrifice itself—that is obvious—because that remains Christ's special prerogative. But there is a *mediate* way to sacrifice for other people: what the theologians call *ex congruo* ("by reason of its fittingness"). "When a man," writes St. Thomas," in the state of grace, does God's will and maintains friendship with God, then it is only fitting and in keeping with the laws of friendship (*secundum amicitiae proportionem*) for God to fulfill the individual's desires with respect to the salvation of his neighbor."

Gerlich, in his work on Therese Neumann, offers the following explanation of reparatory suffering as presented by Therese Neumann (1,300): "I once felt the need to discuss this phenomenon with her in the state of elevated calm; it was something completely new to me and difficult to grasp. I openly admitted that I did not understand the whole affair. Then she gave the following answer (equivalently): 'You see, our Savior is just. And so he's got to punish. But he's kind too, and he wants to help. The sins that have been committed he's got to punish; if someone else takes over the suffering and punishment, then God's justice is satisfied, and our Savior is free to exercise his kindness.'

"In the same conversation I also asked her what her interior attitude towards suffering was. I felt that I had noticed that she was afraid of suffering and did her best to bear up under it with great will power and only out of obedience to the will of God, who laid these crosses on her shoulders. This was her answer: 'No one can really like to suffer. I don't like it either. No man likes pain and I'm just as human as anyone else. But I also love our Savior's will, and when he sends me some suffering, I'm happy to accept it, because he wills it so. But suffering itself I really don't like'."

In Father Naber's journals there are many notes about reparatory suffering, from which the following excerpts have been selected. Others are recognizable in the reports that are reproduced elsewhere in this book.

Friday, March 23, 1928. Father Naber's notes: First there is a list of the names of five visitors: two bishops, two theology professors, and a professor of medicine. "Friday sufferings as usual. Extremely difficult breathing after the crucifixion. Towards evening, Therese sees a vision of Lazarus' resurrection, as recounted in the Gospel of the day. Later she was suffering terrible pains in her right shoulder for someone who had been present that day, and, as she put it, was unwilling to accept the wound in the shoulder."

Father Naber's journal: "August 10, 1928.... This week Therese suffered a lot from blood poisoning caused by an insect bite; she was offering it up for a priest who had begged her to help him overcome the curse of drink. Despite Therese's earnest begging and his own firm proposal, he had fallen into his temptation once again and sunk into such a state of despair that he had taken poison. Therese's sufferings were supposed to save his life and merit the grace of final repentance and conversion for him."

Father Naber's journal: "August 24, 1928: Visit from Cardinal Faulhaber. Therese is still suffering intensely from this blood poisoning. The poison had localized in two abscesses, one in the bowel and the other on the left side."

Father Naber's journal: "September 20, 1928. Today Therese was visited by the religious for whom she had been suffering the blood poisoning. His account of what had happened corresponds perfectly with what Therese had said about him in her states of ecstasy."

Father Naber's journal: "February 15-17, 1931. Today, and especially during the night, Therese had to suffer considerable pain once again in her eyes, head and feet, and also a terrible thirst and temptations from the devil, as a reparation of the sins committed in the Mardi Gras celebrations. In these days, according to what she said in a state of elevated calm, the writer of the insulting post cards was also converted."

Father Naber's journal: "May 9, 1931. Recently I was suffering a crippling attack of rheumatism resulting from a cold I caught. With a zeal and dexterity that would have put the best hospital nurse to shame, Therese tried to cure the ailment with the best of natural means; during the night she went to the church and offered our Savior to take over the suffering herself, promising him that she would be particularly kind to her visitors during the month of June. Next morning Therese could not get up; she did not get to Church for Holy Communion until about nine o'clock, her rheumatism was so bad, with all its crippling effects—twice as painful as what I had been suffering. (She once mentioned in a state of elevated calm that she felt all these sufferings twice as much as others.). But I was able to get around without any trouble at all and hardly felt a single trace of pain."

Recognition of Relics, Consecrations, and Blessings (Hierognosis)

Friday, March 22, 1929. "Today, and on Thursday preceding, Cardinal Archbishop Karl Kaspar, from Prague, was in Konnersreuth. He had witnessed the whole experience of her vision of the passion and made the following statements (*Impressions of Konnersreuth,* page 66):

"34. *Vision:* Resl suddenly leans forward, then backwards,

and wrings her hands violently. A painful sight. She blows her nose—and then she sinks back onto the pillows. The procession has arrived at Calvary.

"Many of those present were already beginning to cry. Therese herself was groaning and wailing. Someone gave the priest a relic: it was supposed to be a portion of the true cross. He held it against her hand, but she showed no reaction: the relic was not genuine. Then I held my pectoral cross (with its relic of the cross) against her hand. Immediately she experienced a terrible pain; she cried out and raised her hands, so that I was sorry I had forced this proof upon her. But then she quickly said: 'Gladly Savior, Gladly Savior!' " [28]

A further example: Professor Wutz related that a priest came to Konnersreuth with different relics, and Therese classified all of them in her state of prepossession: some of them genuine, some of them only touched to genuine relics, some of them absolutely not genuine. When the priest got back home and told the story, they decided to send another religious with the very same relics, to see whether or not the classification would be the same the second time. While this priest was standing outside the door, during the Friday sufferings, intending to ask permission to present his relics as soon as he had got into the room, Professor Naber was given the following message in the state of elevated calm: "There is someone standing outside, who wants to ask me some questions that have already been answered. Tell him that our Savior does not welcome experiments."

Father Naber looked out the door, saw the priest there and asked him if he had any relics with him. When the priest

---

28. Mayr's note: "Father Richstatter, S.J., was scandalized at the fact that Therese should experience any pain upon touching a particle of the cross. But everything that caused our Savior any pain had the same effect on her in her state of prepossession. If the particle of the cross was put completely into her hand, she would kiss it."

acknowledged the fact, he took him aside and delivered Therese's message. This made a much greater impression on this priest, and on the other priest who had previously visited her, then if the same answer had been given in both cases.

Ferdinand Neumann (her brother) relates the following experience. "Time, somewhere near 1932. Friday sufferings. Eight persons at a time were being admitted to the passion vision in Resl's room. After a new group had entered her room, Therese was suddenly interrupted in the middle of her vision and said, 'There's something from Mother.' Everyone looked around in wonder and disbelief, but she would not give in. Then a Franciscan priest stepped forward—from Rome as it turned out—and told Father Naber, 'She's right, I've got something here and I was going to ask your permission to present it. But now I see that I've already got my answer.' He took something out of his cowl and tried to hand it to Father Naber. But Father Naber said he could bring it to Therese himself. Even before the priest put the relics in Therese's hand, she started up from her bed violently, took the relics tightly in both hands [29] — in a state of prepossession—and was unwilling to give them back. Then she said that it was a piece from our Blessed Mother's veil and ended up giving an account of the way in which the relic had come into the hands of its present owners. The priest said that in Rome, despite the evidence of an old document that accompanied it, they had considered it most improbable that the relic could be genuine. He was particularly happy and, when Resl was in her normal state again, he gave her a piece of the veil to keep. Therese had some smaller sections cut from it, at St. Walburg's in Eichstätt, and gave them as presents to some particularly close friends."

---

29. This was contrary to her general reaction; she generally remained passive and expressed her judgment over a relic only when it was touched against her finger — Author.

Kardiognosis - (Reading of Hearts)

This area of intuitive knowledge of her visitors' state of soul is evidenced in the accounts of Father Fahsel and Archbishop Teodorowicz by a whole series of examples, a few of which are presented below:

Father Fahsel (pp. 53f): "In addition to her faculty of distinguishing consecrated things and persons, she also possesses the gift of the discernment of spirits, or, as it is called, the gift of reading hearts. This gift, too, shows up much more strongly when she is in her state of prepossession. She can tell whether or not the person before her is in the state of grace, whether he is an honest person or not, and the relationship between his heart and our Savior's. She has a particularly fine sense for the two sins of pride and lack of love, a faculty which she also has in her natural state as well. . . .

"It also happens that, in her natural state, she suffers a bodily weakness whenever she is confronted by people who have a spiritual condition of absolute pride or unforgiving hate. She always tries to increase her distance from such people. When she was once asked about this extraordinary behavior, she answered: "Our Savior has no way to get close to them." She also shows a very peculiar reaction to persons who are involved in immoral sexual relationships. She cannot bear to be alone in the same room with such persons. When visitors who were in any way unworthy happened to be present during her ecstasies of suffering, it sometimes happened that she would be interrupted in her vision of the passion and ask the priest or her parents to have all visitors leave the room at once. When she was asked why, she always said something like this: "Our Savior does not allow any such thing in the room. He drives out everything that can hinder him in any way." In time they clearly learned that her bodily reactions were strongest in the case of sins of pride and lack of love. As a rule she would faint and develop a fever that showed strongly in her face. This corresponds fully with Christian morality, which regards these two sins of the spirit as the most serious of all sins."

Fahsel presents the following account of a man from Lichterfelde whom he had met through Therese Neumann, brought to Konnersreuth, and there converted (page 98): "When he received the sacraments of penance and the Eucharist for the first time, he was called to Resl, who was already in her state of elevated calm. When he leaned over to listen to her words, he was perfectly amazed to hear her mention two sins from his earlier life. He had not even thought of them for some time, and now he heard them presented in a very concrete statement. Suddenly he began to fear, unnecessarily, that he had been guilty of an incomplete confession, but then Therese told him: "Now don't start poking around in your conscience. Everything has been forgiven. But it's good to realize that everything is known, too.""

On the subject of Therese's charism for discerning human hearts, Archbishop Teodorowicz writes the following: (p. 403ff): "Therese definitely has a very special and particularly acute sense of perception. The penetrating rays of her knowledge of human hearts illuminate the most mysterious and secret ways of the human soul, the ways of grace or the ways of sin, and these ways cannot be spied or discovered by any earthly organ. Everything—the story of their past life, the unveiling of the oppression within each individual soul—serves only as an external but very precious evidence of what constitutes the very heart of the gift of holy wisdom. Therese's clairvoyance unveils the impediments which stand in the way of the soul's interior development and the sins which threaten to choke out the life of grace on one hand, and, on the other hand, it casts light on the secret ways of grace. The truth of this gift is substantiated by strong external evidence."

Teodorowicz then cites examples from Fahsel and continues (page 404): "I myself was present on the following occasion: Only a few persons were in Therese's room; Therese was in a state of ecstatic vision—it was Friday, about nine in the morning;

suddenly Therese began to wail out loud. When the priest asked her what was wrong with her, she answered with the following complaint: 'An apostate has been here, someone who betrayed our Savior!' Could that be true I asked myself; who could prove it? And my companion, Bishop Lisowski, smiled slyly and whispered in my ear: It's not very safe here, you can easily get caught. At the same moment, a religious stepped up to us. He substantiated Therese's statement: a fallen away priest, who had come to Konnersreuth with him, had just left the room. Unbelievers too, even when they put on the mask of faith, were always recognized by Therese."

On page 407 Teodorowicz relates the following case: "A cloistered sister in Marienbad heard that I was traveling to Konnersreuth and asked me to deliver a letter to Therese Neumann. I was glad to comply; I asked the sister if she knew Therese Neumann personally and the answer was no. This sister was not particularly well known to me, and I knew nothing about the contents of the letter. I delivered the letter to Therese, while she was in a state of prepossession. In a trice she knew the contents of the letter, by merely touching the envelope; she knew much more than if she had read the letter and had been dependent merely on the written words. She also knew what was *not* contained in the letter and what was going on in the secret heart of the letter writer. In just a few words she announced that the person concerned was to be pitied, and in this one word she summed up the whole spiritual life of the sister.

"Naturally I wanted to see whether or not this description of the sister's life was correct and thus, when I returned home, I asked the sister what she had written in her letter. 'I only asked Therese for her prayers, because I want to prepare myself as well as possible for the retreat,' the sister answered. When I asked her if she hadn't written anything more than that, she hesitated with her answer, and it was not until I told her what Therese had actually said that she was very disturbed and admitted: 'That fits me all right, I'm fighting all sorts of battles inside myself, and I'm in precisely the state of soul that Therese described.' And then she told me some more details."

Appearances in other Places - (Bilocation)

When Therese Neumann was in Eichstätt on Easter, 1929, Father Ingbert Naab, who was then the guardian for the Capuchin Monastery there, asked her prayers for the mission he was about to preach.... There he saw Therese, for about three quarters of an hour, standing in the back in her black dress and white head cloth, while he preached his conference. But Resl had never left Eichstätt. She told her sister Ottilie: "Today Father Ingbert begins his mission. We'll have to pray real hard for him." Father Ingbert Naab was anything but a credulous person. And thus the experience, which he also recounted to friends in Konnersreuth, can be considered as absolutely credible (cf. also the following account).

May 8, 1931 (Father Naber's account): "A complete stranger told me yesterday that on Saturday, because of a seemingly unbearable moral and economic crisis, he had been on the point of taking his own life. Then Therese suddenly appeared to him and her warnings were enough to keep him from suicide. Therese, in her normal state, later said that she had suffered very much on Saturday and that she had felt very much like despairing. In the state of elevated calm, she said that her guardian angel had taken her form and appeared to the young man to warn him, because he had taken a decisive stand, on one or two occasions, for what our Savior was trying to accomplish in her."

It also turned out that it had been Therese's guardian angel who was present on the other occasion, the one reported by Father Ingbert in the Rhine country.

When I had occasion to discuss this with Therese during her normal state, she told me that here and there a letter would come with the story of one or another apparition, but that she never paid any attention to them and threw them all into the fire. A religious had written her that he had become indifferent in celebrating Mass, that he had been embezzling Mass stipends, and that he was having an illicit affair with a teacher. Then, when he turned to face the congregation after the Communion, he saw Therese sitting before him, crying bitterly, and even drying her tears with a towel, so that he could see the marks of the wound on her uncovered hand. He was so moved that he could hardly go on; he went into the sacristy without saying the prayers after Mass and without sprinkling holy water, and he had to sit when he got there. At that very moment he decided to break with his former life."

Elevation - Levitation

The only case of this phenomenon that is verifiable by the personal experience of the author has already been reported on page 177 with reference to the vision of the Assumption; regarding the second instance, described on page 59 (in St. Walburg's, Eichstätt), since Abbess M. Benedikta von Spiegel is already dead, there is no available eyewitness to substantiate it.

Mystic Relationship to the Blessed Sacrament

The stigmata involves suffering as a sacrifice for mankind in all its fullness.[30]

The sacrifice on Golgotha was closely related to another act of love which our Savior completed immediately before his death. This was the institution of the Blessed Sacrament. Through the Eucharistic sacrifice the mystery of Golgotha became not just a commemoration of the passion (*memoriale passionis*), but the constantly recurring renewal of Christ's sacrificial death. This community between the passion of Christ and the Blessed Sacrament is mysteriously and profoundly represented in the case of the stigmatic. The stigmatic bears the honorable signs of Christ's own wounds on his body; but in no less a marvelous way

---

30. Teodorowicz p. 313.

his soul is especially enriched by a special sense which gives him an extraordinary feeling for the Blessed Sacrament, far superior to anything that can be explained on merely natural grounds. Just as their wounds are a witness to the passion of Christ, this special Eucharistic sense is evidence of the presence of the Eucharistic Savior on the altar of their souls.

The stigmata would be one-sided and imperfect in its manifestations if the ecstatic visions related merely to past events, if the five stigmatized wounds were only the symbol of Christ's sufferings. Only by the fact that this external and intimate relationship to the Blessed Sacrament is present as well does the whole mystery of the redemptive work arrive at its full expression in the stigmata. Past and present fuse inseparably into each other. The Precious Blood of Christ, symbolically represented in the wounds, finds its hallmark in the Mystical Body of Christ, in the Holy Eucharistic sacrifice, in which Christ's sacrificial death is constantly renewed and realized.

The stigmatic's sensitivity to the Holy Eucharist is not so obvious and it does not create so strong an impression as does the experience of Christ's passion; still in its extraordinary apparitions it is no less significant and comes to our attention just as powerfully as the stigmatic phenomena which achieve their fullest expression and significance only through the intimate conformity between the soul and the Holy Eucharist. For the blood shed on Golgotha and the Mystic Blood of the Sacrament of the Altar are all one indissoluble word of love, the most perfect ever known."

The following extraordinary phenomena made their appearance in the case of Therese Neumann; in this respect too she is a perfect member of the "stigmatic family."

1. Awareness of the presence of the Eucharist even in her normal state.

2. Mystic Communion, with assimilation of the species (consecrated Host) without swallowing.

3. Communion without priest and tele-communion.

4. Preservation of the undissolved species of bread in her body until shortly before her next Communion.

The following individual examples are all without exception the reports of eyewitnesses or else selected from Father Naber's journals. They are a further and most impressive corroboration of the reflections from Archbishop Teodorowicz's book that were presented above as an introduction to this section.

Father Naber tells this story: "Whenever we were together in unfamiliar surroundings, Therese could always tell whether a church was Catholic or not, that is, whether our Eucharistic Savior was present in the church or not. At first we, Professor Wutz and I, used to get out of the car to verify the statement each time. There was never any mistake."

The author of this book had the following experience: I was driving with Resl and my wife to the church (the famous Trinity-Pilgrimage Church near Konnersreuth). We wanted to see whether the renovation of the main altar was finished yet. It must have been about the time of the currency reform, because the pastor from Münchenreuth, in whose parish this chapel belonged, had to bring food along for the workmen so that they would keep working for him. As we approached the altar, I did not see the tabernacle lamp burning, and thus I only bowed my head instead of genuflecting. Therese however made a deep genuflection and said: "The Blessed Sacrament is in there." I said: "But Resl, there isn't any sanctuary lamp there." "But our Savior is in there," was her answer. Then I genuflected too, believing what she said. A short time later the pastor from Münchenreuth came up and told us that, since the tabernacle was finished, he had once again begun to reserve the Blessed Sacrament there, that very morning, but they were out of oil for the lamp.

The following case was related to me by Father Naber, some years ago: Since I was not a witness to the event myself, and since Father Naber now remembers only the event itself, but none of the particulars, I asked Therese Neumann's brother Ferdinand for an eyewitness report.

"The year I can't recall too well any more either. It must have been around 1932. But I do recall that it was a Sunday. I was sitting with my sister Marie in the kitchen at the rectory, and then Resl and the pastor came in; I think the afternoon devotions were just over. Resl was suddenly very excited and said: "Our Savior is in here." Father Naber laughed and said: "Resl, you're surely mistaken this time. Our Savior is surely not here in the rectory." "Yes," she insisted, "I can feel it; he is somewhere very near by." And she went straight to a pile of letters that had not yet been opened. It really did not take very much looking before she pulled out a blue business envelope and handed it to Father Naber. He opened it up and there on a single sheet of white paper lay a host. There was not a single line of text, and no return; only the address: Miss Therese Neumann, Konnersreuth. Postmarked Waldsassen.

"The case was quickly cleared up. A few days later a porcellan painter from Waldsassen came by; he was also a gardener by hobby and used to do a lot of work in the parish garden. He was a very scrupulous person; originally a Protestant; he had been converted several times. On the basis of some incidental comments he made, the people in Konnersreuth began to think that he was the sender of the parcel described above, and took him aside for close questioning. He admitted that he had taken the sacred host out of his mouth after receiving Communion and then begun to doubt whether it was anything more than mere bread, so he sent it to Konnersreuth. He was deeply struck by what had happened with the letter. The real reason for such a sacrilegious and obviously foolish way of removing his doubts about the faith was never really made clear to me, despite the fact that I had several conversations with him. Meantime he died."

The incident became known in Waldsassen too; the man told his own story there. As I heard the story, on the basis of his own account, he had gone into one of the narrow passages between the side niches of the Waldsassen parish church right after receiving Communion and taken the consecrated host out of his mouth and wrapped it in a little cloth. In his later life he was deeply repentant for this act, and did everything he could to make reparation, by good works and almsgiving.

Mystical Communion

Whenever Therese Neumann had entered a visionary ecstasy before receiving Holy Communion and saw our Savior coming in place of the priest, either as a Child (Christmas) or in his resurrection glory (Easter), the sacred host would enter into her body as soon as it was placed on her tongue without any swallowing on her part. This fact is substantiated not only by Father Naber, but also by many other priests and lay people who happened to be present on such occasions. Father Naber records such cases frequently in his journal. Father Fahsel speaks of it in his book as something he experienced himself. And so does Archbishop Kasper of Prague.

Gerlich describes the phenomenon in his usual precise way as follows: (I, 166-7) "The Communion took place in the following manner. When the priest with the ciborium came to the corner of the altar, Therese Neumann, upon looking at the host, would fall into ecstasy and show an intense desire to go up to meet our Savior, but her chair prevented her from rising because its arms closed in the front. Her face beamed, her eyes shown, her hands were stretched forward, her feet were in motion. Her whole body would rise somewhat off the chair, as if she wanted to get up. The priest gave me a sign to kneel down directly in front of him, so that I could look straight into her open mouth. I did. When the host came near, she opened her mouth wide and put out her tongue. She held her hands over her breast. The priest laid a whole host on the front of her tongue and then left. She drew in her tongue a little, with the host still visible on it, but only far enough so that the tip of her tongue still touched her lower lip and only covered the teeth of her lower jaw, so that I could still see the back part of her tongue and gums. Suddenly the host disappeared. Her mouth stayed open for a short time. From the time she first opened her mouth she never closed it, nor did she make any attempt to swallow. Nor could the host be seen in her oral cavity and gums—they had remained open the whole time. After some time of deep interior concentration she began a long ecstatic conversation. During the whole time that followed there were no swallowing motions to be noted. No water was offered to her. I must note that the priest had already contacted me on Friday evening, telling me, after he had listened to Therese Neumann's explanation in her ecstatic state, that I should come and witness her reception of Holy Communion, in order to see the new phenomena. Thus on Saturday morning I was well aware of what I was supposed to pay particular attention to. The spot in the church is very bright."

Professor Wutz told me that he had a habit of pressing the sacred host against the tongue somewhat so that it would remain sticking there and not fall off. And that in giving Communion to Therese Neumann he had already had the experience of seeing the Host disappear and his fingers become moist.

Finally I also had an opportunity to witness this phenomenon personally. Father Naber made a sign to me, while I was kneeling there, that I should get up and have a closer look. I did so. And thus I too can testify that the sacred host I had just seen lying on her tongue had disappeared from her open mouth even before the priest had withdrawn his hand. All that happened was a slight reflex motion of the lower jaw when the host touched her mouth, but it followed so immediately upon the host's touching the tongue that it could hardly be considered a swallowing motion (the muscles beneath the chin had no part in the motion); experience has proven that it takes a while to make the host moist before it can be swallowed.

Communion without a Priest—Telecommunion

At the time of Therese Neumann's First Communion, Pope Pius X's permission that allowed and encouraged daily Communion had not yet been promulgated. Particularly, children were not allowed to receive outside the regular quarterly school Communions. As a result, children were encouraged in their religion classes, and adults in the Sunday sermons, to practice Spiritual Communion. Therese practiced this with great devotion. Whenever she could find time, she went into the church and knelt down at the Communion rail, and insistently begged our Savior in the tabernacle to come spiritually into her heart.

On such occasions it sometimes happened that her spiritual Communion turned into a sacramental Communion. It was not until 1953, and then under oath, that Therese offered this explanation: "On the occasion of such visits, it happened once or twice or maybe three times, or possibly oftener, that, while I was kneeling at the Communion rail the sacred host would come floating towards me . . . and I received the Blessed Sacrament, actually swallowing it."

Thus already in her childhood, according to her own sworn testimony, and not only on the occasion of her First Holy Communion, Therese had mystic experiences. She had kept quiet about them for decades, and would probably have never spoken about them at all if the spiritual commission had not made inquiries about her interior life.

Easter, 1929. Therese was in Eichstätt. On April 29/30 she had severe spiritual suffering, which also caused her such physical torture that they were afraid she was dying. In the house chapel, on account of Therese's state of health, a consecrated host was being preserved. Suddenly Therese passed into an ecstasy and made the gestures she usually made upon receiving Communion. Then she passed into a state of elevated calm. A few moments later came the words: "Resl has received our Savior." When Professor Wutz opened the tabernacle, shortly after, the Host was no longer there. (Report of Professor Wutz, corroborated by Ferdinand Neumann, her brother).

Father Naber reports the following case (page 90f): "Just a short time ago I was an immediate witness to this same phenomenon. On Friday, June 26, 1931, about half past ten, Therese came to the rectory. She looked particularly miserable and felt visibly weak. We realized that she had just been suffering for a dying person. She asked the pastor for Holy Communion; she had received just the day before. I went over to the sacristy with her. Therese had taken the sacristy key with her, but she was so weak she could not open the door. When we got inside and had closed the door, Therese made her way falteringly, to her chair behind the altar.

The pastor asked me very amiably if I would like to give her Communion. I said yes, and we both went up to the altar. While he began the customary *Confiteor* at the foot of the altar, I took the ciborium out of the tabernacle. After the first two prayers I went around the altar to the left, towards Therese's seat, while the pastor went around the right side. I was about a yard away when I began the last prayers; then I noticed, to my great surprise, that she was not facing me and waiting, but sitting quietly in her chair and facing the back of the tabernacle. Her arms were crossed over her breast, her mouth and eyes were closed. It was the same posture she assumed every time she received Communion in the state of elevated calm. I looked over to the pastor in amazement and saw him suddenly come to a stop and then wave me away with both arms. I did not understand at first that he wanted me to turn around and go back; I thought that perhaps she was not in a state of ecstasy and I would have to give her only a small portion of the host. In her normal state she cannot swallow the entire host. At that very moment she showed signs of activity. She turned towards me, her eyes still tightly closed, raised her head a little, and opened her mouth. I saw a host lying on her tongue, clearly visible. Then I understood that she had already received the Blessed Sacrament. I dropped the host I had been holding in my fingers back into the ciborium and went back to the altar. The pastor went with me."

In 1963 Father Naber recounted this same experience in somewhat different words:

January 29/30, 1931 (Father Naber's Journal): "Therese was reading letters last night until half past five. During this time our Savior had strengthened her through the state of elevated calm. About eleven in the morning she came to the rectory to ask me for Holy Communion. I had two clerical visitors who were just leaving and so Therese went on ahead into the church. When I got there I found her in a state of elevated calm. I asked her if perhaps the other priest had already given her Communion in the meantime and she answered "No," but, since she had longed so desperately to receive our Savior that she was on the point of fainting (the wound in her heart had opened and blood was flowing down onto her lap), our Savior had come to her in a miraculous manner: a host had left the tabernacle and come floating through the altar towards her (she was sitting on her chair behind the altar); when it got close to her it disappeared and the glorified figure of the Christ Child, about 40 days old, appeared to her and entered her spirit. Therese told me this later in her usual state, and also commented that the host had been surrounded by light all around its outer edge."

Brother Ferdinand tells the following case: "At the time that I was a high school student and living with Professor Wutz, I used to serve for him in the house chapel and also take care of the sacristy duties. One day, according to my usual practice, when I was dressing the chalice, I put one large host on the paten and three small ones, one for my sister Ottilie, one for my brother Hans, and one for me. During the Mass, which had begun somewhat later that morning, Hans had to leave for school before Communion, there were only two small hosts left. He and I both began to search for the third one, thinking that it must have fallen; but we had no luck.

"After Mass I insisted that I had set out three hosts, and the Professor also agreed that at consecration time he had looked on the paten and seen three hosts. We searched once again, thoroughly, but without result, and we were somewhat disturbed at the fact. Some time later Therese called from Konnersreuth and said that the pastor and the other priest had been away that morning but she had such a longing for our

Savior that she had been privileged to attend the Mass at Eich-stätt. During this experience, right before the *'Domine, non sum dignus'* a sacred host had entered her mouth. As evidence of the fact that she had really been spiritually present, she gave us a detailed description of the altar decorations. We were greatly surprised, but glad to be relieved of our anxiety.[31]

Preservation of the Undissolved Host in Therese's Body
Three Cases in Evidence: Advent an Exception

Therese Neumann had a lively sensation of having the Eu-charistic Bread constantly present, undissolved, in her body, preserving her bodily strength. As soon as the species of bread dissolved in her, she experienced great pain and felt herself growing weaker and weaker, and at the same time there was a marked increase in her longing for a speedy reunion with our Savior, such that she frequently broke out in complaints: "Savior, why have you abandoned me? Come again, please come." The examples of Communion without a priest give a good idea of the degree to which this longing could develop. Whether or not this awareness of the sacramental presence and its dissolution really corresponded to reality we cannot abso-lutely determine.

July 26, 1930, Father Liborius Hartl's account. Confirmed by Father Naber (cf. the following report as well). On Friday, July 25, Father Hartl, the assistant at Konnersreuth at that time, was told that "Tomorrow there will be a small disturbance but there is nothing to get excited about." When he asked whether Father Naber or he would be present, the answer was "You

---

31. Such cases of Communion without a priest have been recorded of other stigmatics as well: "Gorres has described those of St. Catherine of Siena (Gorres, *Die christliche Mystik*, Regensburg 1837, II, 567) and B. Ludwig, *Tugendschule Gemma Galganis*, Kirnach - Villingen, 1926, p. 380).

will be called." On Saturday noon, Therese got sick and she brought up blood and bile. She was exhausted and went to bed at once. When she had to vomit again, she felt, to her great astonishment and embarrassment, that the sacred host she had received that morning was coming up. She did the best she could to swallow it once again, but it was no use. She had to vomit the host out into her handkerchief. She immediately sent her sister Zenzl to call the pastor. He sent for the assistant. Both of them saw the undissolved host, somewhat blood-reddened in one spot.

Therese lay there in bed, shivering all over, and holding the handkerchief in front of her. In tears she complained that our Savior had abandoned her, and that was why all this had happened. There was some little consolation in the fact that the handkerchief was freshly laundered. The pastor and assistant consulted together. After the first fright had passed and they had determined that nothing would have to be burned, they decided to see whether or not Therese could swallow the Host again. Then she had a vision and looked up and down, the way she did when she saw the Savior before her in human stature, and opened her mouth as if she were about to receive. The pastor lifted the handkerchief up, towards her mouth. All of a sudden the host had disappeared, without any swallowing motions. In the state of elevated calm that immediately followed, she said: "Our Savior is now inside Resl again. That was a reparatory suffering for a sick girl. This girl had frequently taken the host out of her mouth after Communion and put it in her handkerchief, then later shown it around and made fun of it." When she returned to her normal state, she was full of joy, because she was once again able to feel our Savior within her, and she begged everyone to thank our Savior for his kindness.

June 1, 1932, Father Naber's Notes: "For some time Therese had been suffering for a deathly sick Dutch priest. From the beginning of his sickness he had been recommended to her by telegram. Yesterday particularly she had a lot to suffer in her stomach and breast and spiritually it was also very difficult for her. The day before yesterday, in the morning, I had received word that the following night I was supposed to be at home because Therese would come to me, very disturbed, and with a bitter complaint. Shortly after the beginning of my devotions, one of the servers suddenly came up to my chair and asked me to come to Therese Neumann. I found her in the sacristy, in great anxiety.

"She told me at once; 'O Father, something terrible has happened! Just a little while ago when I was getting ready to go to May devotions, I suddenly got very sick and had to throw up. Finally the sacred host started to come up too, and I couldn't keep it down, so I held my left hand in front of my mouth. The rest of the vomit trickled through my fingers, but the Host stuck on the fingers. (Resl actually did have a whole, moist host sticking to her fingers.) I began to cry: Oh dear Savior, dear Savior, what can I do with you now? Then something said very clearly: The Savior isn't there at all; that's just bread; look at it! Just throw it away. First I had to sit down for a while, on account of my fright, then I rang the bell and since no one came to answer it, I went out into the yard where I met my brother August. He was pale when I told him what had happened and he escorted me almost all the way to the rectory. No one answered the bell there so I came straight over to the sacristy. Oh what have I done to our Savior, that made him go back out of me? I'm lost. If the bishop hears of how I'm carrying our Savior around, he'll throw me out of the Church.'

"Since it was impossible to stay in the sacristy and I was counting on our Savior taking a hand in the business himself (remembering the events of July 26, 1930), I told Therese to come over to the rectory. With her eyes glued on the sacred host which was still in the hollow of her left hand, she came over to the rectory at my side. There, from the very first step, she called to me: 'Father, our Savior is back inside me.' As a matter of fact, the sacred host had disappeared from her hand.

Therese went with me into the rectory, washed her hand, and asked that the water in which she had washed her hand be poured into the sacrarium. Upon her urgent request—she always had great anxiety over any irreverence to the sacred host—I went out in front again to see if any particle of the host had fallen to the ground.

"This reverent anxiety for the Sacramental Presence was being suffered for the priest mentioned at the beginning of this report, as a reparation for his irreverent handling of the Blessed Sacrament."

Holy Saturday, April 4, 1942. Dr. Franz X. Mayr's report: "On Holy Saturday Father Naber, Father Kraus from Eichstätt, and I were visiting with Therese about eight in the evening. We found her sitting in bed and suffering from an upset stomach. From time to time she had to vomit and she brought up some frothy matter, as well as some gall (as she said), onto a small napkin which she held in her hand. While we were chatting with her and watching her, she suddenly had a vision. She saw Joseph of Arimathea imprisoned in a tower cell and being freed by an angel. When the vision and the state of childlike pre-possession which immediately followed it had both passed, her nausea returned—it had been interrupted by the ecstasy. Suddenly, when the vomiting was partcularly intense, she uttered a cry of fright and held the hand with the napkin before her in front of her mouth, which was half opened. As well as she could without closing her mouth, she uttered the words: "The Savior, the Savior," in a tone of lament.

Then she put her tongue out a little to show us what had happened. On the tongue, lay a pure white object of the form and size of a small host, but all puffed up and wet. There could be no doubting the fact that it was the sacred host which Therese had received Holy Thursday morning at Holy Communion. Thus it had remained within her for three days and two nights without dissolving and now it had risen to her mouth again because of her vomiting. Therese simply did not know what to do and could find no way to help herself out of this painful situation.

Strangely enough, she did not make the least attempt to swallow; instead she kept making motions as if she were trying to take hold of the Host with her finger, so that Father Naber, as a precautionary measure, took both of her hands and held them tight. Then he begged her to be calm and advised her to ask our Savior to come back into her again. Therese quickly agreed to this advice and began to pray with very moving gestures, the way children do, with outstretched hands. Suddenly she was very calm and her mouth closed again, for only a short time, and her hands crossed on her breast and her face took on a blessed and peaceful expression, as it always does in the state of elevated calm. When she opened her mouth again, we could clearly see that the sacred host had already disappeared. We did not, however, observe even the slightest swallowing motions. The sacred host had thus returned into her body in the same way that it always does in the case of her ecstatic Communion. The state of elevated calm lasted for some time. During this time the pastor was informed that the severe nausea and vomiting would not recur, and this proved to be the truth. The whole event appears to have been a reparatory suffering.

The sacred host was clearly visible as it lay on her tongue. During the proceedings her brother Ferdinand had come into the room and he made the same observations as the rest of us.[32]

Early Dissolution of the Species of Bread during Advent Season

Father Naber's diary: "December 25, 1930. Towards the end of Advent, Therese had to suffer very much. It seemed to her that the Savior no longer loved her, that she was lost, while her heart was flowing with love for him and she would love him even in hell, if only our Savior would show himself to her once

---

32. (This report was completed by me during the Easter vacation of 1942, read to Father Naber, and judged to be completely accurate by him.)

again. The Sacramental Presence of our Savior ended, on most days, before the regular time, and left her heart desolate and empty and dead; she no longer saw our Savior before Communion and no longer enjoyed the state of elevated calm afterwards, nor could she any longer feel the priest's blessing."

The first of the three cases is described by Father Hartl and Father Fahsel in 1930, and Father Fahsel also published it in his book (page 98) which appeared in 1931. We should like to take this occasion to show how lightly the opponents of Konnersreuth treated the explanation of such phenomena. The Catholic Head Doctor, Dr. Deutsch, of Lippstadt, privately published the following pamphlet in 1938: "Medical Critique of Konnersreuth: Miracle or Hysteria?" On page 86, after some pages of biting sarcasm and mockery, he writes. "... How can the happenings observed there be explained in any natural way? Very simple: Therese takes care of the sacristy work [as if there were no other sacristans or servers in Konnersreuth!—Author], and she is thus in a position to make off with unconsecrated hosts. She lies in her bed, moistens a host a little, smears a little blood from her gums on it, lays it on the napkin and then starts the histrionics with a loud cry of lamentation which brings all her family rushing in. But it does seem positively excluded that all these theatrical goings on with the sacred host could be willed and worked by God...."

When a doctor, in a scientific publication, attempts in this manner to find or invent explanations, without any autopsy (personal eyewitness observation: Dr. Deutsch was never at Konnersreuth), and expects the dozens of serious people who are working and observing on the spot to go along with such wholesale deceit, and even support or cover up for it wherever possible, not only is he obviously giving notice of the fact that he has no respect for the judgment and scientific exactness of other men, but in view of his arrogant underestimation of the basic principles of all human relations and all historical investigation, he also forfeits the right to be taken seriously by others in any of his pretended scientific conclusions. A like fate awaits every author who presumes to base his statements on such shaky footing.[33]

Dr. Gerlich, who was cruelly murdered in the concentration camp at Dachau in 1934 for the sake of his convictions (he had been converted to the Catholic Faith in Konnersreuth), was attacked by Dr. Deutsch in 1938, when he was no longer there to defend himself, in the same article that attacked Archbishop Teodorowicz. Peter Radlo, M.D., in his book *Truth or Deceit*, has already supplied a satisfactory rebuttal to all of Dr. Deutsch's theses. As regards the special case of July 26, 1930, he has the following to say (page 294):

"Dr. Deutsch also makes fun of Resl's description of the case in which the host was vomited up—and as usual he confides only a portion of the whole event to his readers; he would much prefer to keep the whole heart of the matter secret. But it is precisely what he passes over in silence that affords the key to the proper understanding of the account and forces us to look for a solution somewhere else.

"And what does this critic actually pass over in silence? Precisely the fact that this was a reparatory suffering for a person who was completely unknown to Therese Neumann...."

The other two cases of a host being vomited up were also reparatory sufferings on Therese's part, but they are better catalogued in the treatment of her mystical relationship towards the Blessed Sacrament, since they offer a proof of the fact that

---

33. Father Naber recorded in writing the following statement made by one of the visitors (May 20, 1950):

"When I came back to the concentration camp, I met a Vincentian nun who had worked for Dr. Deutsch in the Holy Trinity Hospital at Lippstadt. She told me that shortly before his death Dr. Deutsch had confided in her that the only thing he was afraid to answer for to God was his fight against Konnersreuth. And that if he had it to do all over again, he would never write against Konnersreuth."

The genuinity of this information is attested by (handwritten signature of the visitor).

the Sacred Species had remained undissolved in her body for several hours, and, in the third case, for days.

Mystical Relationship towards her Guardian Angel

Belief in guardian angels has become a pious legend for many people of our times, even for Christians who are outside the Catholic pale. Even faithful Catholics make something of an effort to play down the discussion of this dogma, even though, in every Credo, they confess the preexistence of an invisible world of spirits and acknowledge God as its creator. The technological advances of our age and the imposition of a materialistic or at least a rationalistic picture of the world onto the Christian philosophy of living naturally tend to keep us from thinking about the guardian angels with whom the more interior-oriented man of times gone by had a much more direct contact. Perhaps the vast number of angels and cherubs and seraphs that appear in the late Baroque period produced something of a surfeit, and the somewhat effeminate and sugar-coated representation of the guardian angel in the nineteenth and early twentieth centuries could easily have led to a reaction against the concept as a whole.

But in Konnersreuth we find our way right back to the angel world, and there it is a strong and wingless figure of the angel: radiant, luminous bodies who live and work invisibly in our midst. The Michael figure, suggesting the inviolability of God's omnipotence and the Gabriel figure, representative of the powerful announcing of the divine Word, are enlarged upon here by the Raphael figure and its loving guidance through life and death.

An initial reference was already made in the beginning of this book to the special relationship between Therese Neumann and her own guardian angel; the specific subject under question was her bilocation. The following excerpts from Father Naber's journals are a documentary evidence to enlarge and round out the whole picture.

"May 24, 1931 (Pentecost Sunday). During the main parish Mass Therese Neumann was together with the rest of the parishioners, back in the nave of the church. She did not feel well immediately after the first vision; her heart no longer wanted to work properly. We had all left the room and she was lying there on the settee. Then we suddenly heard her call from downstairs. Her father went running up and found her lying in bed, wearing her night clothes and protesting that someone had put her to bed. On the other side of the room, on the sofa, her clothing was all arranged as if she were still in it, even the watch chain was still fastened around the neck. Therese afterwards told us that she had felt suddenly as if someone were touching her on both shoulders and then her clothing all fell away immediately; then she felt the same touch again and all at once she found herself lying in bed, quite contrary to her own will. In her state of elevated calm she later said that it was her guardian angel who had done all this, to keep Therese from coming to any harm.

Before this experience it frequently happened that Therese, in a moment of severe suffering, would fall out of bed and then would have to lie there helpless on the floor, but that finally, without anyone coming to help her or without being in a position to help herself at all, she was lying back in bed again. In 1927 when Therese was in the rectory for a time, the devil used to come and try to make her leave every night. She would come half way down the stairs but have to stay there; in her weakened condition she could go no further. No one came to help her, and she certainly could not get up by herself; but suddenly she would find herself back in her own bed. In such cases, as she reported it in a state of ecstasy, her guardian angel had come to her assistance.

Her guardian angel—as she reports it in her state of ecstasy—frequently spoke to her too, but only she could hear his voice, and it always came from the right side, during her normal state as well as during her state of prepossession. There were instructions for herself or other people. In her state of prepossession Therese cannot understand High German and thus she repeats the angel's words in a mechanical way, like foreign words; she looks in the direction the words are coming from and complains, in the childlike way she has during her state of prepossession, that she can't grasp him, that he is talking so "differently," and why can't he start talking in a way that she could understand (in this state she does not realize that it is her guardian angel). (Moreover, in her state of prepossession she says that there is a "luminous man" standing at everyone's right hand side, and that the pastor, as she once mentioned, had a more powerful one at his side than she does—probably because he is a priest.

At first, until I heard the explanation in her state of ecstasy, I thought that it was the Little Flower who was speaking to her. Her picture used to hang on the right side of Therese's bed.

Therese had a vision of the healing of the woman with the hemorrhage and the raising of Jairus' daughter. Father Hartl and I were familiar with that much of her vision from the Gospels. But then Therese also had a vision of the healing of two blind men and the driving out of a devil.

While Therese was lying there, afterwards, in a state of prepossession, we were discussing whether or not that part of the vision was also to be found in Scripture. Neither of us could recall. Suddenly Therese began talking again, telling us that someone said it was in Matthew, 9. I had the Bible brought from the Church and we looked it up and found it, in Matthew, 9.

Another time, in the Fall of 1929, I was on a mission in Cham. When I got back home, Father Hartle told me (in the presence of Resl who was in her state of prepossession—it was Friday) that something was bothering him and would give him no peace. That morning, while Therese was having her Passion ecstasy, he had shooed away the flies that were bothering her and made a motion like the sign of the cross. Then Resl had cried out: "Something from our Savior," as she always likes to say whenever she receives a priestly blessing during her state of prepossession. He had been very struck at the fact because he had not intended to give Resl any blessing. Then Resl suddenly began to speak: "Someone said: his doubts will be removed when he learns that it was his 'cooperator' who gave the blessing, standing at the doorway."

I was with Resl once on Good Friday and then I had gone downstairs. I had hardly got into the downstairs room when the bell in Resl's room started ringing. Since there was no one else there, I went back up to Resl's room and was greeted with these words: "Someone just said: He should put on a coat so he doesn't catch cold." I had completely forgotten my coat, which was lying there on the sofa.[34]

Once Resl said that she had misplaced some written notes that she needed right at the moment. She had already prayed in church that they would turn up again, and she had even said some prayers for that same purpose at the stove in her room. Then all of a sudden she heard someone talking and thought it was sister Crescenz, but she saw nothing. The voice said: "Go into the little closet under the roof alongside your room and take a few of the letters away there and you'll find what you're looking for." Therese did as she was told and the notes she wanted were lying there.

At the rectory they were making honey. The housekeeper, Therese's sister Marie, wanted to lift a kettle with about 35 pounds of honey from the floor to the top of the stove, but she could not lift it because shortly before she had had to have a finger amputated when blood poisoning threatened. Therese stooped over, picked up the heavy kettle *from the side,* and lifted it onto the stove top without any effort at all. Later she said that she had heard a voice telling her: "Go right ahead, try it once; it won't hurt you at all." In her weakened condition,

---

34. In her state of prepossession — (it was Good Friday!) — Resl was unable to see anything, and thus could not herself have been aware of the fact that the coat had been left behind — Author.

Therese is completely incapable, by all merely natural means, of lifting 35 pounds, particularly in the manner described.

Mystical Relationship towards the Dead

In many parts of this book we have already spoken of Therese Neumann's mystical relationship with the departed souls, whether in the state of glory (All Saints) or the state of purgation: in the account of her First Holy Communion (see page 62), her reparatory sufferings, and in many other instances.

Archbishop Teodorowicz writes as follows (page 384): "Therese's reparatory sufferings for the souls of the deceased is nothing new in the story of mysticism. St. Catherine of Siena suffered for her father; Catherine of Ricci suffered terribly for 40 days for the conversion and later penance of the famous Medici. Margaret Mary Alacoque, Blessed Catherine of Raccognini, and the Stigmatic Veronica Juliana all experienced similar sufferings. Doctor Imbert Gourbeyre (*La stigmatisation*) says that especially stigmatics are likely to undergo such reparatory sufferings."

"November 1, 1928. At six this morning Therese was privileged to have a vision of heaven. In the first picture she saw our Savior, surrounded by Mary, Joseph, the Apostles, the 24 elders, the 7 archangels, and a great retinue of other angels. In the second picture she saw the Savior standing among the virginal souls, and in a third among the other saints. She recognized many of them whom she had seen in her other visions or known on earth herself. All of them appeared as pure, luminous figures; in addition to our Savior there were two of them with glorified bodies, Mary and Elias. She was so enraptured over the visions that she began to long for death and for the rest of the day she was beside herself."

"November 2, 1928. Today Therese spent the whole day in quiet pain and suffering; she felt completely abandoned, like the poor souls. Twice today, in the morning and in the evening, she was privileged to pay a visit to purgatory. With indescribable sadness she saw the souls there as luminous bodies that are not yet completely pure. Here too she saw many acquaintances, and some of them came to beg her for help.

"The normal Friday sufferings were omitted today."

"November 9, 1928. Usual Friday sufferings and ecstasies, offered up for a soul in Purgatory. The soul is freed and speaks to Therese afterwards and she then sees him going up to heaven, before her very eyes.

"During this same time, Therese had to suffer very much for the city of Vienna where they were holding a big mission at the time."

"November 23, 1928. The usual Friday ecstasies. Today Therese was able to redeem from Purgatory the last Catholic pastor of Arzberg before the definitive introduction of Protestantism there. Because of his intemperance in drink and his negligence in offering Holy Mass, she said, he had to suffer a very long time in Purgatory. On account of his childhood he was finally able to be redeemed."

"December 30, 1930. At about nine in the morning, Therese was suddenly set upon by an unbearable suffering, bodily pain and anxiety of spirit, and finally this interrupted her state of elevated calm. At about the same time, as we later discovered, her Aunt and godmother Forster had died in Waldsassen."

"June 4, 1931. (*Corpus Christi*). Therese has a vision of the washing of the feet and the institution of the Blessed Sacrament. She is particularly struck by the fact that our Savior spoke so gently and lovingly to Judas before washing his feet.

"In the night after Corpus Christi, Therese's recently departed godmother Forster appeared to her while she was awake and in her normal state. Our Savior had given her the grace, she said, to make this visit, since she was completely abandoned. At least Therese ought to say some more prayers for her and try to help her.

"Therese seemed to feel that her godmother did not look the way a person on earth looks any more, but very calm and quiet spoken and gentle. She appeared as a luminous form, but dark.

"For Corpus Christi Therese was unusually zealous in decorating the Church, especially in honor of our sacramental Savior."

In conclusion let us once again quote from Archbishop Teodorowicz (page 389): "The mystery of the dogma of the Communion of Saints seems to be particularly enlightened here. It approaches very close to us, in an almost tangible way; we can feel its living pulsebeat. Most of all, we can only marvel at the harmonious union of the freedom of the human will and the divine activity; we experience the transformation of suffering, the spiritualization of the cross through love, the love of souls and the love of Christ."

Part Three

Evaluation

Conclusion

The following evaluations of Therese Neumann are all taken from men who knew her over the course of many years and were closely connected with her. In selecting these references, we naturally avoided those evaluations which owe their origin to mere literary preoccupations. Also, those visitors who came to Konnersreuth only once or twice and had no opportunity to observe Therese's various states and conditions cannot form any valid judgment. Even though the mystical phenomena were frequent, they were not an every day occurrence, and certainly they were not to be suggested. As a first precaution, those people were to be excluded from the list who felt they were not sufficiently honored or well received at Konnersreuth, and who based their judgments on a certain feeling of animosity. My investigations have uncovered no single negative judgment on the part of any person who really knew Therese Neumann over the course of the years.

One of the chief sources is Father Naber. He was forced to take a stand in 1938, when Konnersreuth was under attack; otherwise this man, who was so reserved in his expression and writing, would certainly never have made a public statement about Therese, particularly while she was still alive. His testimony is joined by that of very sober men, such as the then chief editor of the Munich paper, Dr. Fritz Gerlich, or bishops who had sharp powers of observation and were particularly trained in mystic problems, such as Archbishop Teodorowicz of Lemberg.

State Counsel, Dr. Fritz Michael Gerlich
1929 (I, 172; II, 405-506)

The closer I study Therese Neumann, the more my findings and experiences force me to admit that, at least as far as I am concerned, the explanations offered to date are insufficient, but this is not the only thing that has made such a strong impression on me. The strongest impression I got came from the fact that this person is absolutely oriented towards the Christian religion. I have never before experienced a more perfect fulfillment of the demands of Christianity in any person.

My investigations into Therese Neumann's credibility have arrived at the following result: There is no serious grounds for considering her as an hysteric and thus a conscious or unconscious liar. Quite the contrary, we must, from the very outset, credit her with the reliability of any person who is sound in mind and soul. In assessing the degree of credibility there is one further significant fact: she has an extraordinary degree of religious orientation, feels that she is responsible to God for everything she does, has no greater ambition than to work for his good pleasure, and knows that God looks upon any untruth as a serious sin. The spiritual stimuli which arise from such a strong religious life as that of Therese Neumann, also intensify her love of truth, and thus her credibility, far beyond the normal degree.

These incentives to truthfulness, namely spiritual and mental health and a strong interior religious life, are also to be encountered in the whole Neumann family, especially the parents, and in Therese's confessor and spiritual director, Father Joseph Naber. Obviously any human being can make a mistake. And Therese Neumann, in her normal state, is easily subject to error. The same is true of the other persons named above. But there is no conceivable grounds for accusing them of deliberate deceit. Their religious conceptions are far too developed to permit the mere thought of serving God by some pious deceit. They cannot believe that God, who is truth for them, could have any pleasure in being "served," the way a chieftain of some primitive community is "served," by deceiving his followers and those outside his camp.

On all these grounds I find myself bound in conscience to declare that so far as I am concerned, in accord with every method of historical investigation that I have learned in my university studies and in my later scientific work, that the events which I have accumulated in the story of Therese Neumann's life are historically and critically well established facts. And thus I am forced to the conviction that the case of Therese Neumann, taken as a whole, is not to be explained on any natural grounds.

Cardinal Archbishop Dr. Karl Kaspar, Prague (1930)
(Loc. cit. page 108)

I must honestly confess that I have observed not the least sign of hysteria in Therese Neumann, no suggestion or auto-suggestion, hypnosis or deceit, or for that matter, possession by the devil. The young lady gives the impression of being a perfectly sound and normal person, in the opinion of everyone who has ever had an opportunity to see her and speak with her in her normal state. She is open and pious, and she suffers most from the fact that strangers keep bothering her and that she cannot simply live and work, quietly and with an innocent heart, for those she loves.

Does this make Therese Neumann a saint?

"No man should ever be called blessed before his death." In my own personal judgment Therese Neumann is a highly favored young lady. She strives, as every person should, to be a saint. Not only does she go to confession every week and strengthen her inner life in Holy Communion, with the Sacred Body of our Savior, and not only does she keep herself from the merest trace of sin, but she lives in constant union with our Divine Savior. What is more, she is patient in bearing the crosses he sends her, even cheerful, and she wants nothing but what he wants for her.

Will she remain this same way until her dying breath? We must certainly hope so. But so long as the soul has not departed from the body, the Holy Church will have nothing to say about Resl's person nor about the events at Konnersreuth. I also submit, wholly and entirely, to her infallible judgment.

Our dear Lord has favored Therese Neumann with such extraordinary graces, in this time of indifference and open lack of faith, only in order to show her, and through her the whole world, the way that leads to love for our crucified Savior and hatred for sin.

Archbishop Teodorowicz on Therese Neumann (1936)
(loc. cit. p. 65 ff)

As an introduction to my investigation, I cannot avoid speaking of the overall impression that Therese Neumann makes on all her visitors. She shows herself to be a person of strong will and full vitality; she is just the opposite of a calm and insensitive nature. I know very well that she once dreamed of the vocation of a missionary sister. Activity in the world she lives in, and an urgency to be doing something, are a vital need for such a strong and active temperament. She has a remarkably clear spiritual vision, she has a sharp intellect; she is neither verbose nor laconic . . . she grasps every spiritual problem, even the most serious ones, and then expresses them in a short, meaty, and very definite form.

Naturalness, love of truth, but especially simplicity—these are the three principal qualities I have noted in Therese. But simplicity of soul does not consist, as do some other virtues, in special activities which are verfied only on the proper occasion. Simplicity is the whole cast of her soul, her spiritual health; it streams out of her very person and is shared by everyone who speaks with her or observes her. Her simplicity is in her eyes, in her every motion, and it rules over the exterior as well as the interior of her soul: it resides in her deepest thoughts and feelings. Other virtues, such as humility and patience, could all be artificial, but every artificial attempt to feign simplicity quickly betrays itself. It is also possible for a person to have this blessed gift of simplicity by nature, but this virtue is the foundation of the spiritual and supernatural life, according to the Gospel principle: "Unless you become as children, you cannot enter the kingdom of heaven."

This simplicity brings Therese into a relationship with God that could not possibly be more intimate, no matter how many severe mortifications she were to practice.

Simple in all her behavior, she is not only free from all artificiality, but also from all embarrassment, simply because of the fact that she is unconcerned about herself. She is simple, brief, direct and pointed in what she says, uncommonly simple in treating any subject of conversation.

In the smile that constantly plays on her face, and in her words as well, there is a mirror of her inner joy, a joy that is not without a certain sense of humor. Humor is always a welcome guest in the spiritual life. Father Doyle, a very saintly man who lived a life of strictest mortification, used to say that humor was a great support for the spiritual life. And we are all familiar with the words of St. Francis de Sales, rooted so firmly in his clear Gallic wisdom, that a saint who is sad is a sad saint. Anyone who reads the life of the Little Flower can see this little saint exuded joy all about her, a joy that was evident even in her innocent and jesting words.

A person who had to spend the whole week weaving a mourning cloak out of the threads of her own powers of imagination and interior feelings in order to wear it fresh every Friday, would certainly look much different. Because all her thoughts and feelings would then be thoughts of blood and sorrow and shuddering; her inner eye would shun every ray of joy and her words would preach a continual crusade against joy to all the world, under the standard of blood and suffering.

But here what do we see? Here everything is a song in accompaniment to the choirs of birds, singing for joy, and this joy is never afraid to sound a jesting and humorous note. Everything breathes calm and peace of soul; everything is wrapped up within a mantle of childlike simplicity and everyone who comes to look is struck by it. But are investigations such as these sufficient? Is it not true that the same phenomena regularly occur in the case of hysterics and psychopathic people? And do not such people regularly display great calm as long as their own ego remains free from attack by a horde of imaginary delusions and "fixed ideas"?

I patiently wait for Therese to begin speaking about herself. The visit of two bishops who came primarily for the purpose of gaining some personal experience in Konnersreuth was the propitious moment. In the way that a person speaks about himself or turns a conversation to himself, we can immediately catch a glimpse of his fundamental attitude towards his own ego. The "ego" is always loquacious; it is pleased with self in brisk energetic tones, and likes to take the first step to call attention to itself and steal the limelight, and it is clever enough not to stop playing the role it has to play for even a single moment, whether it speaks or is silent or decks itself in false humility.

It was precisely this that made the greatest impression on me in my meeting with Therese Neumann: the ticklish note of self love that creeps in so easily everywhere, was not to be noticed here in the least, no matter how hard I tried to find a trace of it in her conversation. Therese was well aware of this purpose behind our visit—I had come with Bishop Lisowski. She knew that whatever she told us about herself would go a long way towards influencing our opinions. And still she was absolutely silent on that subject, nor did she ever let herself be led into conversation about herself; when we asked her anything, she confined her answers to the bare essentials, and used only the simplest and shortest words.

Then without any subterfuge, I began forcing her to speak about herself. I set the key myself, and spoke in tones immediately suggesting her fame and the world-wide notice she had attracted: "But now you have become famous throughout the whole world!" Without even thinking, without having a moment's notice to hide behind a cloak of false humility, she smiled and gave an answer that speaks well for her real state of soul. I have already quoted it before but I will repeat it here: "Oh yes, that's really something. Some of them praise me and the others call me a faker; but I pay no attention to either one; it doesn't bring me any closer to God." How simple, how deep, how honest, even from the mystic point of view, are these few words. If John of the Cross had been present, he would have welcomed them with joy, because the point of departure and yardstick that he used to measure all his visions and ecstasies and everything that was in any way connected with them was simply his favorite motto: "Does it bring me closer to God or not?"

Just like a doctor making his clinical investigations, I kept poking and thumping about, trying to find some place where the soul was sick and sensitive. But I could not find such a spot. Her love has contracted her whole soul, her innermost sensitivities and her strongest feelings, all into one single focal point; our Savior. She speaks of him, and of everything that has even the least connection with him, with such a glow of joy and such a burst of sentiment and love that every word is steeped in what she feels towards him; she thinks constantly of him, and she thinks of him because she finds her joy in everything only insofar as it is related to him; and in him she seeks her exclusive happiness.

After this preparation and investigation I decided to acquire a firsthand acquaintance with the question of Konnersreuth. Prior to this I must confess that I had certain reservations, a certain mistrust of the whole affair.

When I clothe the overall impression that I received in such brief words, the spiritual life of Therese Neumann appears harmonious and balanced, despite the variety of her moral and spiritual characteristics. Thanks to this simplicity and straight-forwardness of her whole being, the supernatural world, as she describes it in answer to our questions seems to be reduced to a natural world, or to put it much better, it seems as though the partition between these two worlds has disappeared under the breath of this simple and childlike soul.

No matter which standpoint we assume in examining her life, and no matter which of her characteristics and traits we weigh and investigate, we constantly keep falling back upon the basic key to her soul, the soul of a child of God. She is and remains a child in everything, in her simplicity and humility, in her whole bearing, in her prayer, in her relationship to our Savior, and in her mystic union with him. The graces she receives are also proportioned to these peculiar characteristics of her soul: and for example, in a manifestation of her temperament that is a source of some irritation to many people, namely the fact that she always evidences a certain childlike attitude and manner of grasping things in her ecstasies, I find a proof of the fact that the Holy Spirit has set a visible seal on the childlike simplicity of this child of God.

This spirit of being a child of God, as it is evident in Therese Neumann in all the many facets of her being, even in the most insignificant expressions of her interior and exterior living, seems to me to be the principal touchstone of sound and healthy mysticism.

Evaluation of Dr. Franz X. Mayr, Counsel to the Bishop, Professor of Chemistry, Biology and Geology

The following document was submitted to ecclesiastical consideration on October 18, 1937.

I have known Therese Neumann for almost eleven years. During this time I had frequent opportunity to observe her in the most divergent circumstances. The first time, I came to

Konnersreuth with my college Professor Franz X. Wutz, on December 2, 1926, and stayed there until December 5. Since then I have visited her every year, generally several times a year, either in Konnersreuth or in Eichstätt. In 1928 I spent some eight days in Konnersreuth after Easter, and some two weeks during the long vacation. In the course of the year 1937, I spent three whole weeks of my summer vacation there, recuperating, from August 29 until September 20.

Since I am a natural scientist, from the very outset of our acquaintance, Therese greatly enjoyed talking about birds and flowers with me and asking me all sorts of questions about the natural sciences. Frequently I was able to observe, and even help, her taking care of the birds and flowers in her room and in the garden. And on such occasions the conversation never remained merely on the subject of science and nature. Therese always showed a perfect confidence in me and I knew that she always acted towards me as she really is inside, Therese's family also came to me openly and friendly, and besides that Father Naber gave me every possible opportunity to learn more about all the extraordinary phenomena of Konnersreuth.

In my judgment, Therese Neumann has an uncommonly clear mind and judges her own person and her own personal graces with amazing objectivity and sobriety. Her will is powerful, masculine even, and oriented solely towards fulfilling the will of our Savior in all things, out of love for him, and bringing all men everywhere closer to him. This basic orientation of her spiritual attitude finds clear expression in even the most unintentional expressions. She experiences a constant pain at having been denied the fulfillment of her childhood dream: to work for our Savior as a missionary hospital sister, unknown to the world. Her particularly active and buoyant nature finds a very heavy cross in the fact that she is condemned to external inactivity as a result of her stigmata and her many reparatory sufferings, and in her love of being alone and hidden from the world she finds it hard to put up with the fact that her whole life has been made so public by the special graces she has been favored with.

Only the thought that all this is our Savior's will gives her the strength to bear up under everything with resignation.

Anyone who has had the chance to spend some time with Therese Neumann is constantly amazed at her great simplicity and the straightforwardness of her whole being and her unsurpassed love of truth. Every kind of untruthfulness and hypocrisy is an abomination to her and I have had frequent opportunity to observe that she cannot bring herself to tell even the smallest lie.

On these grounds all *conscious and deliberate* deceit on her part is completely excluded, nor would she ever suffer such deceit on the part of her friends and family.

But neither is there any questions of *unconscious* deceit. Therese Neumann is as psychically sound as anyone else and she is completely free from every trace of hysteria. Moreover, she is completely inaccessible to any form of suggestion, either from her own self or other people—I have had frequent occasion to observe this fact.

The Observation and Investigation of 1927

Both Dr. Seidel and Dr. Ewald, as well as the current episcopal authorities, were fully aware of the fact that the four nurses who helped conduct the clinical observation under oath, were above reproach and fulfilled their task most conscientiously. The Bishop's Office of Regensburg examined into the methods and concludes, according to an official statement of October 4, 1927, that a "clinical observation in a hospital or a clinic [which had been the object of their original efforts] could not have produced any more successful results." Despite the personal views of Ewald, Deutsch, and others, there was no possible way to impugn the objective truth of the following points, on grounds of the doctor's reports:

1. In the period from July 14 to 28, 1927, Therese Neumann took no natural nourishment at all, either liquid or solid.

2. During this whole period, Therese Neumann produced

only 525 ccm of urine. There were no bowel movements at all.

3. Her weight at the end of the examination, despite the considerable variation after her Friday sufferings, was the same as at the beginning of that period.

4. Neither during the period of examination, nor at its end, did any special states of exhaustion make their appearance.

Points one and three are also expressly referred to in the (already quoted) statement issued by the Regensburg Ordinary on October 4, 1927, and in the article on Therese Neumann in the *Lexikon für Theologie und Kirche* (VII, 513f).

Points two and four are also recognized in both cases, in the very high praise bestowed on the four sworn nurses for their conscientious work during the clinical observation; because the claims made there are all based, in the last analysis, on the accounts furnished by these nurses.

In forming a judgment on the points mentioned above we must always keep in mind the fact that a period of eleven days was officially declared by the specialists to be the longest interval over which man could possibly survive without food and drink. And in such cases, naturally, there needs to be absolute quiet, avoidance of all exertion, loss of blood, etc. The possible life expectancy must otherwise be greatly abbreviated. And at all events under natural conditions when a person has completed fifteen days of this total abstinence, if he is still alive at all, he will have shrunken to a mere skeleton and dried into a mummy and be very close to death.

I should like to run through these four points individually, and call particular attention to the following facts that seem to have been overlooked by Dr. Deutsch.

1. The total amount of urine produced by Therese Neumann during the whole time of the observation was only a little more than half a liter, whereas a normal man produces a liter to a liter and a half every day. Furthermore, since many bodily wastes are regularly removed by the urine, such a small urine output would very soon involve very serious and very dangerous symptoms of uremia: acute headache, dizziness, etc., at the

outset, and eventually even death. But in Therese Neumann's case there was not even a single hint of such disturbances.

2. When mediums of any kind, on the basis of their own or outside suggestions, have spent some time in a trance condition, they are always completely exhausted afterwards. If Therese Neumann's ecstasies were the result of merely natural strength of any kind, then a state of immense exhaustion would necessarily have followed immediately upon her Friday sufferings during the time of the clinical observations, and particularly on the second of the two Fridays involved, after eight full days had passed without her taking a single bit of nourishment. But on Saturdays there was not a trace of any such exhaustion to be noticed in Therese Neumann. On the contrary, the weight that she had lost on Friday was always recovered in the course of a few days—something that would be quite impossible in the case of a really exhausted organism.

3. The rapid gaining of weight observed in Therese Neumann's case, sometimes as much as five or six pounds within the course of a few days would be conceivable in a normal person, only in the case of extreme nourishment intake. Even the most refined impostor could not possibly manage to take enough nourishment to account for such an increase in weight without being observed by the four watchful eyes of the nurses.

4. Frequently there is not enough attention focused on the fact that Therese Neumann did *not drink anything* either, during the course of these 15 days. After even a few days, under normal circumstances and with normal physical nourishment requirements, she would certainly have begun to suffer from terrible pangs of thirst. And what is more, the observation took place in the hottest time of the year. Especially after the first Friday suffering and its consequent loss of blood she must have been nearly dying of thirst. And a second such experience, the following Friday, she could not normally have survived. Probably she would have died already before this. But in Therese's case, throughout the whole period of the observations, there was not a trace of any feeling of hunger or thirst: nor is there any record

of the fact that she suffered from a drying out of the gums and tongue, not even on Friday after the suffering.

On the basis of the evidence cited above it is absolutely impossible that Therese could have (as some people like to believe) abstained from food and drink during the time of the observations, but eaten and drunk immediately before and after. No hysterical person or impostor would have been able to live to the end of the observation time under like circumstances, to say nothing of maintaining normal weight and remaining fresh and healthy. On the other hand, we might also point out that a person who came through a fifteen-day test period with such flying colors is certainly not accustomed to taking normal nourishment at other times and that we can easily trust her when she claims that she regularly lives without food.

Thus, in my opinion, the fifteen-day examination was *quite sufficient* to prove that Therese Neumann's continuous lack of nourishment intake is not to be explained on natural grounds. People who are not willing to believe this would no doubt also find some "hole" in any new examination that might be attempted, in order to quiet their conscience.

When we turn to the *other phenomena* that were and are still observable at Konnersreuth, it is obvious that we have more than sufficient criteria for a reliable judgment on the facts involved.

This is already true of the *history of Therese Neumann's sickness and miraculous cures.* As far as her accident in the fire of March 10, 1919, is concerned, it is my firm conviction that hysteria cannot possibly be seriously mentioned as a casual factor. A diagnosis like *hysteria traumatica* [35] are decidedly false. All a person had to do is (as I did) have Therese Neumann

---

35. Dr. Seidel had originally fixed upon *hysteria traumatica* as the diagnosis of her disease, but under the influence of later developments in Konnersreuth he expressly repudiated his original diagnosis (cf. Boniface, 1963 edition, pp. 66 ff) and thus collapsed all the opinions that had been built up on the basis of his original diagnosis.

and her family give a description of the events that preceded and immediately followed the fire and call to mind Therese Neumann's perfectly natural and normal mental and psychic endowments. During the fire Therese had only one goal; she completely lost sight of her own person in her efforts to be of service to her employer and help put out the fire, no matter what it cost; and after her accident she wanted nothing more than to be able to work again and later to join the missionary sisters. The danger consisted not in the fact that she talked herself into a non-existent physical ailment and suffering, but much rather in the fact that, in her restlessness to be doing something active, she paid too little attention to the existing physical ailment and suffering and thus grew steadily worse.

This is clear to everyone who really knows Therese Neumann. There was definitely some disorder in the spinal column after the fire. The hours of steady work lifting the heavy buckets of water, together with the constant and strenuous bending, turning, and extending of the spinal column, could easily effect such a severe strain in the muscles around the vertebrae, and particularly in such a young organism as Therese Neumann's, it would result in a complete organic disorder, even dislocation of the spine. Her mother can substantiate under oath that according to her personal observations she could both see and touch two small lumps through the skin, in the lumbar region—certainly spinal processes—and that they had been wrenched out of place towards the right.

Moreover, we can claim sufficient certainty in establishing the fact, even today, that the big bedsores Therese developed during this period of confinement to her bed were really there and that on May 17, 1925, they were suddenly healed and whether this healing can be naturally explained or not—because the witnesses to this event all are still alive.

Therese Neumann's *ecstasies* all clearly evidence a whole complex of important characteristics which manifestly and essentially distinguish them from all natural trance states, raptures, etc.

As for the *stigmata*, we must once again point out that wounds which remain the same for almost eleven years, never becoming inflamed or infected, and on the other hand resisting the application of any medication or treatment, are not the wounds known to the world of medicine. Anyone who really thinks that Therese Neumann's stigmata might have arisen through a process of autosuggestion needs only to look at the compresses which lay directly over the heart wound on Good Friday, 1936; they have been preserved by her sister Marie. The blood clotting that built up in the wound remained sticking on the compress and it gives a clear picture of the size of the wound. In comparison to such a wound, all the wounds and bleedings that are produced by a process of suggestion (psychogenic) can only be called ridiculous. This argument has even greater weight when we consider the sum total of the wounds from which Therese Neumann bled on last Good Friday: their size can still be clearly judged from the blood stains on her bed jacket and head cloth.

In the area of her *visions*, too, examining particulars that cannot be naturally explained. For example, Therese Neumann distinctly hears our dying Savior say the word *"aes-che"* (I'm thirsty) on the cross, instead of the word *"sachena"* or some other similar form as Professor Wutz and the other investigators had originally expected. No one even thought of *"ase-che"* because it is a neo-Hebrew word. There can be no natural explanation for this phenomenon.

Further criteria for the eventful definitive judgment on the phenomena of Konnersreuth are furnished by the manifold and often very extraordinary reparatory sufferings Therese Neumann underwent, as well as her ecstatic Communions, her unerring feeling for the presence of the Eucharistic Savior and the presence of her own or other people's guardian angels, her feeling for absolution, priestly blessings and consecrations, cardiognosis, prediction of actions and events that are dependent upon the freedom of human will, her ability to recognize all kinds of relics, the extraordinary assistance on the part of her guardian angel, the special temptations from the devil, etc. A further point to be examined into, on a purely factual basis, are the accounts of miraculous cures accomplished through Therese's intercession, the cases of bilocation, clairvoyance, and other similar phenomena which have, in large part, not yet been made public.

Gerlich and Archbishop Teodorowicz particularly have done some very valuable work towards arriving at a final judgment of the above mentioned areas.

Finally we must stress the fact that the sum total of all these phenomena forms a *remarkably significant unity*, which in my opinion, can be completely fitted into the dimensions of Catholic dogma and morality. Many, many people who have come into contact with Therese Neumann have thereby experienced a new deepening of faith and trust; they have become happier and more joyful, and learned a healthy piety from her. No one of them ever experienced any harm to his faith or morals. This fact is also of the greatest importance in evaluating her case.

Naturally it cannot be denied that certain particulars of the Konnersreuth story do present some *difficulties* in explanation. But everywhere in the world of nature, and in Christian revelation, we meet with phenomena that are difficult or perhaps unexplainable and even seem to involve inherent contradictions. In his way of working, God does not ever mean to resolve all difficulties, and if only the broader outlines of divine activity are manifest in a given case, we must generally be content.

Finally, we have all experienced the fact that many of these "difficulties" tend to resolve themselves when we make a thorough on-the-spot investigation. With so many people writing and speaking about Konnersreuth, it is difficult to represent a clear and objectively correct picture. And thus it is hard to believe how many inaccurate and mistaken statements are being spread abroad, even in good faith, and coming to be accepted as truth. Long-distance diagnosis is never highly thought of in scientific circles, and particularly in such a very complicated case as this no honest man can let himself form any serious judgment until he has had a chance to study the whole affair thoroughly and on the spot.

Open Letter from Father Naber to Dr. Joseph Eberle

Dr. Eberle was chief editor of the *Schönere Zunkunft*, Vienna: the letter appeared in the Salzburg *Katholische Kirchenzeitung* Nov. 6, 1938.

Dear Mr. Editor,

In the January 23, 1938 number of your weekly, *Schönere Zukunft*, I read an article entitled "Konnersreuth at the Bar of Theology and Medicine." The writer of this letter is Father Naber: for 28 years now I have been confessor and spiritual director to Therese Neumann; I know her from her school days and I have observed everything extraordinary that has ever occurred in her case, up to the present day, at close range and as exactly as possible. I have also maintained the utmost reserve and sobriety in expressing myself—those who know me will bear me out on this—and apart from a very brief statement to establish the truth of the matter in the very beginning of these extraordinary phenomena, I have written nothing, even though it could easily have turned into a very profitable business for me.

My basic principle has always been this: to make exact observation of all these extraordinary phenomena, in order to discover whether they contain anything contrary to Church dogma or repugnant to Catholic morality. If they do, then to take a merciless stand against them; but if not, then merely to let things run their natural course, and thus not run the risk of going counter to the plans of God. I have deliberated over every single word I have spoken regarding Therese Neumann, in order not to say too much; but neither am I afraid to stand up and be counted as a witness to the truth. Without the least reservation or hesitancy, I would stake my very life on the truth and genuinity of these extraordinary experiences of Therese, as I have observed them, and particularly her lack of nourishment intake. When we consider the simplicity, naturalness, and openness of this "big child" (in the sense in which our Lord uses the term), when we see the fire of her love and inspiration for our Savior shining in her eyes, when we have seen how all these extraordinary states, visions, etc. come upon her without any activity on her part, and all this pure and natural simplicity and perfect historical truth, then we cannot escape the conviction that thousands of people have already arrived at, on the basis of similar observations: "This is genuine." And then we tend to be irritated at the prospect of a pharisaical observation and examination of blood and urine, and intravenous feeding etc., that the world of science wants to undertake.

Unfortunately, and quite contrary to the frequently expressed will of Therese Neumann and her parents, much has been written about Konnersreuth, including much that is deformed and incorrect and in bad taste. And as if this were not enough, some gentlemen are making a joint effort to turn it into a caricature of Konnersreuth—an attack with anti-clerical overtones as well. I cannot reproach anyone for simply believing in Konnersreuth without further ado, but I can and do reproach anyone who forms a definite opinion about the affairs here without having carefully oriented himself in the actual experiences. If you want to understand the poet you've got to visit the poet's home land. And how much truer this is when we are speaking of such extraordinary matters.

Look, I'm just a simple country priest, no doctor or anything like that, but I'm not afraid of all these learned gentlemen either, because I've experienced all these things.... What Dr. Deutsch, for example, has written up about Konnersreuth is based solely and completely on false premises. Dr. Deutsch was never here in Konnersreuth. Dr. Heermann, and Fathers Masoin and Richstätter, S.J., were never there either.... And you, editor of this paper, with the estimate you make of the whole affair in your weekly, were you ever here in Konnersreuth? And your Dr. Pius Havemann? For a decade now this old pot-pourri

Vision during First Mass celebration. During the banquet Therese had a vision, just after a child had climbed onto her lap and offered her some food.

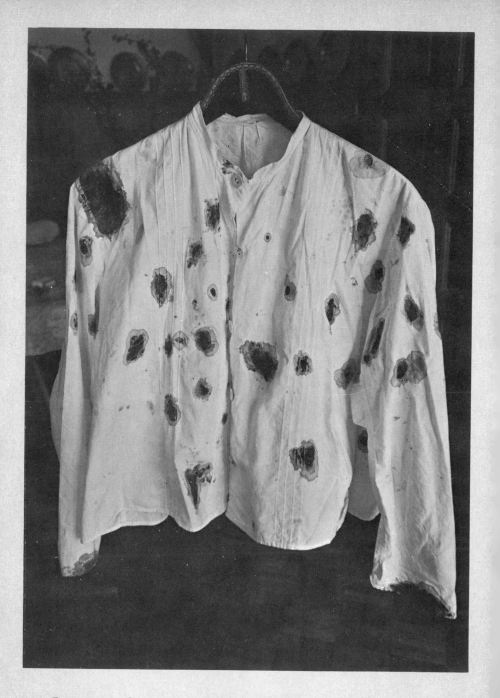

Documentary photographs: front and back of the bed-jacket which Therese Neumann wore on Good Friday, 1959. Taken in 1963.

Visionary participation in the Sunday Mass at Konnersreuth, while Therese is in Eichstätt. Both pictures taken in the library of Professor Wutz, Eichstätt. above: Therese prays together with the priest.
below: the moment of consecration.

Therese passing from her visionary state to her normal condition.

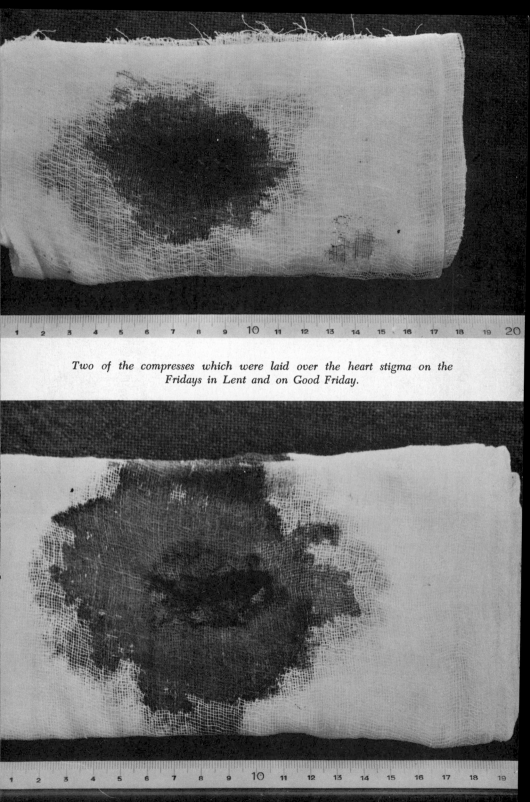

*Two of the compresses which were laid over the heart stigma on the
Fridays in Lent and on Good Friday.*

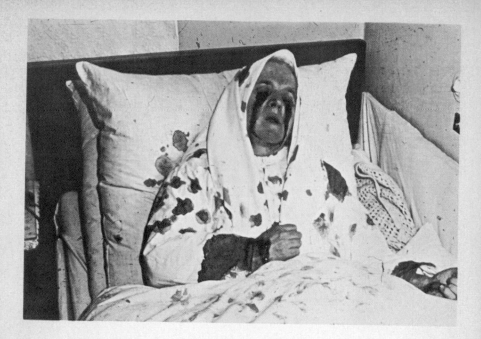

Good Friday, 1953. After the vision of Jesus' death.

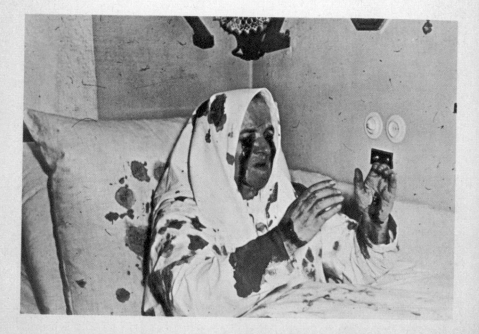

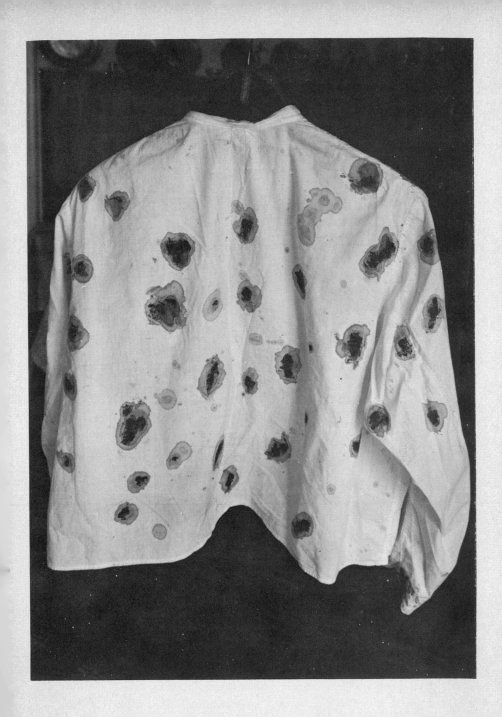

An unexpected Friday vision (St. Wolfgang's Day, October 31, 1941).

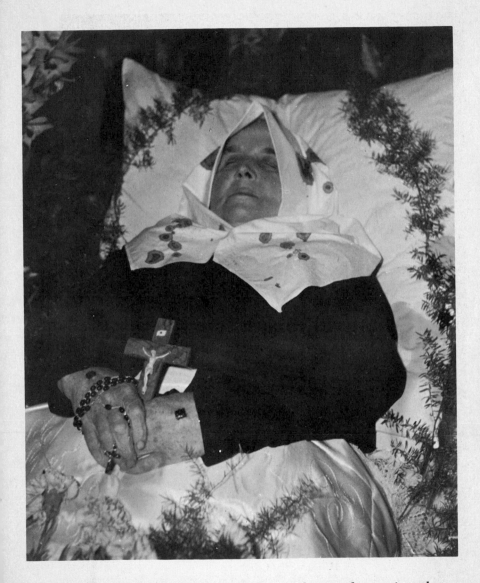

Therese Neumann in death. She was laid out in the room that was formerly her father's work room, from Sept. 18 to 22, 1962.

Father Naber and Ferdinand Neumann pay respects. Taken by Hilmar Pabel, Rottau/Chiemsee.

Headcloth worn by Therese Neumann on Good Friday, 1959.

Resl's room in the Neumann home.

One of the thousands of prayer cards that Therese Neumann used to give her visitors in the course of her years of suffering. The reverse reads: "Savior, gladly every sacrifice for love of you. United in holy prayer. Therese Neumann."

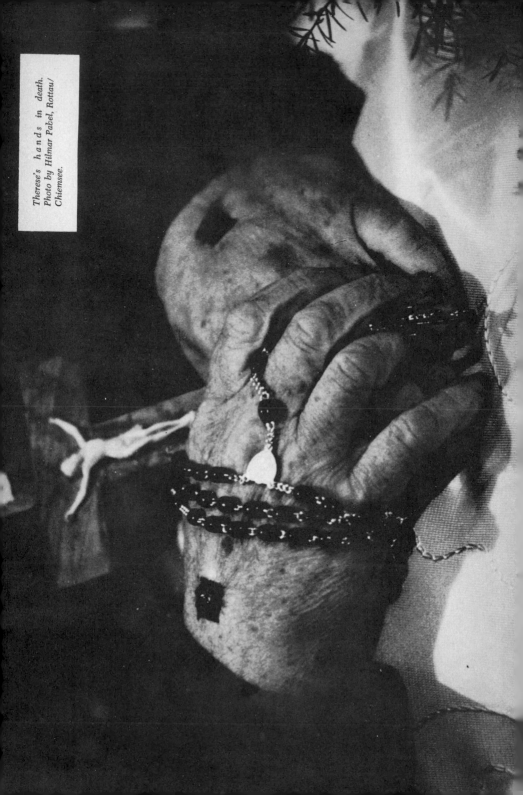

Therese Neumann's grave, near the cemetery cross which was erected on her initiative.

Therese Neumann's handwriting. A postcard addressed to the author.

of lies has been warmed up over and over again—by the opponents of Konnersreuth; one after another they're writing all about it and they call it a science.

Why don't they ask the opinion of those who know Therese Neumann, her character, her religious and normal behavior and the true story of these extraordinary experiences. Her priests, her very modest parents and brothers and sisters, her neighbors, the whole parish, the many, many bishops and priests and competent lay people who have visited the place and doctors who have made their examinations and observations. At present Therese has been in Eichstätt for three weeks now, with Professor Wutz who is ill—one of her sisters is his housekeeper. The professors from the school come to visit here, and frequently the bishop too. All of them, especially the bishop, have a great interest in Therese Neumann. A like interest was always evident in the former bishop of Eichstätt, who is now the bishop of Berlin.

Professor Wutz is already famous for the objectivity and sobriety of his statements. Since 1926 he has frequently visited Konnersreuth and Therese Neumann has often been to Eichstatt. Certainly, if there were any deceit or imposture, he would long since have managed to smell it out. Another of the Eichstätt professors, a member of the chemistry and biology faculty, has sent a lengthy report of his experience and evaluation of Therese Neumann to Bishop Buchberger in Regensburg, I am enclosing a copy of this report.

In 1927 the episcopal ordinariate inquired among the competent authorities on the subject of how long a human being could be expected to survive without any food and drink at all. Answer: about eleven days. Then they ordered a fifteen-day clinical observation of Therese Neumann. Just read what Archbishop Teodorowicz has to report on the subject, how careful they were in the examination. (This Archbishop, who was here several times obviously counts for nothing in your eyes, just like Cardinal Kaspar and Bishop Waitz, because they are not opposed to Konnersreuth either.)

15 *Therese Neumann*

The results of the examination were officially published with the note that they could not possibly have been carried on any better in a clinic and that thus the scientific approach to an understanding of the situation had been done full justice. Therese Neumann's father is prepared to swear under oath that the then vicar general of the diocese, in an effort to win his consent, had promised that after this first examination he would not be troubled again by any further demands. "Now," says her father, "I've kept my word and given consent to the examination; and now the bishop's people have to keep their word too." In the explanation published by the bishop's office in December 10, 1937, we read that the examination of 1927 was sufficient to establish only the current (1927) state of affairs in Konnersreuth. Naturally; even a clinical examination in the year 1938 would be sufficient only to establish the present state of affairs for the two weeks in which it was conducted.

But if the sworn statements of those who are both trustworthy and in a position to make a judgment about the extraordinary events Therese Neumann has experienced are to be accepted in any way, then their oath is certainly valid before both the Church and the world tribunal. And the phenomenon of nourishment intake, or its lack, is a matter that any person with normally sound faculties can easily make a personal judgment on. Therese's father has come in for much criticism on the part of the doctors because of his intransigent refusal to allow a new clinical examination. As for the fact that her father, an old artilleryman, has such a hard head, the Bishop of Berlin says that he is glad he does; if her father were to give in to a new examination, Therese would never see the outside of a clinic again, because one doctor would never take another doctor's word, and one clinic would never accept the findings of another.

This I am convinced, is the result of a higher plan and disposition. So you really believe that our Savior means to let himself be questioned before the tribunal of natural science, and asked to substantiate his miracles? He comes and works his miracles, not for the world of science, but for the simple human good will. When our Savior was hanging on the cross, the scientists of his day kept crying: "Come down from the cross and show us that you are the Son of God!" But our Savior did not come down from the cross; shortly afterwards, though, he did arise from the dead and ascend into heaven and none of these learned gentlemen was privileged to witness it.

What would our Savior meet with today, if he came back to earth and worked his miracles again? What, after all, is the real source of our religious collapse today? It comes, we say, from our semi-rationalism. A ministry counsel, formerly Protestant, who was converted to Catholicism by visiting Therese Neumann, and is now very happy with his new religion, recently wrote these words to me (he was very upset about the way Therese Neumann's case was being handled): "Christianity is not *ratio*, but *mysterium*—not reason but mystery."

On April 29, 1937, the anniversary of her beatification, St. Therese of the Child Jesus appeared to Therese Neumann and said: "You have to fulfill your vocation completely, you have to try to be more like our misunderstood, despised, and persecuted Savior." Therese Neumann was frightened at these words, and so was I. I prayed to our Savior: "Oh, never let me be a tool of this misunderstanding, and despising and persecution!" I can believe that many other people had grounds to offer the same prayer. The theologians are doing the work of Caiphas, but it all helps Therese to grow closer to our Savior in his terrible sufferings. "Has the Church already persecuted her?" a university professor asked, on the occasion of his first visit to Konnersreuth. "That's the only grounds on which I could believe in her genuinity."

We face the future without anxiety. Therese prays: "Savior, you know that we have never thought of anything like this at all. You're the one who started it and you will have to see it through."

Your article, sir, is a monstrous accusation; you know the

eighth commandment. Therese can wait until the day of judgment, as our Savior did, with Caiphas.

All best wishes — Naber, Pastor

Letter of the Head Doctor, Leo Ritter, Regensburg, to Father Naber

Regensburg, April 15, 1949
Prüfeningerstrasse

Reverend and Dear Father,

On Good Friday my thoughts make their way to Konnersreuth; I had very much wished to be able to experience the events there today. But the somewhat quiet day, less demanding than usual, does at least allow me time to write a note to you, extending you the heartiest wishes for the Easter holidays and hoping that Resl, after the difficult days of the Passion, will be richly compensated by her joys in contemplating the risen Savior.

In the meantime I have had opportunity to think over many things and I have met with many young theologians in my professional activities, who have been exposed to Professor Waldmann's contrary influences. I take a very firm and resolute position against Waldmann: there is *no trace* of hysteria here. For me, Resl's stigmata has no "natural" explanation, and Professor Tschermak von Seyssenegg is in perfect accord with this position, to say nothing of the lack of nourishment intake which a few other stigmatics besides Resl have also experienced

Particularly I held up to these young theologians the fact that Waldmann's position and lectures have been working out favorably for the Church. Resl's influence at Konnersreuth is something I have already experienced. The Friday I was there more than 200 people received Holy Communion. And there was not one among them that I didn't see coming out of Therese Neumann's house with a look of genuine conviction on his face.

All who were there were led to the serious reflection about the really important things in life. It is true that some are influenced for a short time, others for a longer time, but one thing is definitely true: the events in Konnersreuth are working out only to the advantage of all really Christian minded people. I pass over Therese Resl's home life in silence, as well as her constant efforts to be of service to other people.

For myself, Konnersreuth leaves me wishing I could pay more frequent visits there. I must thank you once again for your very friendly reception and cooperation.

Best wishes once again for the Easter holidays, both for yourself personally, and for the Neumann family. My daughter sends her best wishes too. Very respectfully yours,

Your devoted Dr. Leo Ritter

Three Accounts of
The Effects of Konnersreuth

Through Konnersreuth to the Church

Ministry Counsel, Paul Schondorf (written in 1936)[36]

Therese Neumann, whom I had previously known only from good books and bad pictures, I finally met personally on August 6, 1931. On that occasion I learned to esteem and love her childlike piety, in no way ostentatious or pietistic, her sharp and lively and at the same time humorous and happy temperament. Her sufferings in the ecstasies which I had witnessed on August 7, 1931, made a deep and lasting impression on me. With these feelings I returned back to my home in northern Germany, purely Protestant country. Months went by. I thought a lot about Konnersreuth, and the images which the terrible Passion of our Savior had left in my mind. I also prayed a good deal in the spirit of the promise I had made Resl. My wife and youngest son were Catholics. Even though I had, for decades, been taking a strong Protestant stand against Catholicism, as is the practice of my church, there was always Konnersreuth as a bond to weld our family together. On this theme we saw eye to eye; we were united.

---

36. The author has since died — Author.

My thoughts went back more and more to the personality of Therese Neumann. They always came to rest on the undeniable fact of her stigmata. This was the one fact I could not possibly get around. I read somewhere that over the course of the centuries there had been a few hundred stigmatics, but never outside the Catholic Church. This too made me think. I was not a rationalist. I did not deny the possibility of miracles. I was also of the conviction that the phenomena I had experienced in my visit to Resl, her stigmata, her lack of nourishment, etc., which are a violation of the laws of nature and all scientific principles, were to be regarded as miracles. I told myself that it would mean denying the existence of God to deny the possibility of miracles. I also realized that precisely our materialistic modern world, which is oriented so much more towards so-called knowledge than faith, and towards nature rather than super-nature, had a deep and pressing need to see a tangible and mighty miracle held up before its eyes and draw the ultimate conclusions from the experience, as happened so regularly and with such telling force in the days of Christ, with all his miracles.

It made me think that miraculous phenomena of such proportions were never at home in my own Lutheran church. Then my thoughts began ranging about in the broader area of the history of the saints and the Catholic Church. Whether Therese was a "saint" or not, or had ever been spoken of as "holy," was of no particular interest to me; but as a Protestant who had previously had no clear conception or close connection with any form of "sainthood" I merely told myself that in Konnersreuth I had seen examples of a union with Christ and phenomenal experiences which had given me such an understandable picture of the concepts and characteristics of holy personalities that it was absolutely impossible to deny them or merely dismiss them as an "imposture."

How foolishly men are inclined to speak about things they know, and want to know, absolutely nothing about. I have heard many such statements made in my circle of friends and acquaintances. And who made up this circle? Christ's coming into the world was absolutely unnecessary, a good friend of mine once declared in my presence—one of the highest public officials of our country. And who of all my acquaintances ever went to Church? All of them, every one, were Protestants who no longer believed in Church or Christ, or they were fallen-away Catholics, or Freemasons or the like. Was it ever possible to even bring up a religious subject for discussion among them? Only once did I dare to touch on the subject of Konnersreuth. The knowing smiles I got for an answer choked off the subject from further conversation. As a result, I began to dis-associate myself more and more from my circle of acquaintances, and almost completely cut off my dealings with them. There finally came a time in which I would go out all alone on quiet walks and try to be left alone with my thought. I had become much more reflective in religious matters.

From the story of Therese Neumann's life and sufferings I knew the role that St. Therese of the Child Jesus played in her eyes. The name Therese struck close to home. It was the name of my mother who had died an early death. I got a copy of the *Autobiography of a Soul* for myself, the story of this saint's life. I read the book and then set it aside; it was too "sugary" for me, and not according to my taste. But I did want to have a much clearer picture of Catholic thinking. So I turned to Catholic literature. The book by Johnson Vernon, *One God, One Faith,* made a lasting impression on me. Here I once again ran across the Little Flower and read of the immense influence that her life had had upon the one-time Anglican convert and author of the book. Once again I read the autobiography of the Little Flower, in the weeks that followed, and this time I managed to achieve a much better understanding of the tenderness and purity of this saintly flower. In my prayers I even dared to beg a single blossom from the rain of roses that she had promised to let loose after her death.

In Konnersreuth I got a very vivid and eyewitness picture of the concept of suffering, suffering for others, reparatory suffering, and now in the cold Protestant sermon service, after everything that lay behind me, I could no longer find any interior satisfaction. Something was drawing me to the Catholic Mass service. I no longer went to my own church. Even though there was still very much that was strange and hard to understand in the Catholic services, I still had a strong feeling that I had somehow come back to the primitive fountainhead of all Christian religion. My Catholic church attendance became more and more frequent and even regular. I began to join my wife and youngest son, but I could not bring myself to tell them about my inner experience. I became concerned about getting rid of my sins and faults, meditating on the Ten Commandments, and I also had a very bad characteristic trait that I had despaired of ever improving at all. It really was not a difficult task: it was something I took more or less for granted, something that seemed to happen all by itself. At Konnersreuth I had stood beneath the cross and said, *Mea culpa, mea maxima culpa.* I had become a different person. The reverent recollection of the congregation at the Catholic services and their spiritual unity with the priestly ministry at the altar, especially at the moment of consecration, never failed to touch me anew. With tears in my eyes I took part in these church ceremonies, and a hunger seized upon the depths of my soul when I saw the faithful approach the Communion rail.

What was I really, inside? Lutheran or Catholic? What should I become? I also had an older son, who had become Lutheran only because I had allowed it. Did I now have the right, as his father, and as the party solely responsible for his religious future, to leave him in the lurch now, while I became a Catholic myself? That would be abandonment of duty and I could never bring myself to that. During this time of inner turmoil I also thought a good deal about my sixty years. Somewhere deep within my heart there was still an extraordinary sense of mistrust, particularly towards the "political" side of Catholicism, a mistrust I could not manage to overcome. What was really waiting for me if I should finally decide to become a Catholic? Was the tree already too old to be transplanted? Could such an old tree really hope to strike roots in new ground? Might it not grow sick and even die? Was there any way back, any way out? Was the long-sought religious life destined only to die out again. In this time of doubt and despair I kept offering one prayer over and over again: "Lord, abide with me, for it is towards evening, and the day is already far spent."

In the course of late summer of 1931 my oldest son, who had a job in Berlin, was discharged from his work as a result of economic conditions. He found a new job in an Austrian resort. There he found lodging in a pension conducted by Catholic nuns. This was the first opportunity he had ever had, in his whole life, to experience Catholic life in a Catholic country. Over his bed hung a picture of the Little Flower, St. Therese, whom he had never heard of before. He stayed there only four weeks, but this brief stay was enough to awaken an interest in the religious life he had witnessed and a desire for a deeper religious activity. Then he moved into a house in Dresden that was near the Catholic parish church. His artistic and musical interests brought him to church and to High Mass on Sunday, in the parish church, and he developed a real attraction. Towards the end of 1932 the local branch of his business firm dissolved. Once again he was without work.

But before returning into his home in north Germany he had a great desire to see Therese Neumann and talk with her. Accordingly he made a trip to Konnersreuth, met Therese Neumann (he got a most friendly reception), and witnessed her Passion ecstasy, which made a deep and lasting impression on him as well. Shortly after his return to our home, he asked me a really astonishing question: "Father, would you have anything against my becoming Catholic?" I could only give one answer: "If it is the result of a deepseated conviction on your part, no." After a most thorough and excellent instruction, my son finally entered the Holy Church, at the age of 28, on May 17, 1933. The interior happiness that radiated from him, pure and tangible, was an unending source of real peace to me, even with respect to his future. The future was hidden, of course, but a great stone had been taken out of the road. I had been almost miraculously delivered from my responsibility for him, through the intervention of Divine Providence.

"I will get up and go to my father." These words kept forcing their way deep inside me. There had to be an end to these halfway measures. I had to, and wanted to, see it all through to the end. I wanted to get the strength I needed from Konnersreuth. I knew that my last doubts and reservations would all disappear there. I had not yet discussed all these inner struggles of mine with my wife, since I could not predict where their final outcome would lead me, but now I suggested to her that we take our vacation in Southern Germany that summer (1933) and take the opportunity to visit Konnersreuth again. On Tuesday, August 22, 1933, we started our trip and got to Konnersreuth that evening. There we learned that Therese and Father Naber had left on an auto trip for Trier to see the shroud, and were not expected to be back until the evening of the next day.

On Thursday, August 24, I was received by Father Naber about noon. He told me that he was prepared for my arrival, because Resl had spoken about me that very morning after Holy Communion (in her ecstatic state of elevated calm) and said that someone was coming that day that he should be especially friendly in receiving. We chatted together for a while, and I was most interested to learn of many particulars of Resl's life that I had not heard previously, especially her childlike recollection at prayer and her lively conversation with our Savior. About one o'clock that afternoon my wife and I went to see Resl at the family home.

I was very happy and deeply moved as I entered Resl's room and said "Hello." Her joy was just as great, but grew even greater when I told her that this time I was coming with quite different ends in view than the previous visit some few years ago. "I know," she said, "you want something whole." These words gave me great joy and made me very hopeful. Therese was still happy and excited in recalling the beautiful trip that lay behind her, and the deep impressions the Cathedral at Trier left upon her. She spoke of the many people she had seen during the veneration of the holy shroud, and how some of them recognized her here and there and she had to make her way through the crowds sideways in order to find a place to hide. (Later I heard from another source that when Therese first saw the great iron nail that had been used to crucify our Savior, she had broken out in the most painful cries, and they had to take her quickly out of the church).

On Friday, August 25, in the morning, there were some forty people outside the Neumann house, waiting to be admitted to the Passion ecstasy. Between ten and ten-thirty my family and I entered Resl's room. We saw her bleeding from her eyes and stigmata in her vision of the carrying of the cross and suffering in that one horrible scene in which our Savior is laid upon the cross to bore the nail holes.

When I first witnessed this Passion ecstasy in 1931, I had been moved by fear and repentance. "If you are insensitive to this, then you are worse than a stone!"—"We have become different people once we entered this house." That was what I wrote in my diary on that occasion. But today this picture had lost all its horror for me. Was not the blessing of this reparatory suffering aimed, not only at my son, but me also? Filled with gratitude, I turned to leave the room with the others. But Father Naber quietly asked me to remain for a moment. When the last of the visitors had left the room, there was a brief interruption in the ecstasy, and Therese sank down like a dead person, passing into a sleep-like state which is called the state of prepossession.

Then Father Naber led me to the bed and put my hand into Therese's hand. "Do you know this man, Resl?" he asked her. Then all of a sudden an expression of childlike joy and a happy and radiant smile passed over her blanched and bloodstreaked face. "Yes, that's the man who wants to come to our Savior," she answered. "You know, I had to suffer a lot for him too, but now everything will be all right. Now you will find peace."

In the childlike purity of her joy she kept chatting on like a person half asleep (a state in which she cannot see anything at all), speaking about me and my particular problems, filling me with joy and hope and strength. Then she sank back on her pillows again and lay there like a dead person. One more look at this unforgettable picture of suffering and then we all quietly left the room.

On Saturday, August 26, I walked around the neighborhood, on the surrounding heights, visiting the beautifully laid out and cared for cemetery, with the grave of the convert priest Bruno Rothschild, who met such an early death, and the pious Lina Weiss. My path also took me to the Calvary Mountain, not too far away. That afternoon, at about four o'clock, we met once again in the rectory with Therese Neumann, where we spent a pleasant and relaxing hour chatting together. I was constantly astonished whenever I looked at Resl, taking such a spirited and lively part in our conversation, often taking the lead, and showing what a natural fine wit she had. I thought of how she was so exhausted just yesterday, in suffering and bleeding, and how I had left her looking like a dead person and now, today, she was perhaps a little pale but still in fresh bloom of youth and vitality, sitting there and chatting with us. And this without having had anything to eat and almost without any natural sleep.

On Sunday, August 27, we participated in the parish High Mass. In adoration and thanksgiving, I bowed my knee to our Eucharistic Savior for the very first time in my life, here in the midst of this pious Konnersreuth congregation.

On September 10, we returned home from our vacation. On September 12, I visited the head of our Catholic parish, a man whom I had known well for a number of years; I told him about my visit and experiences in Konnersreuth, and also my new attitudes, and asked him to give me the instructions I needed to enter the Catholic Church; he had also given instructions to my oldest son. He listened to my story very gravely and then answered that he was completely amazed; he had considered everything possible, he said, except for this. My long-lived and thoroughly ingrained Protestant ways of thinking and speaking were only too well known to him and they had positively excluded every hope of my ever coming over to the Church.

Still, before I finally arrived at this goal there was a long and painful path ahead of me. The heights that my son had managed to reach with a few quick strides, his father had to fight for with persevering patience. There were thorns along my path as well. My regular attendance at the little Catholic church in our country capital had not been unnoticed by the local population and many of my acquaintances. Cold stares began to greet me on the street, and many of my former friends reevaluated their judgment of me and began to take a very distant attitude.

When my son had come over to the Church, a lady stopped me on the street and demanded an explanation: such a thing surely was not possible! From open tactlessness I was preserved however, and then (it was October 3, 1933) I received a visit from the bishop of the Evangelical Church. He came upon my sister's request, in an effort to dissuade me from the step I was planning. In the thorough discussion which ensued it was not difficult for me to defend and explain my standpoint and my intentions. He soon realized that any further efforts on his part would be pointless. He said wearily, as he left, that this had been his last official act. The new political disturbances had removed him from his position as local bishop. We parted on the most friendly terms.

Explanations to my own blood relatives, the kind of explanations that the new convert is never spared, were not missing in my case either. In a Protestant country, whenever a person becomes a Catholic, even if he happens to be in his 60's at the time, it is an event that leaves men speechless, and for the well-known and respected family in which it occurs it is equivalent to a scandal. People want to understand the grounds that could lead to such a thing; they think of persuasion from his wife, influence through his acquaintance with a Catholic cleric, or even some form of mental aberration. But no one ever arrives at the possibility that he might have other grounds, different and very impelling motives.

This chapter of the story is such a sad one that I prefer to pass over it in silence. I saw that, against my will and without any of my own doings, a wall was being built around me, made up of sympathy, mistrust, aversion, and lack of understanding, and that in some cases relations were being completely and formally broken off. Still none of this could have influenced me enough to turn aside from my objective; on the contrary, it only riveted my attention even more firmly and more consciously upon my goal.

On December 30, 1933, after thorough instruction, I entered the Holy Church.

Father Ingbert Naab and Konnersreuth

The following report was written by Father Maximilian Neumayr, O.F.M. Cap. (1947).

Eichstätt is 90 miles from Konnersreuth on a straight line. Still Eichstätt was quickly drawn into the closest and most lively connection with Konnersreuth through the activities of Dr. Franz Xavier Wutz, professor of the Old Testament there, who used to say Mass every day at the Capuchin monastery and was on intimate terms with the fathers there.

Thus the extraordinary happenings and events at Konnersreuth could not long escape the notice of Father Ingbert Naab. Still he experienced no particular desire to visit Konnersreuth. He had strong reservations, despite his deep religious spirit and the natural quickness of his sensitivity for preternatural phenomena. He had strong reservations for women in general, and particularly for women who claimed to have extraordinary visions and states. For months something was holding him back, and despite the frequent invitations he never went to Konnersreuth.

He had already received an encouraging answer (from Therese's ecstatic state) to some questions in a letter which he had written after long hesitation.

In Eichstätt he met her in the home of Professor Wutz, in her natural state. There he also made the acquaintance of the then Protestant chief editor of the Munich paper, Dr. Fritz Gerlich (*Münchener Neueste Narchrichte*). And still, despite the urging of his friends, he could not manage to overcome his inner repugnance. He explained this attitude by the fear he had of hearing something terrible about his future from Therese in her ecstatic state, because from his own and his mother's premonitions he already knew how much mental anguish was bound up with such knowledge and premonitions. Finally on July 1, 1928 everything worked out. He was preaching at the First Mass celebration of a young priest in the order. That afternoon "Resl" also appeared. And then Professor Wutz simply took the priest along to Konnersreuth where, for the first time he witnessed the extraordinary goings on there. From that time onwards, the relationship with Konnersreuth was a close and intimate one. In so far as it was possible to speak of a Konnersreuth Circle, (the name was coined by the opposition), the following men were to be understood as members: Father Naber, Professor Wutz, Dr. Gerlich, Father Ingbert, Prince Waldburg-Zeil.

When Father Naab got back from that first visit to Konnersreuth, he told one of his fellow religious everything he had experienced, that very same night. Understandably enough, he had proportionately little to say about the extraordinary phenomena. But the original, natural, childlike, and humble manner of the girl from Konnersreuth had deeply moved him. He stressed one particular thought on that evening after his visit to Konnersreuth: "You can pray so much differently now. You learn to be much closer united with our dear Savior there." He looked upon it as a very great grace, that he had been privileged to be a witness to such things.

He did, however, feel that there would be some great suffering to follow such great grace. He could not possibly imagine what the suffering would be, but one thing was unqualifiedly clear in his mind: he would have to pay for this grace with some new suffering. This was always God's way, and our Savior had used it on the Apostles. From that time on, in his ascetical sermons in the monastery and also in speaking with his students in and out of class, he began using the word "Savior" more than ever before. "The Savior is the one who did this," "The Savior would smile a friendly smile then," "The Savior would have something to say about that," "The Savior wants me to take a stand against these abuses, to warn people against these dangers...."

All his public lectures, and all his work with the students he now brought into a closer and closer connection with our Savior than ever before; he now found a clearer and more moving picture of our Savior in the Gospel stories, and he used this new acquaintance as the basis for a whole series of spiritual exercises based on our Savior's historical life. In his reverence and devotion to the Holy Eucharist, a change also began to manifest itself, in that he now began to speak of it not so much as the "Blessed Sacrament" (as if it were an object), but referred to it more as "the Savior," who is really and truly and essentially present there, recognizing his friends and observing their work and helping them and making them holy. Now he advised the newly ordained deacons to pronounce the words of distribution much more meaningfully at Communion time: "Corpus Domini nostri Jesu Christi custodiat animam tuam in vitam aeternam," and to say them as a special wish for the communicant and a prayer addressed to Jesus Christ: "Savior, give this very aged man the strength to pass over bravely into eternal life ... : give this youthful person the strength he needs to preserve the everlasting life within him, in the hard struggles of our day and age...."

But above all else, in Konnersreuth he rediscovered the incarnation of his old ideal, an ideal which had accompanied his whole thinking and feeling from the first days of his youth;

the ideal of reparation, reparatory suffering and atonement, but this time it was a clearer picture and a more urgent one.

There were also hours in which he put his hands to his head like a person just waking from sleep: Is this reality? Isn't this suggestion and hypnosis? Am I actually a witness of things that are so strange and mysterious? Or am I perhaps only the victim of delusion? "The most painful thing about it all," he explained whenever he spoke about it, "is knowing that it is only a temptation and still not being able to do anything about it." Over and over again he had experienced the fact that he must very carefully weigh whatever was being passed from mouth to mouth as the words of Resl in her ecstasy; he also was familiar with the extraordinary care and reservation which the standard work of Benedict XIV on the subject of the Canonization of Servants of God observes in the face of all private revelations, based on the grounds that no matter how genuinely a private revelation first comes from God, from the very first moment that it is received by a human person it is subject to all human failings and partiality, even on the part of servants of God.

But then too his experiences in Konnersreuth were of such an overpowering intensity that he could rejoice in them with an undivided heart. He had personally witnessed phenomena that appear only rarely in the lives of even the greatest saints, and he spoke of them only in the most intimate circles. He experienced a startling confirmation of the genuinity of Konnersreuth when Resl, contrary to all expectations and predictions on the part of those who were witness to her vision of Lourdes, heard the Blessed Mother speaking, not in pure French, but the Pyrenees dialect: "Sche sui la conceptione immaculade(oe) (I am the Immaculate Conception)." He saw the miracles that had been worked in souls in and through Konnersreuth; Therese Neumann herself had on occasion sent many confused people to him, for spiritual guidance. Then too he found a mighty confirmation of his trust in Konnersreuth in the unaffected, unpretentious, and open manner of this simple girl. Dr. Gerlich had published his two volumes on Konnersreuth. Now he asked Resl whether she was pleased with his book about her. This was her answer: "If I say yes, that is not right; and if I say no then he will be hurt. So I won't say anything." This made a very striking impression on Father Ingbert.

And now he saw Konnersreuth in a different light—pushing all the extraordinary phenomena into the background—as the decision on the essential questions of Catholic belief and life: "What does our Lord God mean to do at Konnersreuth?" His answer: Konnersreuth does not have to be,—but: "If our Savior wants to work some miracles, he knows why, and humanity must receive them with humility and be thankful that they have been worked."

Father Ingbert's position on the new clinical observation was as follows: "If the family refuses, they have a perfect right to do so; they aren't calling anyone to Konnersreuth and the world of science itself will not be led to a recognition of anything supernatural as a result of this repeated examination. Therese Neumann has not ceased to be a member of her family and to exercise her natural freedom just by receiving the stigmata. This is a question of fundamental natural law."

In his numerous sermons to the people he laid much greater stress on the religious and ascetic significance of the events at Konnersreuth than on the events themselves. It was the time in which people were beginning to take a violent position for or against Konnersreuth. But Father Ingbert was the very first to take a vigorous stand against misrepresentation of the facts of Konnersreuth. "Theological science and mysticism must be honored—but in establishing the facts the prime duty is conscientious investigation."

Principle was something primary for Father Ingbert in the case of Konnersreuth. And the principle of Konnersreuth, in his unshakable conviction, was well worth his dedicated efforts in its behalf. Because no matter how openly skeptical and mistrustful of all extraordinary phenomena a person might care to be, it is still a tenet of Christian faith to count on the fact that God can and will continue to stand by his Church and furnish her with miraculous credentials. And it is an essential element of Christian faith to believe in the central significance of the life and sufferings of Jesus and the preeminent position occupied by childlike simplicity and humility. This is the message that emanated from Konnersreuth. And this was the message that he felt an obligation to propagate, no matter how many hours of work and effort it might cost.

Fritz Gerlich and Konnersreuth (1927)

The Baron Erwein of Aretin wrote the following article in 1949.

The author of these pages must beg forgiveness at being forced to make a place for himself, for a moment, in the foreground of this story, in an effort to make it more understandable and perhaps also to give a clearer indication of the grounds and limitations within which he claims to have a legitimate basis for describing things that are, fundamentally, neither exhaustively nor quite exactly amenable to all objective presentation.

The story deals with phenomena that elude human explanation and takes place in the innermost depths of a human heart, and no curious or penetrating eye can quite see into it from without. I am also well aware of the fact that I am speaking of matters on which the Church can set certain limits to what I have to report, and that I must yield to her judgment. And thus this chapter is subject to the human fallibility of its author without, for all that, ever excusing the author from making every possible effort to paint the exact and perfect truth.

To describe for the reader of these lines what is included under the general title of events at Konnersreuth is certainly superfluous: it is the story of a stigmatic young girl, named Therese Neumann, in Konnersreuth, near Waldsassen in Oberpfalz, a girl who was suddenly and unexplainably cured of her lameness and blindness, who, since 1926, that is, for 23 years, has lived only on the Holy Eucharist, without any other nourishment either solid or liquid, and who has experienced rare visions from Sacred Scripture and Church History and particularly, every Friday, terribly moving visions of Christ's passion, in which she suffers together with our Savior. This same girl, born on the night of Good Friday and Holy Saturday morning in 1898, the daughter of needy and impoverished parents, who has only the most elementary education, on certain occasions displays a faculty for seeing into the deepest mysteries of her visitors' souls with crystal clarity, and knowing things whose knowledge is utterly beyond the power of her normal, sharp and very quick grasp, and thus unexplainable.

I made her acquaintance in July of 1927, when I visited Konnersreuth for the first time, in the company of her adviser, the Eichstätt Professor Franz Xaver Wutz (died in Eichstätt March 19, 1938), and spent a few days there. I tried to express the impressions I received in the account I wrote for the Munich paper, *Münchener Neueste Nachrichte*, August 3, 1927. This was the first public account of Konnersreuth to appear in a major paper, and the lead was quickly followed by all the major newspapers both at home and abroad. As a result, Konnersreuth, in that year of 1927, was flooded with thousands of curious people every week and achieved a sensational position that was not always in keeping with the things that happened there. Naturally the Neumann family is in no way responsible for this publicity—they were very unhappy about it and they could be induced only with great difficulty, by the then bishop of Regensburg, to open their door to visitors who had been recommended by the bishop's office.

Returning from this visit, and somewhat confused by what I had just experienced, I was invited by Gerlich to have lunch with him and Professor Cossmann, and to tell them about the trip and decide how I could best express my views on the matter in the language of the newspaper world. The idea did not appeal to me very much. After all, Munich's most famous restaurant, into which Gerlich had invited me, did not seem to be the best place for telling two people whose religious convictions were more or less unfamiliar to me, about Christ's Passion and the visions of a girl: it was a foregone conclusion that my account would strike against a solid wall of skepticism and misunderstanding. And thus it was. After almost every sentence I was interrupted by one of those objections which I have since learned to listen to with patience and resignation; hysteria, suggestion, autosuggestion, doubts as to the validity of my observations, or merely a look—and this was worst of all—discreetly exchanged by my two listeners, which, although well within the bounds of the most extreme politeness, seemed to cast some doubt upon my mental faculties.

Thus it seemed particularly difficult to hope that there would be any room in the newspaper. But they finally went along with me and devoted a whole issue of the supplement to my article. The newspaper did not regret it; the issue had to be reprinted four times within the next ten days, and the article was translated into no less than 32 languages—even in Iriquois—and on August 31, 1937, that is, ten years later to the day, Cossmann wrote me a letter expressing his friendship and kind feeling towards me, in which he did not hesitate to declare that this article—I had really not thought about it on that date—was the greatest journalistic sensation he had ever experienced in the some forty years of his activities in the newspaper field. There was no mention of our luncheon date on that occasion.

What I finally said to my friendly table companions on that former occasion was this: "Yes, gentlemen, you'll have to go and see it all for yourselves." They both followed my advice, both were converted as a result, and both were murdered by the Nazis, Gerlich at Dachau and Cossmann at Theresienstadt. He was more than seventy when he was dragged off to prison there and forced to clean the latrines during an epidemic of dysentery. This order was the immediate cause of his own infection with the same disease and his consequent death, the death of one of the most prudent and noble men I have ever had the good fortune to know.[37]

After the appearance of my article, Professor Wutz had driven from Eichstätt to Munich and looked for Gerlich (whom he had known previously) and me in the newspaper offices. Gerlich was happy to come along in the car and later came and told me "what a fine, free-thinking and wise man this Wutz is." With this irreproachable and priestly personality he gradually developed a deep and devoted friendship. There is more to relate on this subject later.

The success of my article left Gerlich no peace. He was plagued with the anxiety and fear that his paper had published an account of something that would sooner or later necessarily be exposed as a grand imposture to which I had unwittingly fallen victim, and the unfortunate consequences to his newspaper would somehow have to be undone. He thus made a trip on the evening of September 14, 1927. He suddenly appeared in Eichstatt looking for Professor Wutz and the next day they both came to Konnersreuth. Gerlich came into my office to say goodbye and took leave of me, in all friendliness,

---

37. Author's note:

"I too was acquainted with Professor Cossmann, from the days when I belonged to the Munich *Neueste Nachrichten* in 1923-26, even before the end of my student years. In those shameful days in which Professor Cossmann — meantime he had become a Catholic — had to run around with a Star of Sion on his coat and be put away in a Munich detention camp, I used to invite him into my home one day a week. There were only a few such visits, because, unfortunately, he was soon transported to Theresienstadt. On that occasion he told me the following facts: He and Gerlich had been good friends to start with, but before Gerlich left the Munich paper they had become enemies — I also knew this from Gerlich. Then in 1933 they suddenly met once more, and only once, passing among the cells of the police prison. They had embraced and said, 'Now we've found each other again.' They both began to cry, and they quickly forgot everything that had stood between them. Unfortunately, their paths quickly parted once again."

with these words: "I guarantee you: that's one imposture I'll soon enough manage to root out!" I was seized by a certain sense of anxiety. Not that I supposed he would discover some imposture where there was none, but I had a feeling of responsibility of a quite different nature. I had known Gerlich for more than three years now; he was an unnaturally sharp and logically thinking man. It was absolutely impossible to suppose that a head like his could fail to immediately recognize the calm and elevated earnestness of the situation there. He would not be like the less sensitive temperaments and try to explain away something difficult to understand on the facile and superficial basis of hysteria and suggestion. Here was a man who would be forced to deep interior search and faithful observation.

Five days later, on the evening of September 19, 1927, Gerlich came back to my room, immediately upon leaving the station, and asked me if I could come with him. I accepted his invitation at once and we walked up and down Ludwigstrasse together until two o'clock in the morning, through the light cool autumn rain. He never grew tired of telling about new and different facets of his trip to Konnersreuth.

It was a moving experience to hear this man, with whom I had previously discussed only "shop talk" and politics, speaking about "our Savior" and telling how he had been fighting for the truth all his life long—his death will remove the reproach of indiscretion which these lines might otherwise deserve. Evenings, on his way home from the newspaper offices, he would stop and kneel before the closed door of the Frauenkirche, begging God to show him the truth. And thus this trip had been a wonderful and almost miraculous answer to his prayers. Was this the same Gerlich who had taken leave of me just five days before with the perhaps not frivolous but certainly skeptical word "imposture," and a promise to root it out once and for all? Despite all his respect for the person of Therese Neumann, who impressed him, as she had me two months previously, as being a person of childlike purity, incapable of any deceit, he realized that it was not her person that was the essential thing in Konnersreuth, but rather the truth, a truth which she can certainly promote, but which lays hold of a man immediately, addressing his soul. I had gone to Konnersreuth as a Catholic, and thus my overall philosophy of the world was not appreciably disturbed. But with Gerlich it was different. Not only the fact that at Konnersreuth he witnessed, as an almost everyday experience, everything he had ever heard about miracles and listened to with the apologetic expression and half-open ear which the man of the twentieth century feels justified in assuming towards the man of the Middle Ages or the ancient world; but this sudden and deeply moving understanding had come upon him lightning-like and he had seen the earnest truth shining before him, compared to which the reality of our earthly life is only a parable, like the mirror of which Paul speaks in the letter to the Corinthians—Paul, who himself must have suffered a similar experience on the road to Damascus.

This walk in the midnight of September 19/20, 1927, was one powerful moment in my life in which I witnessed the interior transformation God can effect within a human soul, glowing with a real furnace of love for him, when he moulds it for the mission and destiny to which it has been called.

Author's Conclusion

The question everyone asks today is this: Was, or is Konnersreuth a sign from God, graciously offered to a modern world that is weary of its faith? Is it a shining and warming fire in the darkness of the materialism that denies the spirit of God, and in the cold of the rationalism that limits God's powers, and in the fog of liberalism that conceals the very picture and image of God?

"Count no man blessed before his death" (Sir. 11, 28). The reservation on the part of the competent Church authorities was understandable. But now Therese Neumann is dead (September 18, 1962). "Without in any way anticipating the Church's official judgment," said Father Josef Schumann at her funeral in Konnersreuth, "we can safely say that God has done great things through her." Another passage from Scripture might well be applied to her life: "By their fruits you will know them" (Matt. 7, 20). Her fruits are certainly manifold and choice. The deceased Archbishop Michael Buchberger of Regensburg, who certainly does not have a credulous attitude towards the events that took place in Konnersreuth, counted the following among the fruits of Therese Neumann's life in 1953 "They [the visitors] either found an answer here or at least they went consoled. Others found their faith and still others were strengthened in their faith."

The attentive observer who visited Konnersreuth within the last 30 years was interested in more than these undeniable fruits of her life. He inquired primarily into the reasons behind this mystery and his answer would light upon two factors that have special significance for our times: leading people back to the Eucharist and finding new meaning for suffering in God's plan for salvation.

Her almost forty years of subsisting on nothing but the Holy Eucharist, her intuitive recognition of the Eucharist, her visions of Christ coming down from heaven at the moment of consecration, the mystical entrance and undissolved presence of the species of bread in her body all seem to be a new proof of the living presence of Christ in the Blessed Sacrament, infinitely worthy of adoration, a proof designed for our own times, just as in other eras in which the light of faith was dim, Eucharistic miracles appeared to strengthen faith whenever the dogma of the Eucharist was attacked or doubted.

Through her willing acceptance of suffering, physical as well as spiritual, and through her heroic resignation to the suffering of Christ for the good of all humanity, we find new meaning in suffering—and its reevaluation is a great gift of grace, precisely in our day and age. When Therese Neumann began these sufferings—1918—the First World War had just ended. The beginning of her mystic experiences—1926—falls in the period of extreme economic pressures. And the unspeakable suffering that came upon a part of our people in 1933 and in the Second World War upon all the people and many other peoples besides, bitterly needed someone to point out the meaning behind suffering.

In our days too, when we are beginning to turn away from suffering with slogans of ethical indication or euthanasia, it is very important to know that there must always be suffering and sufferers, that in the plans of God they make up an important part of humanity, which can accomplish a great degree of its own reparation by suffering and by activities designed to relieve the sufferings of others. It is forbidden by the fifth commandment to shorten or put an end to a life of suffering; but on the other hand the healthy person has a great obligation to mitigate and alleviate suffering, either through his own personal sacrifices in time of material need (volunteer nursing, for example), or by preventive legislation. Thus these two groups of humanity will be mutually fruitful for each other: the suffering and the non-suffering, in the family, in the community, in the whole nation, and in the whole of humanity. "Through suffering more men are saved then through the most brilliant sermons," was one of the first words that Therese Neumann heard from the mouth of the Little Flower.

We do well to be thankful to God for allowing such a stirring example to take place precisely in our own days, when we needed it so desperately—but were not so willing to admit our needs. It would be a rejection of divine grace for us to let this opportunity pass by unheeded. We must do our best to probe the deeper purposes that are bound up with Konnersreuth, and ponder them carefully in our hearts and minds even after Therese Neumann's death—especially after her death.

The Church, in her centuries old wisdom, will some day take a position on all these events. In other times and in other lands she has found her own sure way to pass a judgment on the *"magnalia Dei,"*—the mighty deeds of God, and when the time has come, the case of Konnersreuth will not be an exception.

Appendix

A letter of Therese Neumann from the year 1960, addressed to the head of children's clinic in Munich on the occasion of the fiftieth anniversary of her profession. It shows Therese's childlike simplicity—unchanged throughout her whole life, and her readiness to sacrifice and help.

Konnersreuth, March 16, 1960

Dear Mother Superior,

Even though it is pretty late, still my best wishes, from the bottom of my heart, for your solemn and rare feastday. I will give my very childlike thanks to our dear Savior together with you, for all the graces of the last 50 years. Yes, our Savior has been really good to you, especially in the hard war years, but that is easy to understand when we just think of all the many guardian angels of all the big and little children there. We can be sure they are standing beside our dear Mother and begging for the strength you need. You no doubt feel all this, dear Mother. In this spirit I will continue to include you and your whole house in my prayers and suffering and sacrifices.

Last year I spent a long time with your sisters in the hospital at Eichstätt where my dear sister Ottilie underwent such terrible sufferings and finally died a saintly death. Sister A. took such motherly care of her, and so did the good Mother Superior there. If only more young girls would realize what a beautiful

life it is to sacrifice self completely for others. In this spirit
I pray our dear Savior constantly.

And now I wish you and yours, once again, all the best,
together with the promise that we think of each other in our
prayers. With thanks and gratitude,

Therese Neumann

Illustrations

The illustrations in this book are meant to serve as documentation together with the text. Possibly one or the other interested reader, particularly one who has taken a critical stand against Konnersreuth, might find fault with Therese Neumann for letting herself be photographed after having taken such a stand against admitting any visitors with cameras. But there is a big difference between meeting the press because you are not adverse to publicity or even looking for it, on the one hand, and allowing pictures to be taken only in the family circle or among close friends, and then only on special occasions. And when, with a view towards subsequent documentation, Therese Neumann's spiritual directors advised her to let herself be photographed in her ecstatic states, assuring her that no use would be made of the pictures as long as she lived, this was certainly not a breach of piety or reverence, any more than it is when we normally take pictures of religious and sacred ceremonies in our churches.

Obviously there could be no question of *disturbing* her under these conditions: Therese was completely insensitive to outside influence during her states of ecstasy. We might also recall that every year she experienced some hundred visions, not to mention the approximately thirty visions of the Passion. For the years from 1926 to 1962, that makes more than four thousand visions. Compared to such a total, the few during which she was actually photographed hardly deserve to be counted. The unprejudiced reader will simply rejoice at the fact that the noble experiences the immediate circle of Therese Neumann's family and friends were privileged to experience is thus available and preserved in film for her contemporaries and for posterity.

In the following catalogue of photographs, those that belong to the Neumann family are marked by the letter N, those taken by her brother Ferdinand by the letter F, those taken by the author by the letter S. Some of the pictures originate from the illustrated paper in Sommerer, Mitterteich/Opf.; these pictures bear the initials SM.

p. 92 ff. Geographical position of Konnersreuth: politically in the area of Tirschenreuth (Oberpfalz), physically between the Fichtelgebirg and the Bohemian Forest. Scale: the distance between Waldsassen and Konnersreuth is 5 kilometers (3 miles). Taken from a map printed in Waldsassen.

p. 92 ff. (S) Landscape of Konnersreuth — cradled in a valley in the Fichtelgebirg spur.

p. 92 ff. (S) Schneiderixenhaus (Neumann family home) decorated for Corpus Christi. Therese was born and died here. The old name for the house (in keeping with Bavarian custom) was still retained, even when the house changed owners. Therese Neumann's great grandfather originally bought the house. He was a tailor by trade (Schneider in German) and his name was Felix. The popular speech easily corrupted this into "Schneider-ixenhaus."

p. 92 ff. (N) Therese Neumann at the age of three. A typical pose for the era (1901). A stuffed cat, a tennis racquet, a ball, and some flowers had to serve as props.

p. 92 ff. (N) Mother Neumann and her ten living children in 1916. The picture was taken for her husband who was in the service. Left to right: Therese, Marie, Anna, Ottilie, Engelbert, Kreszenz, Agnes, Hans, Mother, August.

p. 92 ff. (F) The Neumann parents at work in the field.

p. 92 ff. (N) Therese Neumann after her cure, end of 1925.

p. 92 ff. After receiving the stigmata. Taken in 1928 by Father Ingbert Naab, O.F.M. Cap., for the Gerlich book. A slightly different pose was actually used.

p. 92 ff. (S) The altar dedicated to St. Therese of Lisieux, the Little Flower, in the parish Church, May 17, 1928 (third anniversary of her canonization).

p. 92 ff. (S) Konnersreuth Parish Church — constructed in 1775-1782 (Lake Roccoco).

p. 92 ff. (S) Therese Neumann's spiritual director from 1909 up to her death: Father Joseph Naber.

p. 92 ff. (S) Ferdinand Neumann, Father, chief figure in the discussion of the clinical experiments, 1952.

p. 92 ff. (F) Mother Anna Neumann, a kindly and happy wife and mother (around 1945).

p. 92 ff. (F) On the occasion of Dr. Gerlich's conversion in Eichstätt, Therese experiencing a vision of the man with the palsy (Sept. 27, 1931). Dr. Gerlich on the left.

p. 92 ff. (N) Ordination of the Convert Bruno Rothschild, June 29, 1932. (Died December 24, 1932.) Front row: Father Naber, Bruno Rothschild, Professor Wutz, Father Cosmas, O.F.M. Cap. Back row: Therese Neumann, her sister Agnes, Marie, Ottilie, and her brother Ferdinand.

p. 92 ff. above: (F) Professor Wutz brings some exotic birds.
        below: (F) a little chick.

p. 92 ff. (F) In Eichstätt with M. Benedicta von Spiegel, O.S.B., Abbess.

p. 92 ff. (F) Relaxation with her sisters in Eichstätt.

p. 172 ff. (F) Therese Neumann, the bird-lover.

p. 172 ff. (N) Resl and "Lotte," the horse she bought for her visits to care for the sick (around 1946).

p. 172 ff. (F) Pilgrimage to St. Nickolaus von der Flue (1938). Therese was always well covered and wrapped whenever she went out publicly.

p. 172 ff. (S) The Trinity-Pilgrimage Chapel, 4 km. from Konnersreuth: note the strong symbolism in the three towers, three cupolas, and clover-leaf ground plan.

p. 172 ff. (SM) Konnersreuth after the shelling in 1945.

p. 172 ff. (S) The tabernacle in the parish Church at Konnersreuth, decorated by Therese Neumann in honor of the Church Patron (St. Lawrence). Several thousands of flowers have been arranged with great love and care.

p. 172 ff. (S) Therese Neumann in 1952. Therese asked the author to take this photo for the then obligatory identification card.

p. 172 ff. (SM) In October of 1957 the rusted weathervane was taken down from the Konnersreuth church tower and a great gilded metal cross was put in its place. An American helicopter flew the heavy cross to the tower.

left: Therese helping protect the top of the cross from the cable.

right: the pilot does a masterful job.

p. 172 ff. (SM) Visitors in Konnersreuth, Good Friday, 1950. The crowds are so thick that the Neumann home is not yet in sight. American soldiers in the foreground.

p. 172 ff. (SM) Good Friday, 1957, in front of the Neumann home. Good Friday, 1959. Visitors stream to the Neumann home despite the pouring rain. The Neumann house has been added onto, to make room for Father Naber who planned to resign, at the age of 90.

p. 172 ff. The stigmata shines through Therese's gloves in her vision of light, May 17, 1927. Therese is sitting in her place behind the main altar. In the background, the sacristy door.

Some of the local people wanted to go into the sacristy on this occasion (the second anniversary of the canonization of the Little Flower). There they noticed Therese, in her usual place behind the main altar, in the midst of her vision. She was seeing the same mysterious and beatifying light out of which she had heard the voice of the Little Flower when she was cured in 1925. Some of the people noted that the stigma in her right hand was shining, even through the glove. Father Naber immediately asked Principal Bohm, who happened to be there in the choir, to go and get his camera from the school house next door. The result was the present photograph in which the same clear light is visible in the hand, proving that it could not have been a mere illusion on the part of the observers. Nothing has been retouched on either the negative or the print.

p. 172 ff. (F) Therese Neumann during her Pentecost visions (taken in her room).

above: the wind and flames.

below: the many baptisms.

p. 172 ff. (F) The vision of the Ascension, Easter, 1936. Christ hovering above the ground.

Disappointed at our Savior's disappearance, Therese attempts to seize him and cries out: "Take me along!"

p. 172 ff. (F) Early that Easter morning Therese had an ecstatic communion, after her visions of the Resurrection. Sitting in her place behind the altar during Mass, she is swept into a vision at the words of consecration; with an expression of great joy she sees the risen Savior coming down onto the altar.

p. 172 ff. (F) This was followed, up until the priest's communion, by the ecstatic state known as the "prayer of calm."

p. 172 ff. (F) Ecstatic Communion: (Easter morning, 1936) In place of the priest, Therese sees our Savior coming with the Sacred Host. Taken in Therese's room.

p. 252 ff. (F) Visionary participation in the Sunday Mass at Konnersreuth, while Therese is in Eichstätt. Both pictures taken in the library of Professor Wutz, Eichstätt.

above: Therese prays together with the priest.

below: the moment of consecration.

p. 252 ff. (F) Therese passing from her visionary state to her normal condition.

p. 252 ff. (F) Vision during First Mass celebration. During the banquet Therese had a vision, just after a child had climbed onto her lap and offered her some food.

p. 252 ff. (F) An unexpected Friday vision (St. Wolfgang's Day, October 31, 1941).

When the feast day of the Regensburg Diocesan Patron, St. Wolfgang (October 31), fell on Friday, Therese Neumann generally would not have any Friday vision. In 1941 this was the case and Therese had planned a very necessary trip to Eichstätt for that week. Late Thursday night her brother Ferdinand saw a light in the Wutz chapel, about half past one. He investigated and found Resl sitting on the carpeted floor, streams of blood from her eyes coursing down over her cheeks, in the midst of her Friday Passion vision. She had gone into the chapel to pray and she was surprised there by the suffering and vision, shortly before midnight. Blood trickled down into her prayer book and she then sat down on the floor. Since she had left her home diocese and travelled into another diocese in which St. Wolfgang's Day was not an ecclesiastical feast, this unexpected Friday vision and suffering took place as usual.

p. 252 ff. (F) Good Friday, 1953. After the vision of Jesus' death.

p. 252 ff. (S) Documentary photographs: front and back of the bed-jacket which Therese Neumann wore on Good Friday, 1959. Taken in 1963. The picture of the front side shows the spot on the right shoulder where the blood seeped through during the vision of the carrying of the cross. In the middle are the stains of the blood from the wound over the heart which seeped through to the bed jacket despite the heavy compresses which had been carefully laid over it. The other spots of blood all appeared during the vision of the scourging, excepting for those on the sleeves which came from the bleeding of the stigmata in the hands.

p. 252 ff. (S) Headcloth worn by Therese Neumann on Good Friday, 1959. It shows the traces of the bleeding from the nine large wounds made by the thorns: the cloth had been folded at the time, with the under part facing outside. (Colorphoto taken in 1963.)

p. 252 ff. (S) Two of the compresses which were laid over the heart stigma on the Fridays in Lent and on Good Friday. They give an indication of the size of the wound. The bleeding from the heart wound soaked through these heavy compresses and stained the bed jacket. Photo taken in 1963.

p. 252 ff. (F) Resl's room in the Neumann home, well known to all the hundreds of thousands of people who visited her on her bed of suffering.

p. 252 ff. (F) Therese Neumann in death. She was laid out in the room that was formerly her father's work room, from Sept. 18 to 22, 1962.

p. 252 ff. Father Naber and Ferdinand pay respects. Taken by Hilmar Pabel, Rottau / Chiemsee.

p. 252 ff. (S) Therese Neumann's grave, near the cemetery cross which was erected on her initiative.

p. 252 ff. Therese Neumann's handwriting. A postcard addressed to the author. Text:

> Konnersreuth, August 3, 1937
>
> Dear Dr. Steiner,
>
> How are you and your dear ones? Is the little one well? Everything is fine at our house, for the most part. Our dear Savior helps make everything all right. Let us put our child-like trust in him. Let us hold true to him always, even when it is hard. . . ."

p. 252 ff. One of the thousands of prayer cards that Therese Neumann used to give her visitors in the course of her years of suffering. The reverse reads: Savior, gladly every sacrifice for love of you. United in holy prayer. Therese Neumann."

p. 252 ff. Therese's hands in death. Photo by Hilmar Pabel, Rottau / Chiemsee.

An Invitation

The Episcopal See of Regensburg has been the recipient of various petitions, based on the conviction that Therese Neumann has been blessed by God with an extraordinary degree of grace and shown herself deserving of this special grace by an heroic life in the practice of religion and virtue, and requesting the Bishop of Regensburg to initiate the official process for her beatification. Everyone who has personally known Therese Neumann and shares this opinion, or who has learned the story of her life from other people or by reading it in books, is invited to follow this example and, unless he has some special information to offer, to make use of the formula printed for this purpose on the following page.

Considerable financial contributions have already been received to defray the costs of such an official process, and they are being held in a special account at the bank in Waldsassen (Stadsparkasse Waldsassen): the name of the account is "Funds for the beatification process of Therese Neumann," number 2000, and it is held in the name of the diocese. In the event that anyone cares to send a check for this purpose, he should address it to either "Kreis - und Stadtsparkasse Waldsassen, Konto Nr. 2000," or send it directly to the Episcopal Ordinary at Regensburg.

An das Bischöfliche Ordinariat
zu Händen des Hochwürdigsten Herrn Bischofs

        84 Regensburg, Niedermünstergasse,
           Date _____

Concerning: request for initiating an informative process on
Therese Neumann with the purpose of eventual beatification.

The undersigned is (are) of the conviction that Therese
Neumann, the stigmatic of Konnersreuth, has been blessed by
God in an extraordinary manner, and has shown herself deserving
of this special grace by her heroic life of reparation, her
charitable works in every field of human endeavor, and her
prayers. Consequently I (we) request His Excellency, the Most
Reverend Bishop of Regensburg, to initiate an ecclesiastical
informative process to examine into the life of Therese Neumann.

               Respectfully yours,

    (The signature(s) should be accompanied by an indication
of the sender's occupation, age, and address.)